STOCKTRADESAPP.COM PRESENTS

Stock Trades:
From Beginner to Mastery

The Complete Guide to Analytical Trading,
Risk Management, and Lifelong Market Mastery

By
Patience (Pat) Fuzane, MBA
CGRC • CISSP • CEH • CompTIA Security+

Published by StockTradesApp.com
stocktradesapp.com

DISCLAIMER: This book is for educational purposes only and does not constitute investment advice.
Investing involves risk including possible loss of principal. Past performance does not guarantee future results.

About the Author

Patience (Pat) Fuzane, MBA • CGRC • CISSP • CEH • CompTIA Security+

Patience (Pat) Fuzane is a cybersecurity professional, entrepreneur, educator, and published author across the fields of federal compliance, artificial intelligence, investing, and personal development. He holds a Master of Business Administration with a concentration in Cybersecurity and carries one of the most rigorous credential stacks in the field: Certified Governance, Risk, and Compliance professional (CGRC), Certified Information Systems Security Professional (CISSP), Certified Ethical Hacker (CEH), and CompTIA Security+.

Pat spent years as a Principal Classified Cybersecurity Analyst at Northrop Grumman, managing security frameworks, compliance programs, and risk management processes for defense and federal systems at the highest classification levels. That career built in him something most trading authors do not bring to the subject: a professional-grade expertise in structured process, evidence-based decision-making, and systematic risk management under conditions where the cost of a wrong call is real and consequential.

Those disciplines translate directly to markets. Risk management, position sizing, stop-loss discipline, process adherence under pressure, and the systematic review of performance outcomes are not just trading concepts. They are the daily vocabulary of anyone who has built and operated a security compliance framework for a major defense contractor. When Pat writes about the 1% rule or structural stop-loss placement, he is drawing on the same intellectual discipline he applied to federal risk management frameworks.

Pat is also the founder of Cert Training Hub LLC (certtraininghub.com), a federal cybersecurity training platform offering RMF, FISMA, and ATO readiness content for professionals preparing for federal compliance roles. His experience building an educational platform from the ground up, producing textbooks, developing curriculum, and teaching complex technical material to diverse learners, is woven directly into the pedagogical structure of this book.

As an instructor and adjunct faculty candidate at the collegiate level, Pat has a documented record of producing high pass rates by combining structured curriculum with the kind of disciplined, step-by-step skill-building that this book applies to trading. He understands from direct teaching experience that the gap between knowing something and being able to do it reliably under pressure is a pedagogical problem with pedagogical solutions, and he has designed every chapter of this book with that gap explicitly in mind.

Pat is also the founder of StockTradesApp.com, the retail trading terminal that serves as the live analytical environment for this book. The platform was built on the same core conviction that drives his educational philosophy: that most people who fail at trading or investing do not fail because they lack intelligence. They fail because they lack a systematic process. StockTradesApp.com was built to give retail traders the professional-grade analytical tools that process requires, and this book was written to teach them how to use those tools effectively.

His published works reflect the full range of his expertise. His cybersecurity title RMF & ATO Readiness: A System for Government Contractors has become a go-to reference for federal contractors, IT professionals, and compliance practitioners navigating the NIST Risk Management Framework and the Authority to Operate process. Artificial Intelligence Is Here to Stay, You Better Learn It Now! brings the same accessibility and structured thinking to the subject of AI for professionals and entrepreneurs who need to understand the technology without a computer science background. And The Hidden Treasures of Married Life: Seven Things I Wish I Knew Much Earlier reflects Pat's belief that the same discipline, intentionality, and process-thinking that builds professional excellence also builds the relationships that make that excellence worth having.

Pat holds an active Top Secret security clearance from his defense contractor work and is based in the Inland Empire region of Southern California, where he continues to build educational platforms, develop curriculum, and pursue his mission of making rigorous, evidence-based education accessible to every serious learner, whether in a federal compliance office, a college classroom, or a retail trading account.

ALSO BY PATIENCE (PAT) FUZANE

RMF & ATO Readiness: A System for Government Contractors

The definitive practitioner guide to the NIST Risk Management Framework and Authority to Operate process for federal contractors, IT professionals, and cybersecurity practitioners navigating the DoD and civilian agency compliance landscape.

Artificial Intelligence Is Here to Stay, You Better Learn It Now!

A practical, accessible introduction to artificial intelligence for professionals, entrepreneurs, and lifelong learners who need to understand what AI means for their careers, their industries, and their daily decision-making without a computer science background.

The Hidden Treasures of Married Life: Seven Things I Wish I Knew Much Earlier

An honest, experience-driven guide to the principles, habits, and mindset shifts that build a strong, enduring marriage, written for couples at every stage who want to go deeper than surface-level relationship advice.

Stock Trades: From Beginner to Mastery

The complete guide to analytical trading, risk management, and lifelong market mastery. This book. The companion text to StockTradesApp.com.

CONNECT WITH PAT AND THE PLATFORM

StockTradesApp.com: The retail trading terminal featured throughout this book. Free to start. Full Terminal, Watchlist, Paper Trading, Dashboard, AI Screener, Compare tool, Price Alerts, and Learn Hub.

Cert Training Hub: Federal cybersecurity training for RMF, FISMA, and ATO readiness. Visit certtraininghub.com.

Platform Support: support@stocktradesapp.com

PREFACE

"In investing, what is comfortable is rarely profitable."
— Robert Arnott, Research Affiliates

I built StockTradesApp.com because I was frustrated. Not with markets, but with the tools available to ordinary retail investors who wanted to approach those markets seriously.

I had spent years working within one of the most rigorously process-driven environments that exists: federal cybersecurity compliance for defense contractors. In that world, you do not make decisions based on gut feel. You build frameworks. You define risk parameters before you act. You document your reasoning. You review your outcomes honestly against your pre-defined criteria. You iterate based on evidence, not emotion. And you protect the system from catastrophic failure above everything else.

When I looked at the retail trading landscape, I found almost none of that. I found platforms optimized to generate transaction volume, not investor outcomes. I found educational resources that taught technical indicators in isolation from risk management, or that discussed position sizing without connecting it to actual stop-loss discipline. I found no consistent, authoritative framework that walked a serious learner from zero market knowledge to a fully functioning, evidence-based trading practice.

So I built the platform. And then I wrote this book.

The framework in these pages comes from two sources. The first is the accumulated wisdom of the practitioners who built modern trading and investing: Graham and Buffett on fundamental analysis, O'Neil on growth stocks, Murphy on technical analysis, Tharp on position sizing and expectancy, Douglas on trading psychology, Bogle on the honest case for passive investing. Every one of them is cited directly in these pages because every one of them contributed something essential to the framework.

The second source is my own professional background. The systematic risk management, process discipline, and evidence-based decision-making that federal cybersecurity requires are directly applicable to trading. The 1% rule is not different in principle from a maximum acceptable risk threshold in a security compliance framework. A structural stop-loss is not different in principle from a documented control that limits the blast radius of a system compromise. The weekly performance review is not different in principle from a formal after-action report. I designed this book to apply the same discipline I developed in federal cybersecurity to the domain of financial markets, because the discipline is the same discipline.

Several things make this book different from others in the trading education space.

It is honest about difficulty. Trading is genuinely hard. The 70 to 80 percent of retail traders who incur losses are not losing because they are unintelligent. They are losing because they entered a complex, competitive, emotionally demanding domain without adequate preparation. This book prepares you adequately rather than promising shortcuts.

It is evidence-based. Every statistic, every methodology, every psychological framework in these pages is sourced from peer-reviewed research, authoritative practitioner texts, or verifiable platform data. You will find full citations in the References section.

It integrates the analytical and the psychological with equal weight. The most sophisticated analytical framework in the world fails in the hands of a trader who cannot honor a stop-loss. Both matter equally and this book treats them as such.

It is platform-specific in the right way. Every platform callout uses the actual names, buttons, and navigation paths of StockTradesApp.com as verified from the live platform. When I say open the ANALYSIS tab, I mean the specific tab that exists in the Terminal right now. The platform instructions in this book work.

And it is complete. Fifteen chapters cover the full journey from beginner to mastery. This is a curriculum, designed to be read in order, with each chapter building on the chapters before it.

I want to be direct about one more thing. This is an educational book, not a guarantee of investment returns. Markets are genuinely uncertain. Even the best-designed frameworks produce losing trades. The goal of this book is not to eliminate losses. It is to give you the process, the discipline, and the analytical vocabulary to make your wins larger than your losses, your capital more protected than it would be without this framework, and your long-term trajectory pointed in the right direction.

The traders who apply this framework consistently, who do the daily practice, who review their performance honestly, and who maintain the discipline these chapters describe, improve measurably over time. I have seen it. I built the platform to support it. And I wrote this book to accelerate it.

Welcome to the work.

Pat Fuzane, MBA
Inland Empire, California
June 2026

STOCK TRADES, FROM BEGINNER TO MASTERY: A COMPLETE FRAMEWORK FOR ANALYTICAL INVESTING

CHAPTER-BY-CHAPTER SUMMARY

The following summaries provide a concise overview of each chapter's core content and the key skills or frameworks it delivers. Use this section as a quick-reference guide when you want to revisit a specific concept without re-reading the full chapter, or as a navigation tool for identifying where a particular topic is covered.

Chapter 1: The Anatomy of a Stock and the Market Ecosystem

- Defines common stock as fractional ownership in a corporation, with rights to residual assets and earnings
- Explains the primary market (IPOs) and secondary market (NYSE, NASDAQ) distinction
- Covers market participants: retail investors, institutional investors, market makers, and specialists
- Introduces price determination through supply and demand; explains why stocks move
- Covers market capitalization (large, mid, small-cap), major indices (S&P 500, NASDAQ-100, Dow Jones), and bull vs. bear markets
- Introduces the StockTradesApp.com Terminal for the first time; shows how to search a ticker and read basic quote data

Chapter 2: Setting the Mindset and Defining Your Financial Goals

- The DALBAR research on the average investor gap: 6.8% average return vs. market returns, explained by behavioral factors
- Kahneman and Tversky Prospect Theory (1979): loss aversion and its practical consequences for trading decisions
- Trading vs. investing: the spectrum of holding periods and their implications for strategy selection
- The power of compounding: numerical illustration of long-term wealth building across 10, 20, and 30 years

- SMART goal framework applied to financial objectives: specific, measurable, achievable, relevant, and time-bound
- Risk tolerance spectrum: conservative, moderate, and aggressive profiles with their practical portfolio implications
- The Investor Identity Statement exercise: a written framework capturing goals, rules, and behavioral commitments

Chapter 3: Navigating Your First Platform: A Complete Tour of StockTradesApp.com

- Platform philosophy: built to make you a better trader, not to make you trade more frequently
- Six roles framework: Trader, Analyzer, Decider, Tracker, Performer, and Winner, each mapping to a platform section
- Complete account registration walkthrough using exact platform language
- Nine navigation items: Terminal, Dashboard, Screener, Watchlist, Alerts, Compare, Paper, Learn, Admin
- Terminal anatomy: AI signal banner, quote grid, chart with SMA20/SMA50, RSI (14), MACD (12,26,9), five analysis tabs
- Dashboard: equity metrics, performance analytics, SPY benchmark, equity curve, Watchlist Live Signals
- Paper Trading: Order Ticket (BUY/SELL toggle, Symbol, Quantity, Place Order), Positions, Trade History
- Alerts: Crosses Above/Below, checked every 5 minutes during market hours
- AI Screener: natural language input against ~55 curated tickers
- Learn Hub: seven categories, 43 lessons plus Glossary, AI-refreshed content

Chapter 4: The Language of Price: Reading a Stock Quote

- Complete 21-field stock quote annotation using AAPL as the example security
- Bid-ask spread mechanics: why the price you see is not always the price you get
- Market hours: regular session (9:30 AM to 4:00 PM ET), pre-market, and after-hours trading
- Volume analysis: four scenarios (high volume up, high volume down, low volume up, low volume down)
- The 1.5x ADV (Average Daily Volume) threshold for confirming price moves (Murphy)
- 52-week range as a psychological reference point: George and Hwang (2004) Journal of Finance research

- Percentage vs. dollar change: which to use and why percentage is the more meaningful comparison metric
- Dividend basics: ex-dividend date, record date, and their effect on stock price
- Platform callout: reading the Terminal quote grid for every field described in this chapter

Chapter 5: Fundamental Analysis: Evaluating the Business Behind the Ticker

- Three financial statements: income statement (revenues to net income), balance sheet (assets, liabilities, equity), and cash flow statement
- Apple FY2022-2023 income statement as the worked example: 13-row annotated breakdown
- Apple FY2023 balance sheet: full sectioned layout with working capital and debt structure
- Free cash flow: the most important fundamental number for growth company analysis
- 13-ratio reference table: P/E, Forward P/E, PEG, P/S, P/B, EV/EBITDA, ROE, ROA, ROIC, Gross Margin, Net Margin, Debt-to-Equity, Current Ratio
- Peter Lynch's PEG ratio: growth-adjusted valuation that corrects for the P/E's blindness to growth rates
- Intrinsic value and margin of safety: Benjamin Graham's foundational framework
- Six moat types: network effects, switching costs, cost advantages, intangible assets, efficient scale, and regulatory protection
- Five-step fundamental analysis framework: moat, growth, profitability, valuation, and risks

Chapter 6: Technical Analysis: Reading the Story in the Charts

- Dow Theory: the foundational principles of trend analysis and market structure
- Stan Weinstein's four stages: Accumulation (Stage 1), Advancing (Stage 2), Distribution (Stage 3), Declining (Stage 4)
- Candlestick anatomy: open, high, low, close, body, and wicks; history from Munehisa Homma (18th century Japan), introduced to Western markets by Nison (1991)
- 11-pattern candlestick table: Doji, Hammer, Shooting Star, Engulfing patterns, and more
- Support and resistance: definition, psychological basis, and role reversal principle
- Six moving average types: SMA-20, SMA-50, SMA-200, EMA-12, EMA-26, EMA-9
- Golden Cross (SMA-50 crosses above SMA-200) and Death Cross (SMA-50 crosses below SMA-200)

- 9 chart patterns: Head and Shoulders, Inverse H&S, Cup and Handle, Double Top/Bottom, Triangles (ascending, descending, symmetrical)
- RSI (14): Wilder (1978); overbought above 70, oversold below 30
- MACD (12,26,9): Appel; momentum crossover and histogram interpretation
- 9-step pre-trade checklist for every entry decision

Chapter 7: Building Your Watchlist and Conducting Routine Research

- The watchlist as a tiered research pipeline, not a flat list of interesting tickers
- Five sourcing methods: AI Screener, Compare tool (relative strength), earnings season calendars, sector/industry news, personal observation (Peter Lynch's approach)
- CAN SLIM framework: seven criteria (Current earnings, Annual earnings, New product/service, Supply and demand, Leader vs. laggard, Institutional sponsorship, Market direction); AAII named it top-performing strategy 1998-2009
- Three-tier watchlist system: Tier 1 (Ready to Trade), Tier 2 (Under Study), Tier 3 (Watch and Wait)
- Blended Signal usage: OVERVIEW tab (scores), SIGNALS tab (technical breakdown), BLEND tab (component weights), ANALYSIS tab (AI briefing)
- Four categories of financial news by signal quality: company fundamental (highest), macro data, analyst actions, commentary (lowest)
- Tetlock (2005) research on expert forecasting accuracy: marginally better than chance over long horizons
- Daily research routine: pre-market (15 min), active session (alert-driven), evening (15-30 min), weekly (45-60 min)

Chapter 8: Risk Management: The Art of Not Losing Money

- Drawdown recovery asymmetry: a 50% loss requires a 100% gain to recover; a 90% loss requires 900%
- 85% survival rate for 1-2% risk rule traders vs. 88% failure rate for 10% risk traders (QuantVPS, 2025)
- The 1% Rule: never risk more than 1% of total account equity on any single trade; start at 0.5% while learning
- Three-formula position sizing system: Dollar Risk = Account x Risk%, Risk/Share = Entry - Stop, Max Shares = Dollar Risk / Risk Per Share
- Portfolio heat: total combined risk across all open positions; cap at 6% of account equity (Van Tharp)

- Five stop-loss types: Structural (below support), Percentage (O'Neil's 7-8%), Moving Average, ATR Volatility, Time
- Never place stops at round numbers; structural stops only at chart-based levels
- Minimum 2:1 Risk-Reward Ratio before any trade qualifies for entry
- Expectancy formula: (Win Rate x Avg Win) - (Loss Rate x Avg Loss); positive expectancy = sustainable edge
- Maximum daily loss limit: 2-3% of account equity; stop all trading when limit is reached

Chapter 9: Analyzing Your Paper Trading Performance

- Deliberate practice (vs. mere repetition) as the mechanism that produces improvement
- Van Tharp's 30-trade minimum for statistically meaningful metrics; 100-200 trades for reliable edge assessment
- Nine Dashboard metrics: Win Rate, Avg Win/Loss, Profit Factor, Max Drawdown, Sharpe-Like, Realized P&L, SPY Benchmark, Trade Count, Expectancy
- Five-metric cluster analysis: Win Rate + Avg Win/Loss together; Profit Factor + Max Drawdown together; Sharpe + Trade Count together
- Four equity curve patterns: steady upward (ideal), irregular with large drawdowns, flat sideways, volatile with no trend
- Six behavioral patterns and their data signatures: cutting winners too early, holding losers too long, overtrading, revenge trading, FOMO entries, inconsistent sizing
- SPY benchmark comparison: aim to beat SPY return with max drawdown no larger than 1.5x SPY's
- Strategy refinement: change one variable at a time; trade 20 positions before assessing the change
- Seven-step weekly review process; three live trading readiness thresholds

Chapter 10: The Psychology of Live Trading: Managing Emotion When Money Is Real

- Neurological basis of the paper-to-live shift: amygdala threat response, cortisol release, constricted executive thinking
- BIS Behavioural Finance Review: 70-80% of retail traders lose; structured psychological training produces 30% higher survivability
- Seven dimensions of difference between paper and live trading: emotional stake, decision speed, stop compliance, position sizing psychology, news sensitivity, loss aversion expression, recovery time

- NBER research: scant correlation between paper trading and live trading behavior across psychological dimensions
- Six emotional states and their structural defenses: fear of loss, FOMO, greed, overconfidence, despair, anchoring
- Five cognitive biases: confirmation bias, recency bias, sunk cost fallacy, availability bias, gambler's fallacy
- Six psychological infrastructure preparations: written rules, reduced position size (25%), pre-session routine, post-loss cooldown (30 min), updated Investor Identity Statement, return-to-paper protocol
- Losing streak protocol: 2 losses (verify process), 3 (reduce size 50%), 5 (stop for the week), 10 (return to paper)
- Winning streak problem: overconfidence produces exactly the wrong psychological state for the risk environment

Chapter 11: Transitioning to a Live Brokerage Account

- Three readiness thresholds: 50 documented trades, Profit Factor above 1.3 for 4 weeks, zero stop violations in last 20 trades
- SIPC protection: up to $500,000 per customer ($250,000 cash); covers custody of assets, not investment performance
- FINRA registration: verify any broker on BrokerCheck at brokercheck.finra.org
- Seven broker selection criteria: regulatory standing, commissions, platform quality, fractional shares, customer service, interest on cash, style alignment
- Broker comparison: Fidelity and Schwab highest for beginners; Robinhood and Webull for mobile-first; IBKR for experienced cost-focused traders
- Account types: taxable brokerage (recommended for active trading), Traditional IRA, Roth IRA, 401(k)
- Pattern Day Trader rule: four or more day trades in five business days in a margin account triggers $25,000 minimum equity requirement
- Starting capital: $5,000 to $10,000; 1% rule yields $50-$100 risk per trade at these levels
- Six order types: Market, Limit, Stop-Loss (Stop Market), Stop-Limit, Trailing Stop, Good-Till-Cancelled
- Tax events: short-term gains (ordinary income), long-term gains (0/15/20%), wash sale rule, capital loss deduction ($3,000/year)
- First 30 days: Week 1 setup only; Week 2 first trade at 25% size; Weeks 2-3 max two positions; Month-end formal review

Chapter 12: Advanced Horizons: ETFs, Options, and Beyond

- SPIVA research: 92% of actively managed large-cap funds underperformed the S&P 500 over 15 years after fees
- ETF vs. mutual fund: ETFs offer intraday tradability, lower minimums, tax efficiency, daily transparency
- 10-ETF reference table: SPY, VOO, QQQ, VTI, IWM, GLD, TLT, XLK, XLV, DIA with expense ratios and use cases
- Expense ratio compounding: 0.03% vs. 1.0% on $100,000 over 30 years produces $220,000+ difference in terminal value
- Core-satellite framework: 60-80% in passive index ETFs (core), 20-40% in active individual stocks (satellite)
- Sector rotation table: four economic cycle phases and their corresponding sector leaders
- Options warning box: significant risk, OCC and CBOE education required before live options trading
- Options vocabulary table: Call, Put, Strike Price, Expiration, Premium, Covered Call, Protective Put, ITM, OTM with AAPL examples
- Covered call: income generation on existing positions in flat/slowly rising markets; caps upside at strike price
- Protective put: portfolio insurance before high-risk events; cost is the put premium

Chapter 13: The Lifelong Trader: Building a Sustainable Daily Practice

- Five-block daily routine: pre-market (15-20 min), active session (as needed), post-market (15-30 min), weekly deep research (45-60 min), monthly audit (90-120 min)
- Six trading journal entry types: pre-trade documentation, win review, loss review, market observation, pattern recognition, monthly reflection
- Di Stefano et al. (Psychological Science, 2016): structured reflection after practice produces 23% better subsequent performance
- Three levels of continuous education: foundational depth (rereading core texts), domain expansion (new analytical tools), market history (historical cycles)
- 10-book recommended reading list: Graham, O'Neil, Schwager, Douglas, Tharp, Lynch, Bogle, Murphy, Lefevre, Fisher
- Four market regimes: trending bull, choppy sideways, trending bear, high-volatility event-driven; each requiring different approach adjustments
- Five-year development arc: Year 1 (foundation), Year 2 (edge clarification), Year 3 (refinement), Year 4 (maturation), Year 5+ (compounding mastery)
- The primary predictor of development trajectory: consistency of practice, not intelligence or starting capital

Chapter 14: Advanced Strategies: Options, ETF Trading, and Expanding the Toolkit

- Options prerequisites: stock proficiency, position sizing mastery, broker approval (Level 1-3), OCC and CBOE education
- Options approval levels: Level 1 (covered calls, cash-secured puts), Level 2 (long calls/puts), Level 3 (spreads), Level 4 (naked options; avoid)
- Seven options strategies table: Long Call, Long Put, Covered Call, Cash-Secured Put, Protective Put, Bull Call Spread, Bear Put Spread
- Five options Greeks: Delta (price sensitivity), Theta (time decay), Gamma (delta rate of change), Vega (implied volatility sensitivity), Rho (interest rate)
- Three most important Greeks for beginners: Delta (understand position movement), Theta (time works against buyers), Vega (implied volatility crush warning)
- Implied volatility crush: do not buy options in the final week before earnings; the IV premium almost always exceeds the actual move
- Five active ETF trading strategies: index ETF trend following, sector rotation, volatility-adjusted sizing, ETF pair trading via Compare, bond/equity rotation
- 401(k) employer match: the highest guaranteed return available; always maximize before allocating to active trading

Chapter 15: The Mastery Mindset: Trading as a Lifelong Discipline

- Mastery defined: consistent application of a sound process across all market conditions; competence plus character
- Seven mastery principles: Process Precedes Outcome, Humility Is Operational, Losses Are Information, Patience Is a Strategy, Volatility Is Not Risk, The Market Will Always Be There, Continuous Improvement Compounds
- Three compounding engines: Capital (returns on returns), Skill (capability through deliberate practice), Knowledge (each understanding enriching prior base)
- Complete framework integration: Research Layer (Ch. 1-6), Strategy Layer (Ch. 7-9), Transition Layer (Ch. 10-11), Expansion Layer (Ch. 12-14), Mastery Layer (Ch. 15)
- Financial independence as the long-term vision: passive and active investment income sufficient to cover living expenses without employment income
- Letter to Your Future Self exercise: seven prompts covering current assessment, commitments, psychological challenge, five-year vision, and self-encouragement
- Final message: "Go trade well. Review honestly. Improve continuously. Protect your capital."

Table Of Contents

QR Code For Accessing the "https://stocktradesapp.com" WebApp for your practice.

PART I

The Foundation

Zero Knowledge to First Steps

CHAPTER 1

The Anatomy of a Stock & The Market Ecosystem

> *"The stock market is a device for transferring money from the impatient to the patient."*
> — **Warren Buffett**

Every great investor started exactly where you are right now: at the beginning, with more questions than answers, and a healthy mix of curiosity and caution. The stock market can look like an intimidating, fast-moving world full of flashing numbers, cryptic terminology, and financial news that seems designed to confuse rather than inform. This chapter is here to change that.

By the time you finish reading this chapter, you will understand what a stock actually is, why the stock market exists, who the key players are, and how billions of dollars move through the system every single day. More importantly, you will begin to see the market not as a mysterious casino, but as a logical, structured ecosystem built around one simple idea: connecting people who have money to invest with companies that need money to grow.

Let's start at the very beginning; and build from the ground up.

1.1 What Is a Stock, Really?

Before you can trade stocks, you need to understand what you are actually buying when you purchase one. The answer is simpler than most people think.

A stock: also called a share or equity; is a small piece of ownership in a company. When a company decides to sell portions of itself to the public, it divides itself into millions of tiny equal pieces. Each of those pieces is a stock. When you buy a stock, you become a part-owner, or shareholder, of that company.

> **KEY TERM: Stock (Share / Equity)**
> *A unit of ownership in a corporation. Buying one share of a company entitles you to a proportional claim on its assets and earnings. If a company divides itself into 1,000,000 shares and you buy 1,000 of them, you own 0.1% of that company.*

The Ownership Analogy

Imagine your neighbor bakes the most incredible pies in town. Business is booming, but she doesn't have enough money to open a storefront, buy commercial ovens, and hire staff. She has two choices: borrow the money from a bank and pay it back with interest, or invite a group of friends and community members to each contribute money in exchange for a percentage of the future profits.

She chooses the second option. She divides her pie business into 100 equal pieces and sells each piece for $100. If you buy 10 pieces, you own 10% of the pie business. If the business earns $5,000 in profit next year, your 10% stake entitles you to $500 of that profit. If the business becomes incredibly successful and someone offers to buy it for $50,000, your 10% stake is now worth $5,000, which is a $4,000 gain on your original $1,000 investment.

That, in essence, is how stock ownership works. The only differences when it comes to real corporations are scale (millions of shares instead of 100), liquidity (you can sell your shares on an exchange any business day instead of waiting to find a buyer), and complexity (publicly traded companies have legal obligations to report their financial performance).

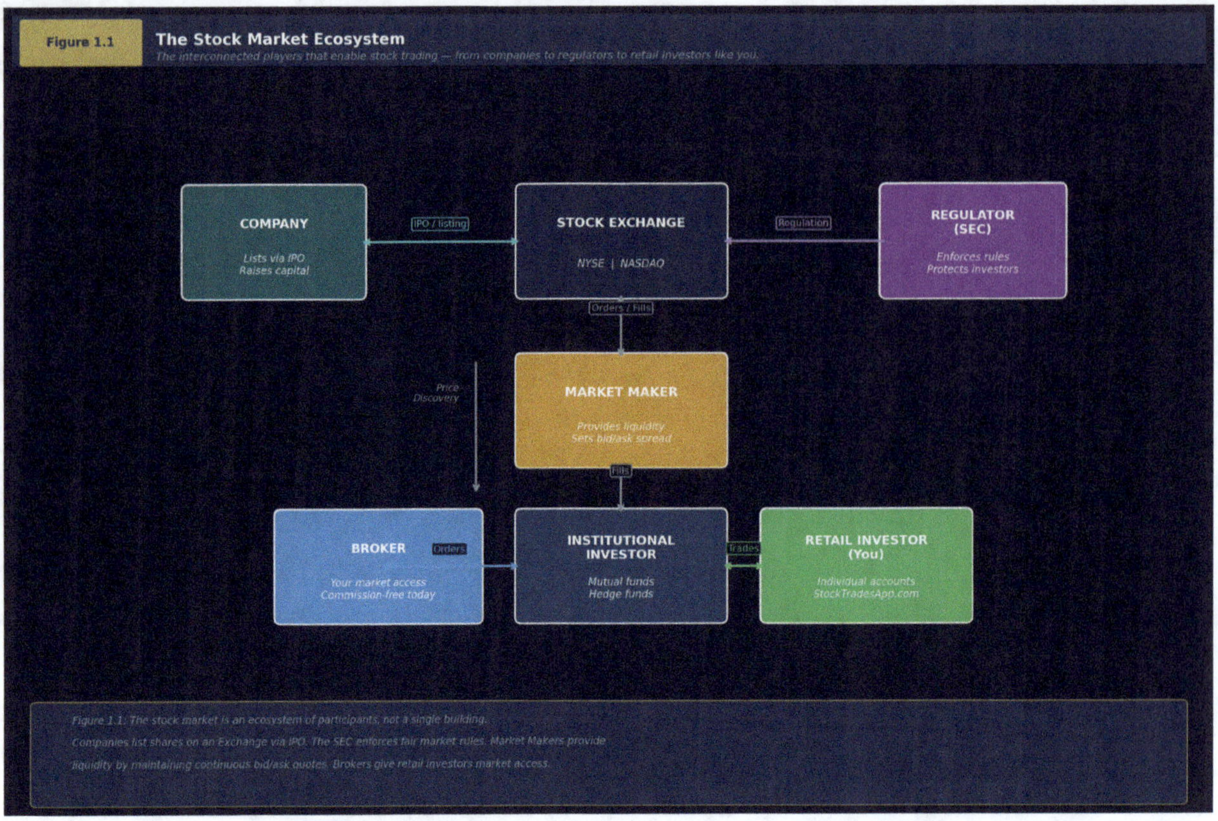

Figure 1.1 - The Stock Market Ecosystem: Exchanges, brokers, market makers, institutional and retail investors; and how they all connect.

Everyday Life	Stock Market Equivalent
Buying a slice of a pie business	Buying shares of a company's stock
The pie business has 100 equal pieces	A company issues millions of shares
You own 10 pieces = 10% of profits	You own 1,000 shares = proportional earnings
Business grows, your slice is worth more	Stock price rises as company succeeds
Business fails, your slice loses value	Stock price falls if company struggles

Two Ways Stocks Make You Money

When you own a stock, there are two primary ways you can profit:

- **The stock price rises above what you paid for it. If you buy a share at $50 and it later trades at $80, your gain is $30 per share. You realize that gain when you sell.** Capital Appreciation:

- **Some companies share a portion of their profits directly with shareholders on a regular basis (usually quarterly). These cash payments are called dividends. A company that pays a $2 annual dividend on a $40 stock has a dividend yield of 5%.** Dividends:

> **DID YOU KNOW?**
> Not every stock pays dividends. Many fast-growing technology companies like Amazon in its early years; reinvest all of their profits back into the business rather than paying shareholders. Investors who buy these stocks are betting entirely on capital appreciation. Mature, stable companies like Coca-Cola and Johnson & Johnson, on the other hand, have paid consistent dividends for decades.

1.2 Why Do Companies Sell Stock?

Understanding why companies issue stock in the first place will help you think about the market as a two-sided ecosystem, not just a place where traders swap numbers, but a fundamental mechanism that fuels economic growth.

When a private company wants to raise large amounts of capital to expand, it can take a significant step called an Initial Public Offering, or IPO. During an IPO, the company works with an investment bank to offer shares of itself to the general public for the first time. The money raised goes directly to the company and is used for purposes like building new facilities, hiring employees, acquiring other companies, paying down debt, or funding research and development.

> **KEY TERM: Initial Public Offering (IPO)**
> *The process by which a private company offers shares of itself to the public for the first time. After an IPO, the company's shares are listed on a stock exchange and can be freely bought and sold by investors.*

Once a company has completed its IPO and its shares are listed on an exchange, the company itself does not receive money from the day-to-day trading of its stock between investors. If you buy 100 shares of Apple from another investor on the NASDAQ exchange, that money goes to the seller, not to Apple. The company already received its capital during the IPO. What the stock price does affect, however, is the company's ability to raise additional capital in the future, compensate employees with stock-based options, and make acquisitions using its stock as currency.

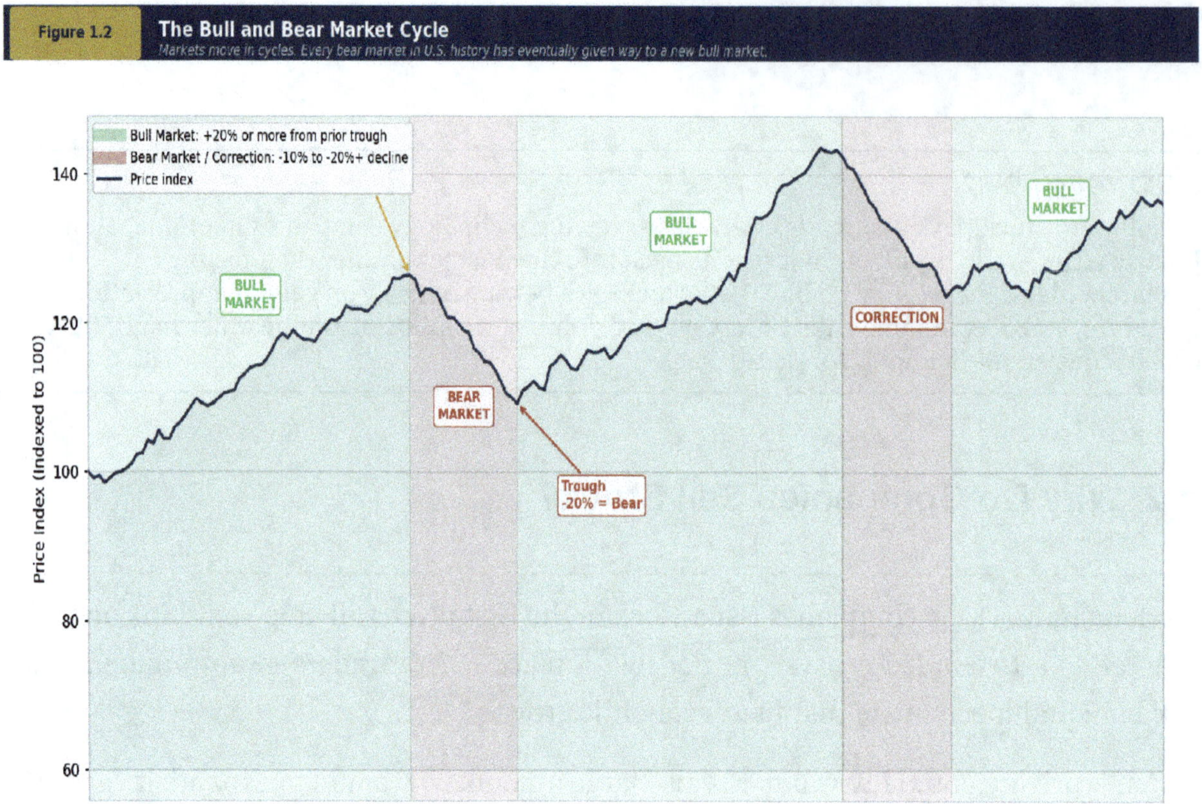

Figure 1.2 - The Bull and Bear Market Cycle: Every bear market in U.S. history has given way to a new bull market. The S&P 500 has been positive over every rolling 20-year period in history.

A Company's Perspective: Equity vs. Debt

Companies have two fundamental options when raising capital: issuing equity (selling stock) or taking on debt (borrowing money through loans or bonds). Each has trade-offs:

- **No repayment obligation. No interest payments. But existing owners give up a percentage of control and future profits.** Equity Financing (Selling Stock):
- **Company retains full ownership. But must repay principal plus interest regardless of how business performs. Too much debt can cripple a company during hard times.** Debt Financing (Borrowing):

Most large companies use a mix of both. Understanding this balance, called a company's capital structure, becomes important when you conduct fundamental analysis in Chapter 6.

1.3 The Stock Market Ecosystem: Who Are the Players?

The stock market is not a single building or a single computer. It is an interconnected ecosystem of participants, each playing a specific role in ensuring that buyers can find sellers and that prices reflect the most current available information. Let's meet the key players.

Player	Role	Analogy
Stock Exchange	Provides the regulated marketplace where stocks are listed and traded	The shopping mall where stores (companies) operate
Broker / Brokerage	Acts as your agent to buy and sell stocks on your behalf	The personal shopper who goes into the mall for you
Market Maker	Stands ready to buy or sell a stock at any time, providing liquidity	The currency exchange booth always open for business
Institutional Investor	Large organizations (mutual funds, pension funds, hedge funds) trading in enormous volume	The bulk wholesaler buying pallets, not single items
Retail Investor	Individual investors like you trading for personal accounts	The individual shopper browsing the aisles
Regulator (SEC)	U.S. Securities and Exchange Commission: enforces rules that protect investors and ensure fair markets	The mall security and management office

The Major U.S. Stock Exchanges

When people talk about "the stock market," they often mean one of two primary U.S. exchanges:

- **The oldest and largest stock exchange in the world by market capitalization, founded in 1792. The NYSE is known for listing many large, established companies like Coca-Cola, JPMorgan Chase, and ExxonMobil. It operates a hybrid model combining electronic trading**

with a physical trading floor in lower Manhattan. New York Stock Exchange (NYSE):

- **Founded in 1971 as the world's first fully electronic stock exchange. The NASDAQ became the exchange of choice for technology companies and is home to giants like Apple, Microsoft, Amazon, Google (Alphabet), and Meta. It operates entirely electronically with no physical trading floor.** NASDAQ:

DID YOU KNOW?

There are actually more than a dozen stock exchanges operating in the United States, though NYSE and NASDAQ account for the vast majority of trading volume. Beyond the U.S., major exchanges include the London Stock Exchange (LSE), the Tokyo Stock Exchange (TSE), the Shanghai Stock Exchange (SSE), and the Hong Kong Stock Exchange (HKEX). Collectively, the world's stock markets represent over $100 trillion in market capitalization.

The Role of the Broker

Individual investors cannot walk onto the floor of the NYSE and start buying stocks. Retail investors access the market through a licensed intermediary called a broker or brokerage firm. Historically, brokers charged significant commissions for every trade. Today, thanks to the rise of technology and competition, most online brokers; including those compatible with StockTradesApp.com, offer commission-free trading on stocks and ETFs.

When you are ready to transition to live trading in Chapter 13, we will walk through exactly how to evaluate and open a brokerage account. For now, understanding that a broker is simply your access point to the market is sufficient.

🖥 PLATFORM FEATURE: Platform Overview, stocktradesapp.com

StockTradesApp.com is designed to be your all-in-one trading education and practice environment. Throughout this book, every concept you learn will be directly tied to a feature or tool within the platform.

In Chapter 3, we will take a full guided tour of the platform. For now, visit stocktradesapp.com and take a moment to explore the homepage. Notice how the platform is organized around three core pillars: Learn, Practice (Paper Trade), and Analyze.

This three-pillar design mirrors the three stages of your journey through this book: building knowledge, practicing safely, and developing mastery.

1.4 How Stock Prices Are Determined

One of the most common questions beginners ask is: who decides what a stock is worth? The answer is both simple and profound. Stock prices are determined by supply and demand which is the same fundamental economic force that determines the price of everything from a cup of coffee to a house.

At any given moment, there are investors who want to buy a particular stock (demand) and investors who want to sell it (supply). The price at which a buyer and a seller agree to complete a transaction becomes the market price for that stock at that moment. Every time a trade is executed, a new price is set.

KEY TERM: Market Price
The most recent price at which a stock was bought and sold. The market price fluctuates continuously throughout the trading day (9:30 AM to 4:00 PM Eastern Time) as new trades are executed. It represents the collective, real-time opinion of all market participants about what that company is currently worth.

What Moves Stock Prices?

Stock prices are constantly moving because new information is constantly becoming available. Broadly speaking, stock prices are influenced by:

- **Earnings reports, new product launches, revenue growth, and profit margins. When a company reports earnings that beat Wall Street expectations, its stock often jumps. When it misses expectations, it often falls.** Company Performance:
- **Interest rates, inflation, unemployment data, and GDP growth all affect investor sentiment and the broader market. When the Federal Reserve raises interest rates, for example, it often puts downward pressure on stock prices.** Economic Conditions:
- **A breakthrough in artificial intelligence lifts tech stocks. A new regulation tightens margins for pharmaceutical companies. Events**

within a sector can move entire groups of related stocks simultaneously. Industry Trends:

- **Markets are driven by human emotion as much as by logic. Fear, greed, optimism, and panic all move prices in ways that sometimes defy fundamental value. Understanding this psychological dimension becomes crucial in Part IV of this book.** Investor Sentiment:
- **Global events: pandemics, wars, elections, trade agreements; can send shockwaves through markets almost instantaneously.** News and Geopolitical Events:

An important concept to embrace early is that stock prices reflect expectations about the future, not a verdict on the past. When investors buy a stock at today's price, they are making a bet that the company will be worth more in the future than it is right now. This forward-looking nature of markets is why a company can report record profits and still see its stock fall; if those profits were already 'priced in' and the market was expecting even better results.

REAL-WORLD EXAMPLE

In February 2022, Meta Platforms (parent company of Facebook) reported its first-ever quarterly decline in daily active users. Even though the company was still enormously profitable, the stock fell more than 26% in a single day thereby erasing over $230 billion in market value. The market had priced in continued user growth. When reality fell short of expectations, investors sold aggressively. This single event remains one of the largest single-day market cap losses in U.S. stock market history.

1.5 Market Capitalization: Sizing Up a Company

Not all stocks are created equal. One of the most important ways investors categorize stocks is by market capitalization which is commonly called market cap. Market cap tells you the total market value of a company's outstanding shares.

The formula is straightforward:

```
Market Cap = Share Price × Total Shares Outstanding
```

So if a company has 10 million shares outstanding and each share is trading at $50, the company's market cap is $500 million.

KEY TERM: Market Capitalization (Market Cap)
The total market value of a company's outstanding shares of stock. Calculated by multiplying the current share price by the total number of shares outstanding. Market cap is one of the most widely used indicators of a company's size and is used to categorize stocks into groups like large-cap, mid-cap, and small-cap.

The Market Cap Categories

- **The largest companies in the world. Examples include Apple, Microsoft, Amazon, and Alphabet (Google). These are typically stable, globally recognized businesses.** Mega-Cap (Over $200 Billion):
- **Well-established companies with significant market presence. Generally considered relatively stable investments with lower volatility. Examples: Nike, McDonald's, Goldman Sachs.** Large-Cap ($10B – $200B):
- **Companies that have moved beyond the startup phase but still have meaningful growth potential. They carry more risk than large-caps but potentially more upside.** Mid-Cap ($2B – $10B):
- **Smaller, often younger companies with high growth potential but also higher volatility and risk. These stocks require more research and carry greater uncertainty.** Small-Cap ($300M – $2B):
- **Very small companies. Often thinly traded with limited analyst coverage. The highest risk category and appropriate only for experienced investors who conduct extensive due diligence.** Micro-Cap (Under $300M):

As a beginner building your first paper trading portfolio on StockTradesApp.com, you will primarily work with large-cap and mega-cap stocks. These companies are well-covered by analysts, have abundant historical data, and tend to move in more predictable patterns and making them ideal teaching tools as you develop your skills.

1.6 Market Indices: The Scoreboard of the Stock Market

You have almost certainly heard a news anchor say something like: 'The Dow was up 300 points today, while the S&P 500 closed at a record high.' But what exactly are the Dow and the S&P 500? They are market indices, and understanding them is essential for any trader or investor.

A stock market index is a hypothetical portfolio of securities representing a particular market segment. Indices are used to benchmark performance; both of the overall market and of individual investment portfolios. If your portfolio gained 8% last year but the S&P 500 gained 15%, you underperformed the benchmark.

- **Often simply called 'the Dow,' this is the oldest and most widely cited U.S. stock market index. It tracks 30 large, publicly owned companies considered representative of the U.S. economy. Despite its fame, the Dow tracks only 30 stocks and is considered a narrower measure of market health.** The Dow Jones Industrial Average (DJIA):
- **The Standard & Poor's 500 tracks the 500 largest publicly traded companies in the U.S. by market cap. It is widely considered the best single gauge of large-cap U.S. equity performance and is the benchmark that most professional fund managers are judged against. When financial professionals refer to 'the market,' they are usually referring to the S&P 500.** The S&P 500:
- **Tracks over 3,000 stocks listed on the NASDAQ exchange, with a heavy weighting toward technology companies. When tech stocks are booming or crashing, the NASDAQ Composite reflects that dramatically.** The NASDAQ Composite:
- **Tracks 2,000 small-cap U.S. stocks. It is used as a benchmark for smaller company performance and is often watched as an indicator of domestic economic health.** The Russell 2000:

PLATFORM FEATURE: Checking Market Indices on stocktradesapp.com

StockTradesApp.com displays real-time index data for the S&P 500, NASDAQ Composite, and Dow Jones directly on the main dashboard.

When you log in, you'll see the current level of each major index, the day's change in points, and the percentage change. This snapshot gives you an immediate pulse of overall market conditions before you examine any individual stock.

Practice: Each morning before any trading session, begin by checking the index panel. Is the broader market trending up or down? This context should always inform your individual stock decisions.

1.7 Bull Markets, Bear Markets, and Market Cycles

The stock market does not move in a straight line. It moves in cycles, alternating between prolonged periods of rising prices and prolonged periods of falling prices. Understanding these cycles will help you maintain perspective and discipline no matter what the market is doing.

- **A period of sustained rising stock prices, typically defined as a rise of 20% or more from a recent low. Bull markets are characterized by investor optimism, economic expansion, and increased trading activity. The longest bull market in U.S. history ran from March 2009 to February 2020; over 11 years of sustained gains following the 2008 financial crisis.** Bull Market:
- **A period of sustained falling stock prices, defined as a decline of 20% or more from a recent high. Bear markets are often accompanied by economic slowdowns or recessions, rising unemployment, and widespread investor pessimism. While frightening to experience, bear markets are a normal part of the market cycle, and historically, every bear market has eventually given way to a new bull market.** Bear Market:
- **A shorter-term decline of 10% to 20% from a recent high. Corrections are more frequent than bear markets and are considered a healthy, normal part of market behavior. They often represent buying opportunities for long-term investors.** Market Correction:
- **A period during which prices move within a relatively narrow range, neither advancing nor declining significantly. This often occurs as the market 'digests' recent moves and investors await new catalysts.** Consolidation / Sideways Market:

THE LONG VIEW

Despite crashes, corrections, bear markets, recessions, wars, pandemics, and every other catastrophe the 20th and 21st centuries have produced, the long-term direction of the U.S. stock market has always been upward. The S&P 500 has delivered an average annual return of approximately 10% per year over the past century (before inflation). This historical resilience is a powerful argument for patient, long-term investing; a theme we will return to throughout this book.

1.8 The Beginner's Jargon Decoder

Every field has its own language, and the stock market is no exception. Before you move into deeper territory in the chapters ahead, here is a quick-reference glossary of the most common terms you will encounter as a beginning trader. These definitions will expand throughout the book, but having them in plain English from the start will make everything that follows much clearer.

Term	Plain-English Definition
Ticker Symbol	A unique abbreviation used to identify a publicly traded company on an exchange. Apple is AAPL. Tesla is TSLA. Microsoft is MSFT.
Portfolio	The collection of all investments (stocks, ETFs, bonds, cash) owned by an investor.
Volatility	A measure of how dramatically a stock's price fluctuates. A highly volatile stock can swing 5–10% or more in a single day. Lower volatility stocks move more slowly and predictably.
Liquidity	How easily and quickly a stock can be bought or sold without significantly affecting its price. Large-cap stocks like Apple are highly liquid. Micro-cap stocks may have very limited liquidity.
Blue Chip Stock	A share of a large, well-established, financially sound company with a long track record of reliable performance. Examples include Johnson & Johnson, Procter & Gamble, and JPMorgan Chase.
Sector	A broad grouping of companies that operate in similar areas of the economy. The eleven primary S&P 500 sectors include Technology, Healthcare, Financials, Consumer Discretionary, and Energy.
52-Week High / Low	The highest and lowest prices at which a stock has traded during the past 52 weeks. These levels often act as psychological benchmarks and areas of support or resistance.
Volume	The total number of shares of a stock that are bought and sold during a given time period (usually a single trading day). High volume on a price move signals conviction; low volume may suggest weakness.
Spread	The difference between the highest price a buyer is willing to pay (bid) and the lowest price a seller is willing to accept (ask). A tight spread indicates a liquid market; a wide spread suggests low liquidity.
Going Long	Buying a stock with the expectation that its price will rise. The standard form of stock investing.

Term	Plain-English Definition
Going Short (Short Selling)	Borrowing shares and selling them, hoping to buy them back later at a lower price and profit from the decline. An advanced strategy covered in later chapters.
Portfolio Diversification	Spreading investments across different stocks, sectors, and asset classes to reduce the risk that any single investment can devastate the entire portfolio.

1.9 Your First Steps on StockTradesApp.com

This book is not just a reading experience, but, it is a doing experience. Every chapter you complete will be paired with hands-on practice inside StockTradesApp.com. The platform is specifically designed to align with your progression through these pages, giving you a safe, risk-free environment to apply every concept before real money is ever involved.

Here is what you should do right now, before moving to Chapter 2:

1. Visit stocktradesapp.com and create your free account. The registration process takes less than two minutes.
2. Once logged in, spend 10 minutes exploring the platform without any objective. Just click around, read the labels, and get a feel for the layout. You don't need to understand everything yet. This is just your first orientation.
3. Find the Paper Trading section of the platform. You will see a simulated account loaded with virtual capital. This is your sandbox and your consequence-free practice environment. We will put it to full use starting in Chapter 4.
4. Locate the Market Overview dashboard. Notice how it displays the major indices (S&P 500, NASDAQ, Dow Jones), sector performance, and top movers for the day. Bookmark this page. You will check it every morning.

PLATFORM FEATURE: Chapter 1 Platform Exercise

STEP 1: After creating your account, use the platform's search bar to look up three companies you are personally familiar with as a consumer. This might be Apple (AAPL), Nike (NKE), Amazon (AMZN), or any company whose products or services you use regularly.

STEP 2: For each company, note three things: the current stock price, the market cap category (large-cap, mega-cap, etc.), and whether the stock is listed on the NYSE or NASDAQ.

STEP 3: Check whether the day's broader market (as shown by the S&P 500 index) is up or down. Do the stocks you looked up appear to be moving in the same direction as the broader market? This relationship, between individual stocks and the overall market, is something you will study in depth as you progress through this book.

Record your observations in a notebook or digital journal. This trading journal will become one of your most valuable tools throughout your journey.

Chapter 1 Summary

You have covered a remarkable amount of ground in this opening chapter. Here is what you now understand that you did not before you started:

- A stock is a unit of ownership in a company. When you buy shares, you become a part-owner and benefit from the company's growth through capital appreciation and dividends.
- Companies sell stock to raise capital for growth. The Initial Public Offering (IPO) is the process by which a private company goes public for the first time.
- The stock market ecosystem includes exchanges (NYSE, NASDAQ), brokers, market makers, institutional investors, retail investors, and regulators. Each plays a specific role in keeping markets liquid, fair, and efficient.
- Stock prices are set by supply and demand and reflect the collective, real-time expectations of all market participants about a company's future value.
- Market capitalization categorizes companies by size: mega-cap, large-cap, mid-cap, small-cap, and micro-cap. Each category carries different risk and reward characteristics.
- Market indices like the S&P 500, NASDAQ Composite, and Dow Jones Industrial Average serve as benchmarks for overall market performance.
- Markets move in cycles: bull markets, bear markets, and corrections are all normal parts of the long-term investing landscape.

CHAPTER 2

Setting the Mindset & Defining Your Financial Goals

"The investor's chief problem (and even his worst enemy), is likely to be himself."

— **Benjamin Graham, The Intelligent Investor (1949)**

Chapter 1 gave you the architecture of the stock market: what stocks are, who the players are, and how prices move. That was the blueprint of the building. This chapter is about something more fundamental because it is about you. Because before you place a single trade, even a paper trade, you need to understand the investor sitting at the keyboard.

The uncomfortable truth that most beginner trading books skip past is this: the stock market is one of the few arenas in life where intelligence, education, and hard work do not automatically translate into success. Brilliant people lose fortunes in the market every year. Meanwhile, patient, disciplined, ordinary investors quietly accumulate life-changing wealth over decades. The difference is rarely their stock-picking ability. The difference is almost always their psychology.

In this chapter, we will explore the science of investor psychology, the critical difference between trading and investing, how to define your personal financial goals with precision, and how to understand your true risk tolerance before the market tests it for you. This is the chapter that will save you from your future self.

2.1 The Psychology Gap: Why Smart People Lose Money

Let's begin with a number that should stop you in your tracks.

6.8%

The annual performance gap between what the S&P 500 delivered and what the average individual investor actually earned, over a 30-year period. The market returned 10.5% annually. Individual investors averaged just 3.7%.

Source: DALBAR Inc., Quantitative Analysis of Investor Behavior (30-Year Study)

According to research conducted by DALBAR Inc., a leading financial research firm known for its Quantitative Analysis of Investor Behavior, the S&P 500 generated average annual returns of approximately 10.5% over a 30-year period. Yet during that same period, the average individual equity investor earned just 3.7% annually. That 6.8 percentage point gap represents more than $1.2 million in foregone wealth for a typical investor over three decades. The market was willing to make them wealthy. They got in their own way.

The market did not fail these investors. Their own psychology did. They bought high when optimism was at its peak and sold low when fear was at its worst. They chased momentum stocks after the gains had already been captured. They held onto losing positions too long, hoping they would recover, and sold winning positions too early, afraid of giving back gains. These are not mistakes made by unintelligent people. They are predictable, documented, scientifically understood patterns of human behavior that emerge when money is on the line.

> *"Investment is 80% psychology."*
> — **Credit Suisse Securities (USA) Research**, *Behavioral Finance: The Psychology of Investing*

This insight from research by Credit Suisse Securities points to a foundational truth: technical knowledge accounts for only a fraction of investment success. The rest is the discipline to apply that knowledge consistently, especially under stress. This book will teach you both; but understanding the psychological dimension first is not optional. It is the prerequisite for everything that follows.

The Science Behind the Mistake: Prospect Theory

In 1979, behavioral economists Daniel Kahneman and Amos Tversky published one of the most consequential papers in the history of economics: Prospect Theory: An Analysis of Decision Under Risk. Their research, for which Kahneman received the

Nobel Prize in Economics in 2002, revealed something profound and unsettling about human decision-making.

> *"Losses loom larger than gains. The pain of losing $1,000 could only be compensated by the pleasure of earning $2,000."*
> **— Daniel Kahneman & Amos Tversky**, *Prospect Theory: An Analysis of Decision Under Risk, Econometrica (1979)*

Kahneman and Tversky demonstrated through controlled experiments that human beings do not evaluate gains and losses symmetrically. We feel the pain of a loss approximately twice as intensely as we feel the pleasure of an equivalent gain. This phenomenon, called loss aversion, is not a character flaw or a sign of weakness. It is hardwired into human cognition, likely an evolutionary adaptation that helped our ancestors survive by avoiding threats more urgently than they pursued rewards.

The problem is that in the stock market, loss aversion becomes a liability. It causes investors to hold losing stocks far too long ("I can't sell now, I'd be locking in a loss"), to sell winning stocks too quickly ("I'd better take my profit before it disappears"), and to abandon diversified long-term strategies during downturns precisely when staying the course would be most beneficial. These behaviors have names in behavioral finance:

- **The Disposition Effect:** The tendency to sell winning investments too early and hold onto losing investments too long, driven by the asymmetric emotional weight of gains versus losses. First documented by researchers Shefrin and Statman (1985)
- **Recency Bias:** Overweighting recent events when making decisions about the future. Investors who experienced the 2008 financial crisis became overly pessimistic about equities for years afterward, even as the market staged one of its greatest bull runs in history.
- **Overconfidence Bias:** Research consistently shows that investors overestimate the precision of their own predictions and the quality of their own information. A landmark study by Barber and Odean (2000) found that the most active traders; typically the most confident, underperformed the market by an average of 6.5% per year.
- **Herd Behavior:** The tendency to follow the crowd rather than independent analysis. As economist John Maynard Keynes observed, it is often professionally safer to fail conventionally than to succeed unconventionally because this is a dynamic that drives bubbles and panics alike.

BEHAVIORAL FINANCE: A BRIEF HISTORY

The field of behavioral finance emerged in the 1970s and 1980s as economists and psychologists began to challenge the dominant theory that markets are populated by perfectly rational actors who always make optimal decisions (the "efficient market hypothesis").

The Nobel Prize in Economics has been awarded to behavioral finance pioneers three times: to Daniel Kahneman in 2002 for Prospect Theory, to Robert Shiller in 2013 for his work identifying irrational exuberance in financial markets, and to Richard Thaler in 2017 for his work on mental accounting and nudge theory.

Their collective work established that markets are made up of human beings with consistent, predictable psychological biases; and that understanding those biases is as important as understanding financial statements.

The First Rule of the Self-Aware Investor

Understanding your own psychological tendencies is not enough. You must build systems that protect you from yourself before the market creates conditions that trigger those tendencies. This is why, throughout this book, you will build trading rules, position sizing frameworks, and journaling practices; not because they are bureaucratic formalities, but because they are the structural safeguards that keep discipline in place when emotion is screaming at you to act irrationally.

> *"Investing isn't about beating others at their game. It's about controlling yourself at your own game."*
>
> — **Benjamin Graham**, *The Intelligent Investor; the foundational text of value investing, first published 1949*

2.2 Trading vs. Investing: Understanding the Difference

One of the most important questions you need to answer before touching StockTradesApp.com is: what kind of market participant do you want to be? The answer will shape every decision you make about strategy, time commitment, risk tolerance, and financial goals. The two primary approaches namely, trading and investing, are fundamentally different philosophies, not just different time horizons.

The Investor: Thinking in Years and Decades

An investor buys stakes in businesses with the expectation of holding them long enough to benefit from the company's underlying growth. Investors study fundamentals; earnings, revenue, competitive position, management quality; and they are largely indifferent to short-term price fluctuations. Their edge is patience and the power of compounding.

The prototype of this approach is Warren Buffett, who has held some of his core positions for decades. His famous maxim, "Our favorite holding period is forever", captures the investing mindset perfectly. Investors do not try to predict what a stock will do next week. They try to understand what a business will be worth over the next decade.

> *"My wealth has come from a combination of living in America, some lucky genes, and compound interest."*
> — **Warren Buffett**, *Berkshire Hathaway Annual Shareholder Letter*

The Trader: Thinking in Minutes, Days, and Weeks

A trader seeks to profit from shorter-term price movements, often using technical analysis such as the study of price charts, volume, and momentum indicators; rather than fundamental analysis of business quality. Trading strategies include day trading (all positions opened and closed within a single market day), swing trading (holding positions for days to weeks), and position trading (holding for weeks to months).

Trading requires more active attention, faster decision-making, and a higher tolerance for frequent losses offset by larger gains. Professional traders typically expect to be wrong on a significant percentage of their trades, but their risk management ensures that winning trades generate enough profit to more than cover the losses.

The Hybrid Approach: Where Most Investors Live

Most serious market participants are neither pure investors nor pure traders. They maintain a core long-term portfolio of carefully selected stocks and ETFs held for months or years, while also allocating a smaller portion of their capital to shorter-term trades when high-probability setups present themselves. This hybrid model allows for the wealth-building power of long-term compounding while still capturing shorter-term opportunities.

This book is structured to serve both approaches. The foundational chapters (1–6) build universal knowledge that every market participant needs regardless of style. The strategy chapters (7–11) help you identify and refine your personal approach. By Chapter 10, you will have enough experience in the StockTradesApp.com simulator to know instinctively which style suits your personality and schedule.

🖥 PLATFORM FEATURE: Trading vs. Investing Settings on stocktradesapp.com

StockTradesApp.com supports both trading and investing approaches within its paper trading simulator. When you set up your paper trading account, you will be prompted to select a primary approach: Short-Term Trading, Swing Trading, or Long-Term Investing.

This selection customizes your dashboard to surface relevant tools because traders see more technical chart indicators and order type options prominently; long-term investors see more fundamental data, dividend tracking, and portfolio growth projections.

You can switch between modes at any time. In fact, we recommend experimenting with both approaches in your paper trading account before committing to a primary style with real capital.

2.3 The Power of Compounding: Time Is Your Greatest Asset

Albert Einstein is widely credited with calling compound interest "the eighth wonder of the world. He who understands it, earns it, but, he who doesn't, pays it." While researchers at Quote Investigator note that no verified primary source confirms Einstein said this, the mathematical truth it captures is beyond dispute. Compounding is the mechanism by which patient investors build extraordinary wealth from ordinary monthly contributions.

Compounding is simple in principle: your returns generate returns. If you invest $10,000 and earn 10% in Year 1, you have $11,000. In Year 2, if you earn another 10%, you earn it on $11,000; not the original $10,000. You earn $1,100 instead of $1,000. That extra $100 is compounding at work. It seems trivial in Year 2. Over 30 or 40 years, it becomes the dominant driver of your wealth.

> *"The nature of compound interest is that it behaves like a snowball of sticky snow. The trick is to have a very long hill, which means either starting very young or living to be very old."*
> — **Warren Buffett**, *The Snowball: Warren Buffett and the Business of Life by Alice Schroeder (2008)*

The Cost of Waiting: A Concrete Illustration

The following table illustrates the profound impact that starting age has on long-term wealth accumulation. All scenarios assume the same $300 monthly investment and a 7% average annual return which is a conservative estimate below the historical average of the S&P 500.

Starting Age	Monthly Investment	Total Contributed	Value at Age 65 (7% avg.)	Compounding Gain
Age 25	$300/month	$144,000	$913,000	**+$769,000**
Age 35	$300/month	$108,000	$454,000	**+$346,000**
Age 45	$300/month	$72,000	$189,000	**+$117,000**
Age 55	$300/month	$36,000	$59,000	**+$23,000**

Assumes 7% average annual return, compounded monthly. Hypothetical illustration for educational purposes only.

The numbers are striking. An investor who begins at age 25 and invests $300 per month ends up with more than $913,000 by retirement at 65, despite contributing only $144,000 over that period. The remaining $769,000 is pure compounding. An investor who waits until age 45; just 20 years later, ends up with less than $189,000, having contributed only $72,000 less. The cost of those 20 years of delay is not $72,000. It is $724,000.

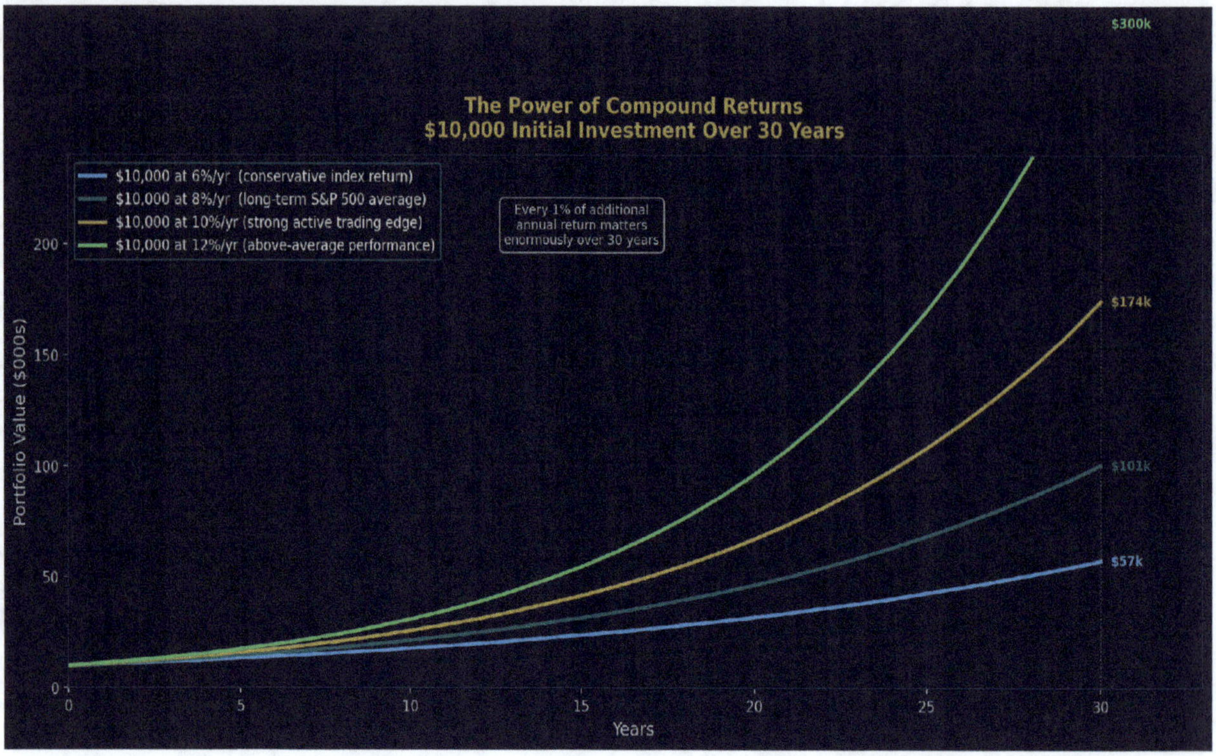

Figure 2.3 — The Power of Compound Returns: A $10,000 investment at four different annual return rates over 30 years.

This is why; regardless of whether you ultimately prefer trading or investing, every dollar you start working in the market earlier rather than later has a compounding value that is almost impossible to recapture later in life.

> **WARREN BUFFETT AND THE COMPOUNDING TIMELINE**
>
> Over 99% of Warren Buffett's wealth was accumulated after his 50th birthday, not because he became a better investor in his fifties, but because the compounding snowball he had been building since age 11 had finally reached the steep part of the hill.
>
> Buffett bought his first stock at age 11 and had accumulated approximately $1 million by age 30. At 93 years old, his net worth exceeds $130 billion. The mathematics of compounding, not a change in strategy, explains the extraordinary wealth created in his later years.
>
> This is the most powerful argument for beginning your investment journey as early as possible; not because you need to become Warren Buffett, but because even a fraction of that compounding effect, applied consistently over decades, produces life-changing results.

2.4 Defining Your Financial Goals with Precision

One of the most consistent mistakes beginners make is entering the stock market with a vague goal: "I want to make money." That is not a goal. It is a wish. Effective financial goal-setting requires specificity, time horizons, and an honest accounting of your current financial position. Without clear goals, every market move will feel equally relevant, and you will be at the mercy of noise, headlines, and emotion.

Effective financial goals follow what financial planners call the SMART framework: Specific, Measurable, Achievable, Relevant, and Time-bound. "I want to grow my wealth" is not a SMART goal. "I want to build a $500,000 investment portfolio within 20 years by investing $800 per month in a diversified mix of large-cap stocks and index ETFs" is a SMART goal.

> **KEY TERM: SMART Financial Goal**
> *A goal that is Specific (clearly defined), Measurable (quantified in dollars and percentages), Achievable (realistic given income, expenses, and time horizon), Relevant (aligned with your life priorities), and Time-bound (with a clear deadline or milestone schedule). SMART goals transform vague financial ambition into an actionable investment plan.*

The Three Tiers of Financial Goals

Most investors benefit from organizing their goals into three distinct tiers based on time horizon. Each tier carries different risk implications and calls for different investment strategies.

- **Short-Term Goals (0–3 Years):** Emergency fund, debt elimination, down payment on a vehicle, travel savings. Money needed within 3 years should generally NOT be in the stock market, which can be volatile in the short term. High-yield savings accounts and short-term certificates of deposit (CDs) are more appropriate.
- **Medium-Term Goals (3–10 Years):** Down payment on a home, funding a business, education expenses. These goals can tolerate moderate risk. A balanced mix of stocks and bonds, shifting more conservative as the deadline approaches, is a common approach.
- **Long-Term Goals (10+ Years):** Retirement, generational wealth, financial independence. Long time horizons can absorb market volatility and benefit most from equity investing. Historical data strongly supports higher stock allocations for goals more than 10 years away.

THE EMERGENCY FUND RULE IS A NON-NEGOTIABLE PREREQUISITE

Before you invest a single dollar in the stock market; even in paper trading with an eye toward eventual live trading, financial experts universally agree on one prerequisite: a fully funded emergency fund.

An emergency fund is 3 to 6 months of essential living expenses held in a liquid, insured account (such as a high-yield savings account). This fund serves as the financial buffer that prevents you from being forced to sell investments during a market downturn to cover unexpected expenses; a scenario that turns temporary paper losses into permanent realized losses.

The Certified Financial Planner Board of Standards recommends that investors assess emergency fund adequacy before allocating capital to higher-risk assets. This is not optional. It is the foundation upon which every other financial goal is built.

A Sample Financial Goals Framework

The table below illustrates how a disciplined investor might structure multiple concurrent financial goals across different time horizons. Use this as a model to build your own framework which is adapted to your income, expenses, and personal priorities.

Financial Goal	Target Amount	Time Horizon	Monthly Savings Needed	Priority
Emergency Fund (3–6 months expenses)	$15,000	18 months	$833	**HIGH**
Down Payment on Home	$60,000	5 years	$1,000	**HIGH**
Retirement (via brokerage + 401k)	$1,200,000	30 years	$1,100*	**HIGH**
Child's College Education	$80,000	15 years	$244	**MEDIUM**
Travel / Lifestyle Fund	$20,000	3 years	$556	**LOW**

**At 7% average annual return, compounded monthly. Hypothetical illustration only.*

Notice that this framework doesn't suggest you need to fund every goal simultaneously at full capacity from day one. The priority column helps sequence your efforts. Most financial planners recommend addressing high-priority goals first, especially the emergency fund and retirement contributions (particularly if an employer matches 401(k) contributions, which represents an immediate 50–100% return on those dollars).

2.5 Understanding Your True Risk Tolerance

Risk tolerance is one of the most discussed and most misunderstood concepts in personal finance. Most investors dramatically overestimate their risk tolerance when markets are rising and dramatically underestimate it when markets are falling. The question is not: "Are you comfortable with risk?" The question is: "How will you actually behave when your portfolio drops 30% in three months and every financial news headline is predicting further catastrophe?"

Risk tolerance has two distinct components that must both be considered:

- **Financial Risk Capacity:** The objective, mathematical ability to absorb losses based on your income, expenses, assets, liabilities, time horizon, and financial obligations. This is a function of your balance sheet, not your feelings.
- **Emotional Risk Tolerance:** Your subjective psychological ability to withstand volatility without making panic-driven decisions that damage your long-term returns. This is a function of your nervous system and temperament, and it can only be truly known when tested by real market adversity.

The most dangerous investor is one whose emotional risk tolerance is lower than their financial risk capacity, someone who can mathematically afford to hold through a 40% drawdown but who will psychologically be unable to resist selling at the bottom. The second most dangerous investor is one whose emotional risk tolerance exceeds their financial risk capacity; someone who feels bold taking large risks but who genuinely cannot afford to absorb significant losses.

> *"Most people get interested in stocks when everyone else is. The time to get interested is when no one else is. You can't buy what is popular and do well."*
> — **Warren Buffett**, *Widely attributed across Berkshire Hathaway shareholder letters and interviews*

The Risk Tolerance Spectrum

Investors are typically categorized into five risk profiles based on the combination of their financial capacity and emotional tolerance. Understanding where you fall on this spectrum is essential before constructing any portfolio.

Risk Profile	Time Horizon	Typical Allocation	Emotional Tolerance
Conservative	1–5 years	20% stocks / 80% bonds & cash	Very low: prefers stability over growth
ModeratelyConservative	3–7 years	40% stocks / 60% bonds	Low: can accept small fluctuations
Moderate	7–15 years	60% stocks / 40% bonds	Medium: understands and accepts market cycles
ModeratelyAggressive	10–20 years	80% stocks / 20% bonds	High: comfortable with significant volatility
Aggressive	15+ years	90–100% stocks / minimal bonds	Very high: can stay calm during sharp drawdowns

These allocations are guidelines, not formulas. Your optimal allocation depends on the specific interplay between your goals, time horizon, income stability, existing assets, and temperament. A fee-only certified financial planner (CFP®) can help you build a personalized allocation strategy when you are ready to transition from paper trading to real capital.

The Market Stress Test: Are You Really as Bold as You Think?

Here is a practical exercise that financial advisors often use to help clients discover their true emotional risk tolerance. Read each scenario and notice your gut reaction; not the rational response you think you should have, but the visceral, immediate one.

1. Your portfolio drops 10% in one month due to broader market uncertainty. How do you feel: Mildly concerned but patient? Anxious but holding? Tempted to sell some positions?
2. Your portfolio drops 25% in three months. A major recession is being discussed on every financial news channel. Multiple prominent analysts are predicting further declines. What do you do?
3. A single stock position you bought on strong conviction drops 40% after a disappointing earnings report. Do you buy more at the lower price? Hold? Sell immediately to limit further loss?
4. Your portfolio is up 35% over 18 months. A friend tells you they've made 200% trading a high-momentum technology stock you don't own. How do you feel about your own positions?

Your honest answers to these scenarios reveal more about your true risk tolerance than any questionnaire. If Scenario 2 makes your stomach lurch, you are probably a moderate or moderate-conservative investor regardless of your age or financial capacity. If Scenario 4 makes you want to abandon your strategy and chase your friend's return, you need to build stronger rules around FOMO; one of the most destructive forces in trading psychology, which we will address in depth in Chapter 12.

2.6 Investing Is Not Gambling: Drawing the Critical Line

A question that genuinely curious beginners sometimes ask is: what is the real difference between investing in stocks and gambling in a casino? It is a fair and important question, and the answer reveals much about the disciplined approach that separates successful investors from those who treat the market as entertainment.

- **In a casino,** the house has a mathematical edge on every single bet. The longer you play, the more certain it becomes that you will lose. The expected value of every wager is negative for the player.
- **In a properly diversified, long-term stock market portfolio,** history demonstrates a positive expected value. The U.S. stock market has delivered positive returns over every rolling 20-year period in history. Properly diversified investors who hold through market cycles have been rewarded by the long-term growth of the global economy.

The distinction becomes blurry, however, when investors engage in undisciplined speculation: buying meme stocks based on social media hype, trading with borrowed money (margin) without understanding leverage risk, concentrating all capital in a single volatile position, or day-trading without an edge or a system. These behaviors begin to resemble gambling not because the underlying instrument is inherently speculative, but because the approach has no probabilistic foundation, no risk management, and no plan.

> *"Speculation is an effort, probably unsuccessful, to turn a little money into a lot. Investment is an effort, which should be successful, to prevent a lot of money from becoming a little."*
>
> — **Fred Schwed Jr.**, *Where Are the Customers' Yachts? (1940): one of the most enduring classics of Wall Street literature*

This book together with the StockTradesApp.com platform; are built around disciplined investment and trading principles, not speculation. As you progress through the chapters, every strategy you learn will be grounded in logic, probability, and risk management. The goal is not to get lucky. The goal is to build a repeatable, evidence-based process.

2.7 Building Your Investor Identity Statement

One of the most powerful tools any investor can develop is a written Investor Identity Statement with a concise personal document that captures who you are as an investor, what you are trying to achieve, what risks you are willing to accept, and what rules you commit to following regardless of market conditions.

This is not a business plan or a legal document. It is a personal compass that you return to whenever the market creates conditions that tempt you to deviate from your strategy. The act of writing it forces clarity. The act of returning to it forces discipline.

Your Investor Identity Statement: A Template

Answer each of the following prompts as specifically and honestly as you can. Save your answers in your trading journal within StockTradesApp.com. We will revisit and refine this statement in Chapter 10 when you prepare for live trading.

5. MY PRIMARY FINANCIAL GOALS: List your top 2–3 specific, measurable financial goals with target amounts and time horizons.
6. MY INVESTING TIME HORIZON: Is most of your investment capital earmarked for goals more than 10 years away, between 3–10 years, or sooner?
7. MY RISK TOLERANCE: Based on the stress test in Section 2.5, which risk profile best describes you: Conservative, Moderate, or Aggressive? What market conditions would genuinely test your commitment to your strategy?
8. MY PRIMARY APPROACH: Am I primarily an investor (focused on long-term fundamentals) or a trader (focused on shorter-term price patterns)? Or a hybrid of both?
9. MY NON-NEGOTIABLE RULES: What rules am I committing to regardless of market conditions? (Examples: I will never invest money I need within 3 years. I will never risk more than 2% of my portfolio on a single trade. I will not check my portfolio more than once per day.)

10. MY BEHAVIORAL WEAKNESSES: Based on what I know about behavioral finance, which cognitive biases am I most susceptible to, is it loss aversion, overconfidence, recency bias, or FOMO? What safeguards will I build to counteract them?

🖥 PLATFORM FEATURE: Creating Your Trading Journal on stocktradesapp.com

StockTradesApp.com includes a built-in Trading Journal; a private digital notebook where you record your observations, strategy notes, emotional reflections, and lessons learned from each trade.

Step 1: Navigate to the Journal section of the platform and create your first entry. Title it: "My Investor Identity Statement" and record your answers to the six prompts in Section 2.7.

Step 2: Every time you make a paper trade in the simulator, create a journal entry capturing: why you entered the trade, what your exit plan was before you entered, what actually happened, and what you learned. This practice, far more than any single trade outcome, is what separates investors who improve from those who repeat the same mistakes indefinitely.

The Trading Journal is one of the most underused tools in the platform. The investors who use it consistently are the ones whose performance improves most dramatically over time.

2.8 The Disciplined Investor's Daily Mindset

Before we move to Chapter 3 and your first full tour of StockTradesApp.com, it is worth articulating what separates the mindset of a disciplined, long-term investor from that of a reactive, emotion-driven speculator. These are not abstract virtues. They are daily practices that compound in value just as surely as your investment returns do.

- **Process Over Outcomes:** A disciplined investor evaluates the quality of their decision-making process, not just the outcome. Even a bad trade can reflect good process if it followed established rules. Even a profitable trade can reflect bad process if it was based on a hunch or a tip. Focus on building and following a repeatable process. Over time, good process produces good outcomes.
- **Patience as Strategy:** Most of the time in the market, the right action is no action. As investor and author Peter Lynch observed, far more money has been lost by investors preparing for corrections, or trying to anticipate corrections, than has been lost in corrections themselves. Patience is not passive. It is an active, disciplined choice to trust your process and let compounding work.

- **Humility as Protection:** The most dangerous moment for any investor is a sustained period of success. Overconfidence following a winning streak leads to oversized positions, reduced research rigor, and the dismissal of contrary evidence. The greatest investors maintain humility about their own limitations and the inherent unpredictability of markets.
- **Continuous Education:** Markets evolve. Strategies that worked in one economic regime may underperform in another. The investor who commits to lifelong learning; reading annual reports, studying market history, understanding macroeconomics; builds a compounding knowledge base that becomes a durable edge over time.
- **Rules Over Impulse:** Your written rules, your Investor Identity Statement, your pre-defined risk limits, all these documents exist specifically to govern your behavior during the moments when emotion most wants to override them. Honor the rules you wrote in your calm, rational state over the impulses generated by your fear or greed in the heat of the moment.

> *"The most important quality for an investor is temperament, not intellect. You need a temperament that neither derives great pleasure from being with the crowd or against the crowd."*
>
> — **Warren Buffett**, *University of Nebraska speech, widely quoted across Berkshire shareholder materials*

Chapter 2 Summary

Chapter 2 has laid the psychological and strategic foundation upon which every practical skill in this book will rest. Here is what you now carry into your trading journey:

- **The Psychology Gap is Real:** DALBAR research shows that over a 30-year period, the average individual investor underperformed the S&P 500 by 6.8 percentage points annually, not because of bad stock picks, but because of predictable psychological mistakes.
- **Loss Aversion is Hardwired:** Nobel laureate Daniel Kahneman and Amos Tversky demonstrated that humans feel the pain of losses approximately twice as intensely as the pleasure of equivalent gains. Recognizing this bias is the first step toward managing it.

- **Trading and Investing Are Different Disciplines:** Both can be profitable, but they require different skills, time commitments, and psychological profiles. Knowing which approach suits you, or how to blend both; is essential before putting real capital at risk.
- **Compounding Rewards the Patient:** The mathematics of compounding mean that time in the market is more powerful than timing the market. Starting earlier, even with smaller amounts, produces dramatically superior outcomes over decades.
- **SMART Goals Replace Vague Wishes:** Effective investing begins with specific, measurable, time-bound financial goals organized across short-, medium-, and long-term horizons. Your emergency fund is the non-negotiable foundation before any market investment.
- **Risk Tolerance Has Two Dimensions:** Your financial risk capacity (what you can mathematically afford to lose) and your emotional risk tolerance (how you will actually behave during a drawdown) may differ, and both matter.
- **Your Investor Identity Statement is Your Compass:** A written personal document capturing your goals, risk tolerance, approach, and non-negotiable rules is the most practical tool for maintaining discipline when markets create emotional conditions designed to test it.

CHAPTER 3

Navigating Your First Platform: A Complete Tour of StockTradesApp.com

"Give me six hours to chop down a tree and I will spend the first four sharpening the axe."
— Attributed to Abraham Lincoln

Chapters 1 and 2 gave you the knowledge to understand the stock market and the self-awareness to approach it with discipline. Now it is time to pick up the tool you will use throughout this entire journey: StockTradesApp.com. This chapter is your complete guided orientation to the platform. By the time you finish reading it and complete the exercises at the end, the platform will feel natural and familiar, so that when Chapter 4 begins building your analytical vocabulary, you are spending your energy on learning, not on navigation.

Think of this chapter as the orientation session before your first day at a new job. You are not yet doing the full work, but you are learning where everything lives so that when it is time to perform, the environment never slows you down. Professional traders who use any platform for the first time invest significant time learning its layout before risking a single dollar. You will do the same.

One important note before we begin: StockTradesApp.com is a living platform. Features are updated and new tools are added as the platform grows. The descriptions in this chapter reflect the platform at the time of publication. If a feature looks slightly different from its description here, check the navigation menu for the current location.

3.1 The Platform Philosophy: Built to Make You Better, Not to Make You Trade More

Most retail trading platforms profit when you trade frequently. They use confetti animations, push notifications, and gamified interfaces designed to maximize transaction volume, regardless of whether those trades are in your best interest. StockTradesApp.com was built around a fundamentally different philosophy, stated plainly on the homepage: "Built to make you money, not to make you trade."

The platform achieves this through transparent signals rather than black boxes. Every Buy, Hold, or Sell rating on the platform shows you the exact RSI, MACD, trend, and momentum inputs behind the recommendation, so you understand why a signal is being generated rather than blindly following an algorithm you cannot see or question. It provides discipline tools rather than gambling triggers: drawdown tracking, win rate truth, and confidence trends that help you face your actual performance rather than the story you tell yourself.

This philosophy matters practically. As a beginner, you are not just learning to use a software tool. You are being trained in a workflow designed by the platform to build the habits that separate retail traders who eventually become profitable from the approximately 70 percent who lose money, as the platform itself acknowledges in its homepage statistics. Every feature you encounter in this chapter was designed with that outcome in mind.

> *"An investment in knowledge pays the best interest."*
> — **Benjamin Franklin**, *widely attributed, reflecting Franklin's lifelong philosophy on self-education*

3.2 The Six Roles: A Framework for Your Development

When you visit stocktradesapp.com, the homepage organizes the entire platform around six roles that describe the complete journey from a beginning trader to a disciplined, profitable one. These six roles are not just marketing language. They map directly to the six stages of your development that this book is designed to move you through, and they correspond to six distinct areas of the platform you will explore in this chapter.

Role	Tagline	What the Platform Gives You
The Trader	Read the tape like a pro	Real candlestick charts with SMA20 and SMA50 overlays built in. A Bloomberg-style terminal layout for every ticker you search.
The Analyzer	Stop guessing what the chart means	RSI, MACD, momentum, and trend fused into a transparent Buy / Hold / Sell rating with every input shown. No black boxes.
The Decider	Get a second opinion before you click buy	AI-written briefings that explain the setup, the outlook, and the risks in plain English before you commit to a trade.
The Tracker	Never lose a ticker again	A unified watchlist where one tap pulls up the full terminal view for any saved ticker, including its live signal and score.
The Performer	Prove the edge before risking real money	A $100,000 paper trading sandbox that tracks your equity curve, drawdown, win rate, and Sharpe-like score in real time.
The Winner	Compound the right habits	Benchmark your paper trading results against SPY, annotate the trades that move the needle, and repeat what actually works.

As you read this chapter and explore the platform, keep these six roles in mind. Every section of StockTradesApp.com serves one or more of them. By the time you complete this book, you will have actively practiced all six. For now, the goal is to understand the landscape before you begin navigating it.

WHAT IS PAPER TRADING?

Paper trading is the practice of simulating real market transactions using virtual money rather than actual capital. The term dates to an era before electronic platforms, when aspiring traders would track hypothetical trades by writing them on paper.

StockTradesApp.com executes your paper trades against real, live market prices. If you buy 10 shares of Apple in the simulator, the platform records that transaction at the actual price Apple is trading at that moment, and your virtual portfolio tracks the real profit or loss on that position in real time.

The $100,000 paper trading sandbox is more than just a practice tool. The platform tracks your equity curve, drawdown, win rate, Sharpe-like score, and SPY benchmark comparison, giving you the same performance analytics a professional fund manager uses, applied to your simulated trades. This is how you prove your edge before you risk a single real dollar.

3.3 Creating Your Account: Getting Started in Minutes

If you have not yet created your free account on StockTradesApp.com, now is the time. The registration process takes less than five minutes and requires only an email address or a Google account. No credit card is required to access the Terminal, Watchlist, Paper Trading, or Dashboard. AI-written analysis is gated to signed-in users to keep platform costs sustainable, but signing in is free.

Account Registration Walkthrough

Step 1: Open your browser and navigate to stocktradesapp.com. You will land on the homepage, which introduces the platform as a retail trader's terminal built around six essential roles: Trader, Analyzer, Decider, Tracker, Performer, and Winner. The homepage showcases real charts, transparent signals, AI analysis, watchlists, and your $100,000 paper trading sandbox.

Step 2: Click the "Open free account" button in the top right corner of the navigation bar, or the large "START FREE" button in the center of the page. Both take you to the registration screen, where you can create an account with your email and password or sign in with Google.

Step 3: Enter your email address and create a secure password. Your password must be at least eight characters long and include at least one number and one symbol. If you prefer a faster setup, click "Continue with Google" to sign up using your existing Google account instead.

Step 4: If you registered with email and password, check your inbox for a verification message from StockTradesApp.com and click the link to confirm your account. If you signed up with Google, you will be taken directly to the onboarding questionnaire without this step.

Step 5: Complete the three-question onboarding questionnaire. There are no wrong answers. Select your experience level (Beginner, Intermediate, or Advanced), your primary reason for joining (Learning the markets, Active trading, Long-term investing, Companion to the book, or Something else), and your initial approach (Investor for multi-month or multi-year horizons, Trader for short-term setups and signals, or Not sure yet). Your answers customize the layout of your dashboard.

Step 6: Click "Continue to Dashboard." You will land on your personalized Dashboard with your paper trading account already funded with $100,000 in virtual capital. This is your practice fund for the entirety of Parts I through III of this book.

THE RESET BUTTON: USE IT WISELY

Inside the Paper Trading section, you will notice a RESET button in the top right corner. This button resets your virtual account back to $100,000 and wipes your trade history.

Use this option sparingly. Learning from a losing paper trading account is far more valuable than resetting to a clean slate every time performance declines. The discomfort of watching a virtual drawdown develop teaches you more about your own decision-making under pressure than any clean account ever will.

There is one legitimate use case for a reset: if you placed several test trades in the first few minutes of exploring the platform and want to start your serious paper trading practice from a clean baseline. Beyond that early reset, commit to living with your paper trading results, just as you will eventually live with your real trading results.

3.4 The Navigation Menu: Nine Doors, One Platform

Once you are signed in, the entire platform is accessible through the navigation menu, opened by clicking the three-line hamburger icon in the top right corner of any page. The menu contains nine items, each opening a distinct section of the platform. Learning what each item does is the fastest way to build an accurate mental map of the platform before you explore it in detail.

Nav Item	What You Do There	Covered In
Terminal	Search any ticker and get a full chart with SMA overlays, RSI, MACD, AI signal, news, fundamentals, and the Blended Buy/Hold/Sell rating with score	Chapter 3 (intro); Chapters 4, 5, 6 (deep use)
Dashboard	View your paper trading performance: cash, equity, win rate, profit factor, max drawdown, Sharpe-like score, SPY benchmark comparison, watchlist signals	Chapter 3 (intro); Chapter 9 (performance analysis)
Screener	Type a plain-English description of what you are looking for and the AI Screener matches it against a curated universe of ~55 large and mid-cap tickers	Chapter 7
Watchlist	Add tickers by symbol or name to your single unified watchlist; one tap launches the full Terminal view for any saved ticker with its live signal	Chapter 3 (setup); Chapter 7 (advanced use)
Alerts	Set price alerts for any ticker; choose "Crosses Above" or "Crosses Below" a target price; prices are checked every 5 minutes during market hours	Chapter 3 (setup); Chapter 7

Nav Item	What You Do There	Covered In
Compare	Add multiple tickers and view their normalized percentage returns side by side on a single chart across time frames from 1 month to 5 years	Chapter 7
Paper	Place simulated Buy and Sell orders with the Order Ticket; track open positions, cash available, and full trade history with timestamps and fills	Chapter 3 (intro); Chapter 4 onward
Learn	Bite-sized, AI-refreshed lessons organized into seven categories: Market Basics, Stocks, ETFs, Options, Retirement, Personal Finance, and Glossary	Chapter 3 (orientation); Ongoing throughout book
Admin	Account settings, profile management, and platform preferences	As needed

Keep this table as your reference point whenever you are looking for a feature. Every platform callout in this book will name the specific nav item you need to open before describing what to do inside it.

3.5 The Terminal: Your Stock Research Command Center

The Terminal is the most feature-rich section of StockTradesApp.com and the one you will use most frequently throughout this book. It is your all-in-one stock research environment: charts, signals, AI analysis, news, and fundamentals for any ticker you search, all on a single scrollable page.

To open the Terminal, click the hamburger menu and select Terminal, or click "Open the Terminal" on the homepage. You will land on a search interface. Type any ticker symbol (AAPL, MSFT, TSLA, BTC-USD, ^GSPC) or company name and the Terminal loads a full analysis page for that security.

What You See on the Terminal Page

The Terminal page is organized from top to bottom in a logical research flow. Here is what each section contains:

- **Search Bar and Controls:** At the top you will find the ticker you searched, an ANALYZE button (green, triggers the AI signal), a SAVE button (adds the ticker to your Watchlist), and time frame selectors spanning 1D, 5D, 1M, 3M, 6M, YTD, 1Y, 5Y, and ALL.

- **AI Signal Banner:** A green bordered box immediately below the controls shows a plain-English explanation of the current Buy, Hold, or Sell signal. For example: "WHY SELL: The stock is rated as a sell because the price is trending downward and recent news coverage has been mostly negative." It shows the timestamp and confirms the signal matches current indicators.
- **Quote Grid:** A four-panel data grid showing Symbol, Last Price, Change (dollar and percentage), Bid/Ask (live during market hours, "Not available / market closed" after hours), Exchange, Blended Signal (BUY/HOLD/SELL in color with a numeric score broken into technical and news components), and 52-Week Range (low in red, high in green, with percentage of range shown).
- **Price Chart:** A candlestick or line chart labeled "PRICE - SMA20 - SMA50" with the number of bars analyzed and a "CLICK CHART TO DRILL DOWN" prompt. SMA20 and SMA50 are overlaid automatically on every chart.
- **RSI Panel:** Labeled "RSI (14) OVERBOUGHT >70 - OVERSOLD <30." An orange line plotted on a 0 to 100 scale with red dashed line at 70 and green dashed line at 30.
- **MACD Panel:** Labeled "MACD (12,26,9) MOMENTUM / CROSS." Green histogram bars with the MACD and signal lines.
- **ETF Profile:** Profile data for ETFs; shows "ETF profile unavailable for this symbol" for individual stocks.
- **Fundamentals:** Balance sheet and earnings data. Shows "Fundamentals unavailable for this symbol" when the data source does not carry the ticker.
- **AI News Digest:** A green "WHAT MOVED [TICKER]?" button that generates an AI-written plain-English briefing of recent news affecting the stock.
- **AI Earnings Briefing:** A green "GENERATE EARNINGS BRIEFING" button that produces an AI summary of the most recent earnings report.
- **Composite Signal:** A circular gauge (red for Sell, amber for Hold, green for Buy) with a CONFIDENCE percentage below it.
- **News Panel:** Tabbed news from Yahoo Finance and Fox Business, with article thumbnails, source, and timestamps.
- **Analysis Tabs:** Five tabs at the bottom of the page: OVERVIEW (blended, technical, fundamentals, news scores, bars analyzed, range), WALKTHROUGH, SIGNALS (full technical breakdown), BLEND (how technical, fundamentals, and news combine), and ANALYSIS (full AI-written briefing of setup, outlook, and risks).

PLATFORM FEATURE: Your First Terminal Search

Open the Terminal from the navigation menu. Type "AAPL" in the search bar. You will see the full Terminal page load for Apple Inc.

Notice the AI Signal banner near the top. It tells you in one sentence whether the platform currently rates AAPL as a Buy, Hold, or Sell, and why. Click the ANALYZE button to generate a fresh signal if you do not see one.

Scroll down past the chart to find the five analysis tabs at the bottom: OVERVIEW, WALKTHROUGH, SIGNALS, BLEND, and ANALYSIS. Click each tab and spend 60 seconds reading what it contains. You do not need to understand everything yet. This first pass is orientation only.

Click SAVE to add AAPL to your Watchlist. Then use the search bar to look up two more companies whose products you use regularly. Notice how the chart and signal sections update instantly for each new ticker.

KEY TERM: Blended Signal

The primary rating on StockTradesApp.com's Terminal. It combines a Technical score (based on RSI, MACD, momentum, and trend indicators), a Fundamentals delta (adjustment based on fundamental data where available), and a News delta (sentiment adjustment based on recent headline analysis) into a single composite score. The Blended Signal is displayed as BUY, HOLD, or SELL with a numeric score (e.g., -29 means a moderately strong Sell). The platform always shows the breakdown so you can see exactly what is driving the rating.

3.6 The Dashboard: Your Performance Headquarters

The Dashboard is where you go to assess the overall health of your paper trading operation. Unlike the Terminal, which is focused on a single ticker at a time, the Dashboard gives you the big picture: how your portfolio is performing as a whole, how individual metrics like win rate and drawdown are developing, and how your paper trading strategy compares to the benchmark.

Navigate to the Dashboard from the hamburger menu. You will see your performance data organized into several distinct panels.

Dashboard Element	What It Shows	Why It Matters
Cash	Your current undeployed virtual cash. Starts at $100,000. Decreases as you open positions, increases as you close them for a profit or receive cash back from closing a loss.	Your dry powder. Having cash available means you can act on opportunities. Being fully invested means you cannot.
Holdings Value	The current market value of all your open positions combined. Updates in real time as prices move.	Together with Cash, this makes up your Total Equity.
Total Equity	Cash plus Holdings Value. The true current value of your paper trading account.	The primary measure of your paper trading portfolio's overall worth.
Return	Your total gain or loss from the starting $100,000, shown in both dollars and percentage.	The single most important number. Are you making or losing money on your overall strategy?
Realized P&L	Profit and Loss from trades you have already closed. This is money you have actually made or lost.	Your track record. Unrealized gains can disappear; realized gains are locked in.
Win Rate	The percentage of your closed trades that were profitable. Shown as a percentage.	Quality metric. A 60% win rate means 6 out of every 10 trades you close are profitable.
Avg Win / Loss	The average dollar gain on your winning trades versus the average dollar loss on your losing trades.	Combined with win rate, reveals your true edge. A 40% win rate can still be profitable if average wins are 3x average losses.
Profit Factor	Total gross profit divided by total gross loss. A Profit Factor above 1.0 means you are net profitable.	A Profit Factor of 1.5 means you earn $1.50 for every $1.00 lost. Professional traders target 1.5 to 2.0+.
Max Drawdown	The largest peak-to-trough decline your account has experienced. Shown in dollars and percentage.	Your worst moment. Tells you how much pain your strategy produced at its lowest point.
Sharpe-like Score	A risk-adjusted return metric similar to the professional Sharpe Ratio. Measures return per unit of risk taken.	Higher is better. Positive means you are being rewarded for the risk you are taking.
SPY Benchmark	Compare your paper trading return against the SPY ETF (S&P 500 tracker) over the same period.	The honest question: are you beating the market? If SPY returned 15% and you returned 5%, a simple index fund beat you.

Dashboard Element	What It Shows	Why It Matters
Watchlist Live Signals	All your saved tickers grouped by asset class (Bonds, Commodities, Crypto, Stocks) with live Last price, Change, Signal (BUY/HOLD/SELL), Score, and an OPEN button.	Your monitoring hub. One tap on OPEN launches the full Terminal for any watchlist ticker.

Below the performance metrics, the Dashboard displays an equity curve chart that plots your paper trading strategy (green line) against SPY (gray line) over time, with green dots marking winning trade closes and red dots marking losing ones. This visual is one of the most instructive things the platform produces: it shows you not just whether you are ahead or behind the market, but exactly when your best and worst decisions occurred relative to market conditions.

🖥 PLATFORM FEATURE: Reading the Dashboard for the First Time

When you first open the Dashboard, most metrics will show $0.00 or 0.0% because you have not yet placed any paper trades. This is expected.

After you place your first paper trade in Section 3.8 of this chapter, return to the Dashboard. You will see the Holdings Value update immediately to reflect your open position, and Total Equity will shift from $100,000 to whatever your current paper portfolio is worth.

The BENCHMARK row allows you to type any ticker symbol (not just SPY) as your benchmark and click SET. Some traders benchmark against QQQ (the NASDAQ-100 ETF) if they trade primarily technology stocks, or against a sector ETF relevant to their strategy.

3.7 The Watchlist: Your Ticker Monitoring Pipeline

The Watchlist is your personal list of tickers you are actively monitoring. It is a single unified list, not multiple separate watchlists. You add any ticker by typing its symbol or company name into the input field and clicking SAVE. The platform supports stocks, ETFs, bonds and rates (such as ^TNX for the 10-year Treasury yield), commodities (such as GLD for gold), crypto (such as BTC-USD), indices (such as ^GSPC for the S&P 500), and international stocks.

Once a ticker is saved to your Watchlist, it appears with the date you saved it and two action buttons: ANALYZE (which opens the full Terminal view for that ticker with one tap) and a trash icon (which removes it from the list). The Watchlist also feeds the live signal panel at the bottom of your Dashboard, so you can monitor all your saved tickers and their current Buy/Hold/Sell signals in one place.

Building Your First Watchlist

Step 1: Open the navigation menu and select Watchlist. You will see the "+ ADD TICKER OR NAME" input field at the top of the page.

Step 2: Type "AAPL" (or the full name "Apple") and click SAVE. Apple will appear in your list with today's date and an ANALYZE button.

Step 3: Add at least four more tickers: one technology stock (try MSFT, NVDA, or GOOGL), one healthcare stock (try JNJ or PFE), one consumer stock (try KO, WMT, or NKE), and one index (try ^GSPC for the S&P 500). This gives you a diversified monitoring list that spans multiple sectors.

Step 4: After adding your tickers, click ANALYZE on any one of them. Notice that this opens the full Terminal page for that ticker immediately, without requiring you to navigate back to the Terminal section. This one-tap access is the core workflow of the Watchlist.

Step 5: Return to the Dashboard and scroll down to the Watchlist Live Signals panel. You will now see your saved tickers listed with their current prices, daily changes, and Buy/Hold/Sell signals. This panel updates in real time during market hours.

Your Watchlist will grow and evolve throughout this book. As you learn to screen for stocks in Chapter 7, you will develop a more systematic approach to what belongs on your list and why. For now, the five or more tickers you have added are your starting monitoring universe.

🖥 PLATFORM FEATURE: Price Alerts: Stay Informed Without Staring at Screens

The Alerts section (accessible from the navigation menu) lets you set price alerts for any ticker. Enter the ticker symbol, select the condition ("Crosses Above" or "Crosses Below"), enter a target price, and click "+ ADD."

Prices are checked every five minutes during market hours. When a stock crosses your target level, you receive a notification. Triggered alerts stop firing automatically until you manually reactivate them, preventing you from being bombarded with repeated alerts on the same level.

As a beginner, use price alerts to notify you when a stock on your Watchlist reaches a level you have identified as a potential entry point. This is one of the most practical discipline tools on the platform: it removes the temptation to check prices constantly and trains you to make decisions based on pre-planned levels rather than real-time emotional reactions.

3.8 Paper Trading: Your Consequence-Free Classroom

The Paper Trading section is where you execute simulated trades. Navigate to it from the hamburger menu by selecting Paper. You will see a clean, professional-grade order entry interface alongside your current portfolio state.

The Paper Trading Page Layout

The Paper Trading page is organized into four distinct areas from top to bottom:

- **Portfolio Header:** Four tiles showing your current CASH, HOLDINGS VALUE, TOTAL EQUITY, and RETURN. These update every time you place or close a trade.
- **Order Ticket:** A BUY / SELL toggle, a SYMBOL field where you type the ticker you want to trade, a QUANTITY field for the number of shares, and a green "PLACE BUY ORDER" or "PLACE SELL ORDER" button. The current CASH AVAILABLE is displayed below the button so you can verify you have enough virtual capital before placing an order.
- **Positions:** Shows all your currently open paper trades with a count ("X OPEN"). When you have no open positions it displays: "NO OPEN POSITIONS. PLACE YOUR FIRST ORDER TO GET STARTED."
- **Trade History:** A chronological record of every paper trade you have placed, labeled "X FILLS." Each entry shows the timestamp, ticker, action (BUY or SELL), quantity, price per share, and total value of the transaction.

Placing Your First Paper Trade

Step 1: Open the navigation menu and select Paper. You will see the Paper Trading page with your $100,000 in virtual cash.

Step 2: In the Order Ticket, make sure the BUY tab is selected (it will be highlighted green).

Step 3: In the SYMBOL field, type the ticker of a stock you added to your Watchlist. For example, type "AAPL" for Apple Inc.

Step 4: In the QUANTITY field, type "10" to simulate buying 10 shares.

Step 5: Check the CASH AVAILABLE amount shown below the button to confirm you have sufficient virtual funds. Then click the green "PLACE BUY ORDER" button.

Step 6: Your order will execute immediately at the current market price. Look at the POSITIONS section: your 10 shares of AAPL should now appear as an open position. The HOLDINGS VALUE tile in the header will update to reflect the current market value of your new position.

Step 7: Return to the Dashboard and scroll down. You will see your new position reflected in the Watchlist Live Signals panel and in your equity metrics.

Congratulations. You have placed your first paper trade. From this point forward, every concept you learn in this book will be practiced in this same environment. The mechanics are now familiar; the next chapters will give you the analytical skills to make those mechanics meaningful.

THE PSYCHOLOGY OF PAPER TRADING: A CANDID WARNING

Paper trading is an extraordinary educational tool, but it has one well-documented limitation: because there are no real financial consequences, the emotional pressure of live trading is completely absent. You may find that you make perfectly rational decisions in the simulator and then discover that fear or greed disrupts those same decisions when real money is at stake.

This is normal and expected. Chapters 2 and 12 address the psychological transition from paper trading to live trading directly.

For now, the most effective way to make your paper trading experience as realistic as possible is to treat every virtual dollar as if it were real. Do not place reckless trades simply because the stakes feel low. Do not reset your account after a losing stretch. Build the same discipline now that you intend to bring to live trading. The emotional habits you practice in the simulator are the ones that will govern your behavior when the money is real.

3.9 The Learn Hub: Investing, in Plain English

The Learn section of StockTradesApp.com is a self-contained educational library designed to work alongside this book. Navigate to it from the hamburger menu by selecting Learn. You will arrive at a page with the headline "Investing, in plain English" and a description that captures its purpose precisely: "Bite-sized, jargon-free lessons on everything from 'what is a stock' to options Greeks and Roth IRAs. Written for humans, refreshed by AI."

The Learn Hub is organized into seven categories, each containing multiple lessons. A search bar at the top lets you find any lesson by keyword (try searching "P/E," "RSI," or "ETF" to see how it works).

Nav Item	What You Do There	Covered In
Market Basics	6 lessons covering how markets, brokers, and orders actually work. Start here if anything from Chapter 1 felt unclear.	Chapters 1, 4
Stocks	7 lessons on reading a stock, valuing it, and understanding what moves the price.	Chapters 4, 5
ETFs & Funds	5 lessons on index funds, ETFs, and mutual funds as the building blocks of most portfolios.	Chapters 12, 14
Options	5 lessons on calls, puts, and the strategies traders use to manage risk and speculate.	Chapter 14
Retirement	5 lessons on IRAs, 401(k)s, Roth vs Traditional accounts, and planning for the long run.	Chapter 14
Personal Finance	5 lessons on budgeting, emergency funds, debt, and the habits that compound wealth.	Chapter 2
Glossary & Abbreviations	10 lessons defining every term, ticker symbol, and abbreviation used on the platform.	All chapters

The Learn Hub also surfaces a Popular Lessons section on its main page. At the time of publication, those lessons include: What is a stock?, How stock exchanges work, Bid ask and the spread, Market vs limit vs stop orders, Bull markets vs bear markets, What is a market index?, The P/E ratio explained simply, and Market cap: small, mid, and large. You will recognize most of these topics from Chapters 1 through 4 of this book. Reading the platform's plain-English version of a concept after working through the book's more detailed treatment is an excellent way to reinforce your understanding.

🖳 PLATFORM FEATURE: Using the Learn Hub Alongside This Book

The most effective way to use the Learn Hub is as a quick reference when you encounter a term or concept during active platform use that you want to clarify immediately, without having to flip back to the relevant chapter of this book.

For example: you are analyzing AAPL in the Terminal and see the Blended Signal score of -29. You want a quick reminder of how the scoring works. Search "signal" or "RSI" in the Learn Hub search bar and the relevant lesson appears in seconds.

The Learn Hub is not a replacement for the depth and structure of this book. It is a companion: the fast-lookup tool you reach for in the moment, while this book is the systematic curriculum that builds your knowledge layer by layer.

3.10 Compare and the AI Screener: Two Tools Worth Knowing Early

The Compare Tool

The Compare section (navigation menu: Compare) lets you add multiple tickers to a single normalized percentage-return chart. Add AAPL, MSFT, and NVDA as chips, select a time frame (1MO, 3MO, 6MO, 1Y, 2Y, or 5Y), and the chart displays each stock's return from the same starting point, so you can compare their performance over that period on equal footing regardless of their different share prices.

This tool is particularly useful for comparing stocks within the same sector before deciding which one to add to your paper trading portfolio, or for benchmarking any stock against a relevant index. Chapter 7 uses the Compare tool as part of your research process for building a systematic watchlist.

The AI Screener

The Screener section (navigation menu: Screener) is one of the most distinctive features on the platform. Rather than requiring you to set up filters for market cap, P/E ratio, sector, and dozens of other variables the way traditional stock screeners work, the AI Screener accepts a plain-English description of what you are looking for and matches it against a curated universe of approximately 55 popular large and mid-cap tickers.

Type a prompt such as "Large-cap tech with low debt and P/E under 25" or "Defensive dividend payers yielding over 3%" or "Stocks under $200 that are down more than 5% this month" into the input field and click RUN SCREEN. The platform processes your description and returns matching candidates from its ticker universe.

Four preset prompt chips are displayed on the Screener page to help you get started quickly. The platform notes clearly that results are AI-assisted and not financial advice, and that the universe is limited to its curated set of approximately 55 tickers rather than the full market. Chapter 7 covers the Screener in full detail, including how to write effective prompts and how to use the results as a starting point for deeper research in the Terminal.

🖥 PLATFORM FEATURE: A Note on the Screener Universe

The AI Screener works against a curated set of approximately 55 popular large and mid-cap tickers, not the full universe of publicly traded stocks. This is intentional: the platform is designed for retail traders learning to trade, and concentrating on the most liquid, well-covered names in the market is a sound pedagogical choice.

As a beginning paper trader, this limitation is actually an advantage. The 55 tickers in the screener universe represent the kinds of stocks that beginning traders should be studying: heavily covered, liquid, with abundant fundamental data and widely followed technical levels.

When you are ready to research outside the screener universe, use the Terminal's direct ticker search. The Terminal accepts any valid ticker symbol, not just the ~55 in the screener universe.

3.11 Chapter 3 Exercises: Completing Your Platform Orientation

Before you advance to Chapter 4, complete each of the following exercises within StockTradesApp.com. These tasks ensure that when Chapter 4 introduces the language of price, you are already comfortable in the platform environment. None of these exercises require any real money.

1. EXPLORE THE TERMINAL. Open the Terminal from the navigation menu and search for three companies whose products you use regularly. For each one, record in a personal notebook: the current Blended Signal (BUY/HOLD/SELL and the numeric score), the 52-week range and where the current price sits within it, and one headline from the News panel. Do not try to understand everything yet. Simply observe.
2. BUILD YOUR WATCHLIST. Open the Watchlist and add at least five tickers: the three companies you searched in Exercise 1, plus one index (^GSPC for the S&P 500

or ^NDX for the NASDAQ-100), and one bond rate (^TNX for the 10-year Treasury yield). These last two additions will help you understand the broader market context as you develop your trading skills. Click ANALYZE on each to confirm they load correctly in the Terminal.

3. SET ONE PRICE ALERT. Open the Alerts section. Pick any stock from your Watchlist. Set an alert for "Crosses Above" a price that is about 5 percent above the current price, and set another for "Crosses Below" a price about 5 percent below it. This creates a simple notification bracket around the stock's current level.
4. PLACE YOUR FIRST PAPER TRADE. Open the Paper section and follow the step-by-step walkthrough in Section 3.8. Buy 10 shares of any stock currently on your Watchlist. After the order fills, open the Dashboard and note how your Cash, Holdings Value, and Total Equity have changed. Then open the Watchlist and notice the live signal entry for your new position.
5. USE THE COMPARE TOOL. Open the Compare section and add three technology stocks (try AAPL, MSFT, and NVDA). Set the time frame to 1Y. Study the normalized return chart. Which stock performed best over the past year? Which underperformed? Write a two-sentence observation about what you see.
6. EXPLORE THE LEARN HUB. Open the Learn section and navigate to Market Basics. Read any two of the six lessons. Then use the search bar to find the lesson on "bid ask and the spread." Reading it now will give you a head start on Chapter 4, which covers this concept in depth.

BEFORE YOU MOVE TO CHAPTER 4

Chapter 4 teaches you the complete language of price: bid-ask spreads, market hours, volume, and every data field packed into a stock quote. It is the vocabulary chapter that makes everything else in the book immediately readable.

You should complete Chapter 4 with the Terminal open on another screen or device. Every concept Chapter 4 introduces corresponds to something visible on a live Terminal page, and seeing each data point in real time on a real stock will accelerate your comprehension far more than reading alone.

Chapter 3 Summary

Chapter 3 has transformed StockTradesApp.com from an unfamiliar interface into a familiar working environment. Here is the complete orientation you now carry forward:

- **The Platform Philosophy:** Built to make you a better trader, not to encourage more trading. Transparent signals with every input shown, discipline tools over dopamine triggers, and a $0 starting cost versus $360 to $2,400 per year for comparable professional terminals.
- **The Six Roles:** Trader, Analyzer, Decider, Tracker, Performer, and Winner. Each role maps to a section of the platform and a phase of your development as covered in this book.
- **Nine Navigation Items:** Terminal, Dashboard, Screener, Watchlist, Alerts, Compare, Paper, Learn, and Admin. Every platform feature in this book lives under one of these nine items.
- **The Terminal:** Your single-ticker research command center. Chart with SMA20 and SMA50 overlays, RSI (14), MACD (12,26,9), AI News Digest, AI Earnings Briefing, Composite Signal, News panel, and five analysis tabs: Overview, Walkthrough, Signals, Blend, and Analysis.
- **The Dashboard:** Your portfolio performance headquarters. Cash, Holdings Value, Total Equity, Return, Win Rate, Profit Factor, Max Drawdown, Sharpe-like Score, SPY Benchmark comparison, equity curve chart, and Watchlist Live Signals panel.
- **The Watchlist:** A single unified list supporting stocks, ETFs, crypto, bonds, indices, and international tickers. One tap on ANALYZE launches the full Terminal. Feeds live signals to the Dashboard.
- **Price Alerts:** Set via the Alerts nav item. Crosses Above or Crosses Below a target price, checked every five minutes during market hours.
- **Paper Trading:** The Order Ticket (BUY/SELL, Symbol, Quantity, Place Order button), Positions panel, and Trade History log. Your $100,000 virtual sandbox. Performance tracked against SPY on the Dashboard.
- **The Learn Hub:** Seven lesson categories totaling 43 lessons plus a glossary. Search any term. Use it as a fast-lookup companion to this book.
- **Compare and AI Screener:** Compare normalizes multiple tickers to percentage return on one chart. The AI Screener accepts plain-English descriptions against a curated ~55-ticker universe.

CHAPTER 4

The Language of Price: Reading a Stock Quote Like a Professional

"In investing, what is comfortable is rarely profitable."

— **Robert Arnott, Chairman of Research Affiliates**

Every piece of information you will ever use to make a trading decision ultimately traces back to price. Charts are pictures of price history. Technical indicators are mathematical calculations applied to price. Fundamental analysis tells you what a company is worth so you can compare that worth to its price. Volume tells you how many times a price changed hands. Even news events are only relevant insofar as they move price.

Before you can read a chart, understand an order type, or execute a strategy, you need to speak the language of price fluently. This chapter teaches you that language from the ground up. Every term introduced here appears directly on the StockTradesApp.com Quote Page, and you should have that page open on a live stock as you read. Seeing each concept in real time, on real data, will accelerate your comprehension faster than any description alone.

By the time you finish this chapter, a stock quote that once looked like a wall of numbers will read like a coherent, information-rich story about what a company's stock is doing, why it is doing it, and what context surrounds it.

4.1 The Complete Stock Quote: Every Number Decoded

A stock quote is a real-time snapshot of a stock's trading activity. When you pull up any ticker on StockTradesApp.com, you are looking at a quote. Professional traders read quotes instinctively and instantly, extracting meaning from each data point within seconds. The table below decodes every element of a standard stock quote using Apple Inc. (AAPL) as a real-world example.

Study this table carefully. Every row represents a piece of information that will appear in your daily workflow on the platform and in the chapters ahead.

Data Field	Example Value	What It Tells You
Ticker Symbol	AAPL	The unique exchange abbreviation for the company. Every publicly traded company has one. Apple is AAPL, Microsoft is MSFT, Tesla is TSLA.
Last Price	$189.42	The price of the most recent completed transaction. Updates in real time during market hours. This is the number most people mean when they say "the stock price."
Change ($)	+$2.87	The dollar amount the price has moved since yesterday's closing price. Positive means the stock is up today; negative means it is down.
Change (%)	+1.54%	The percentage the price has moved since yesterday's close. This is more meaningful than the dollar change because it shows the move in proportion to the stock's price.
Bid Price	$189.40	The highest price any buyer is currently willing to pay. If you sell at market, you will receive approximately this price.
Ask Price	$189.43	The lowest price any seller is currently willing to accept. If you buy at market, you will pay approximately this price.
Bid-Ask Spread	$0.03	The difference between the bid and ask. On liquid large-cap stocks like Apple, the spread is typically just one or two cents. On illiquid stocks, it can be much wider.
Open	$187.65	The price of the stock's very first trade when the market opened at 9:30 AM. Comparing the open to the current price shows the intraday trend direction.
Previous Close	$186.55	The last traded price from the previous trading session. The daily change is calculated from this number.
Day's High	$190.21	The highest price reached during today's trading session. If the current price is near the day's high, buying pressure is dominating.
Day's Low	$186.80	The lowest price reached during today's trading session. If the current price is near the day's low, selling pressure is dominating.

Data Field	Example Value	What It Tells You
52-Week High	$199.62	The highest price the stock has traded at over the past year. A stock trading near its 52-week high signals strong upward momentum and potential resistance.
52-Week Low	$164.08	The lowest price over the past year. A stock trading near its 52-week low may represent value or signal fundamental problems. Context matters.
Volume	54.3M	The number of shares traded so far today. Compare to the average daily volume (below) to assess whether today's activity is unusual.
Avg. Daily Vol.	58.1M	The average number of shares traded per day over the past 30 trading days. Used as a baseline to assess whether today's volume is high, low, or normal.
Market Cap	$2.91T	Total shares outstanding multiplied by the current price. Tells you the total market value of the company. Apple's $2.91 trillion makes it one of the world's most valuable companies.
P/E Ratio	31.2x	Price divided by earnings per share. How much investors are paying for each dollar of earnings. A higher P/E suggests higher growth expectations. Covered in depth in Chapter 5.
EPS (TTM)	$6.07	Earnings Per Share over the Trailing Twelve Months. The company's net profit divided by total shares. The foundation of the P/E calculation. Covered in Chapter 5.
Dividend Yield	0.51%	Annual dividend per share divided by the current price. Apple pays a modest dividend. Stocks with higher yields (3-5%+) are called income stocks and attract different investors.
Beta	1.24	Volatility relative to the S&P 500. Apple's 1.24 beta means it tends to move about 24% more than the market in either direction on any given day.
Exchange	NASDAQ	The exchange where the stock is listed and primarily traded. Apple is listed on the NASDAQ. The exchange affects trading hours, reporting requirements, and listing standards.

This table represents the complete vocabulary of a stock quote. Do not attempt to memorize every definition in one sitting. Instead, keep this chapter open as you use

StockTradesApp.com, and refer back to each row whenever you encounter a data point you want to understand more deeply.

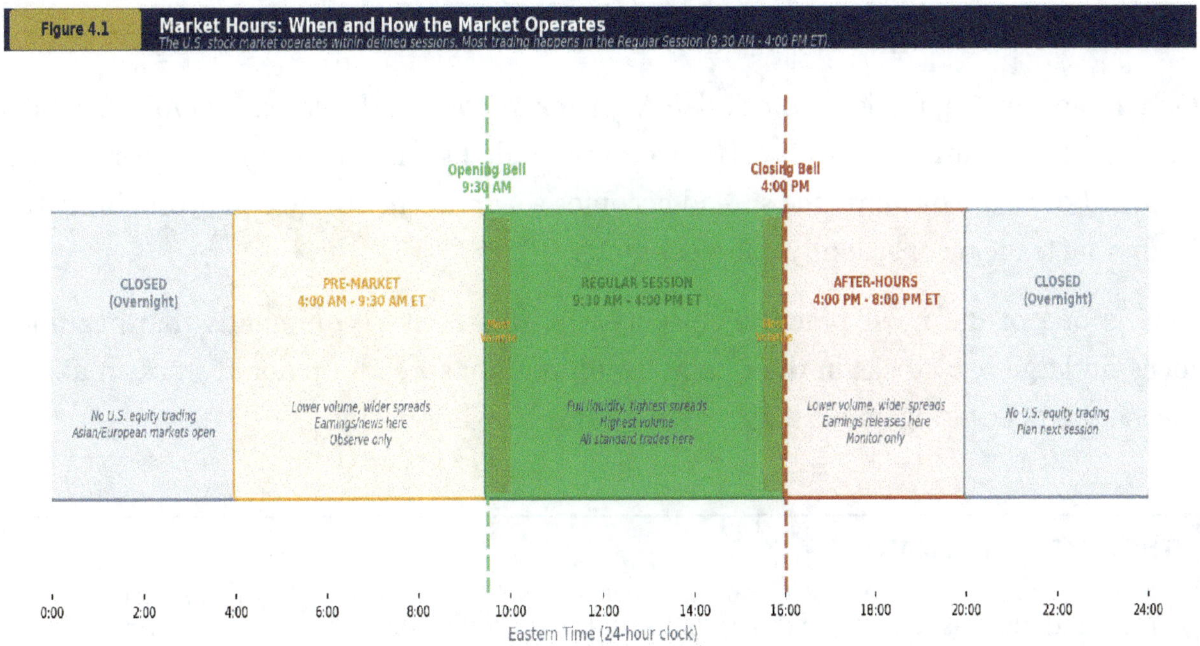

Figure 4.1 - Market Hours: The U.S. market operates in defined sessions. The Regular Session (9:30 AM to 4:00 PM ET) is where all standard trades are placed. The first and last 30 minutes are the most volatile.

4.2 The Bid-Ask Spread: The Hidden Cost of Every Trade

Of all the elements in a stock quote, the bid-ask spread is the one beginners most often overlook and professionals most carefully monitor. Understanding the spread is essential because it represents a transaction cost that exists on every single trade you will ever make, even on platforms that advertise commission-free trading.

> **KEY TERM: Bid-Ask Spread**
> *The difference between the highest price a buyer is willing to pay for a stock (the bid) and the lowest price a seller is willing to accept (the ask). When you place a market buy order, you pay the ask price. When you place a market sell order, you receive the bid price. The spread is the built-in cost of transacting immediately. A tight spread (a few cents) signals a highly liquid stock. A wide spread (tens of cents or more) signals low liquidity and higher implicit transaction costs.*

A Concrete Example of Spread Cost

Suppose a stock has a bid of $20.00 and an ask of $20.10. The spread is $0.10. If you buy 100 shares at market, you pay $20.10 per share, or $2,010 total. The moment your order fills, the stock would need to rise to $20.10 just for you to break even on a market sell. You have already paid $10 in spread cost before the stock moves a single penny.

On a large-cap, highly liquid stock like Apple or Microsoft, the spread is typically one to three cents, making it a trivial cost. On a thinly traded small-cap or micro-cap stock with a spread of $0.50 or more, the spread becomes a significant obstacle to profitability that beginning traders consistently underestimate.

This is one of the most practical reasons why this book recommends that beginners focus on large-cap stocks in their paper trading: tight spreads on liquid stocks make the mechanics of entering and exiting trades cleaner and less costly.

THE ROLE OF THE MARKET MAKER

The bid-ask spread is not an arbitrary number. It is set and maintained by market makers: firms (and, increasingly, algorithms) that stand ready to buy or sell a stock at any time, providing the liquidity that makes orderly markets possible.

Market makers profit from the spread. They buy at the bid and sell at the ask continuously, capturing the difference on each transaction. In exchange for this profit, they provide an essential service: ensuring that you can always buy or sell a stock quickly at a known price, rather than waiting indefinitely for a matching counterparty.

According to research by the CFA Institute, the spread on U.S. large-cap stocks has narrowed dramatically over the past three decades, from an average of $0.125 (one-eighth of a dollar under the old fractional pricing system) before 2001 to fractions of a cent on the most liquid stocks today. This reduction in transaction costs has been a major benefit to retail investors.

Reading Bid and Ask on StockTradesApp.com

On the StockTradesApp.com Quote Page, the bid and ask prices are displayed in real time in the Key Statistics Bar, just below the main price header. During market hours, these numbers will update continuously as buyers and sellers post and revise their orders. Outside of market hours, they reflect the last posted bids and asks from the pre-market or after-hours session.

As you become more experienced, you will develop a habit of checking the spread before placing any order. For your paper trading in early chapters, simply note the spread on each stock you trade and record it in your journal. You will begin to build an intuitive sense of what a normal spread looks like for different types of stocks.

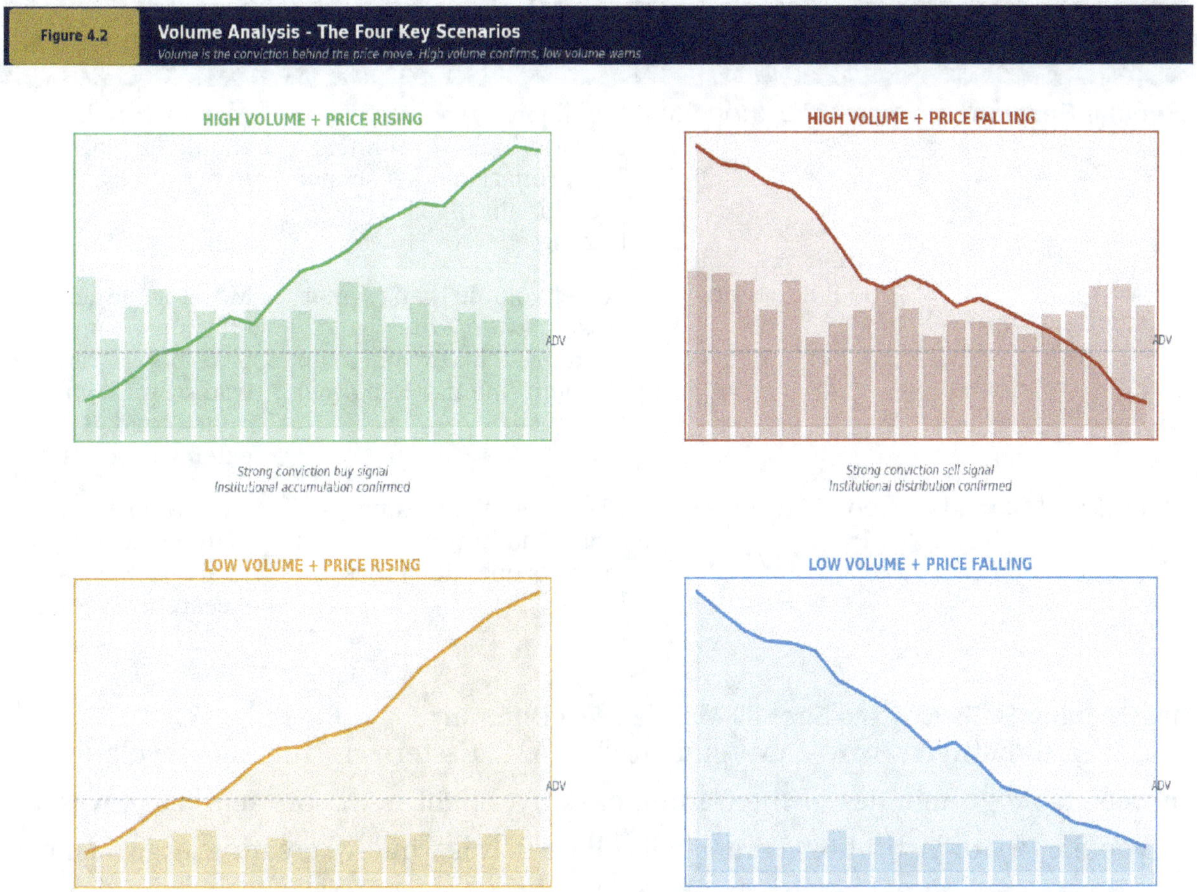

Figure 4.2 - Volume Analysis: The Four Key Scenarios. High volume confirms price moves; low volume warns that they may not hold. Always interpret price movement in the context of volume.

4.3 Market Hours: When and How the Market Operates

The U.S. stock market does not run continuously. It operates within defined hours on defined days, and understanding those hours is fundamental to knowing when your orders will execute, when prices are most active, and how to interpret price movements you see outside of standard trading sessions.

Trading Session	Hours (Eastern Time)	Characteristics	For Beginners
Pre-Market	4:00 AM to 9:30 AM	Lower volume, wider spreads, higher volatility. Major earnings reports and news releases often occur here.	Observe but do not trade. Price moves can be exaggerated and misleading.

Trading Session	Hours (Eastern Time)	Characteristics	For Beginners
Regular Session	9:30 AM to 4:00 PM	Full liquidity, tightest spreads, highest volume. The primary market session used for all standard trading.	All paper trades should be placed here initially.
After-Hours	4:00 PM to 8:00 PM	Lower volume than regular session, wider spreads. Earnings releases and major announcements often occur here.	Monitor for news affecting open positions. Avoid trading until you understand extended-hours risk.
Overnight / Closed	8:00 PM to 4:00 AM	No U.S. equity trading. Asian and European markets operate in these hours.	Review positions, plan the next day's strategy, read research.

The Opening Bell: Why the First 30 Minutes Are Different

The period between 9:30 AM and 10:00 AM Eastern is the most volatile and unpredictable 30 minutes of the trading day. Overnight news, pre-market moves, and the rapid entry of institutional orders all collide in this window, creating large, fast price swings that can be difficult to trade profitably without experience.

Most professional traders either avoid making new entries in the first 15 to 30 minutes of the session, or they have very specific, well-tested strategies for doing so. As a beginning paper trader, the safest practice is to observe the first 30 minutes without placing new orders. Watch how your watchlist stocks behave at the open. Where do they gap up or down from yesterday's close? Do they reverse quickly or continue in the direction of the gap? These observations build an intuitive understanding of opening market dynamics that will serve you throughout your trading career.

> *"The first hour of trading is the most important. It sets the tone for the entire day. I almost never make a trade in the first 30 minutes unless I have a very specific plan."*
> — **Mark Minervini**, *Stock Market Wizard, as cited in Market Wizards by Jack D. Schwager (2012)*

The Closing Bell: The Final 30 Minutes

Just as the opening session is unusually volatile, the final 30 minutes of trading (3:30 PM to 4:00 PM Eastern) also sees elevated activity. Institutional portfolio managers rebalance positions at the close. Options traders manage expiring positions. Mutual funds execute orders to meet end-of-day pricing requirements. The result is a surge in volume that can move prices significantly in a short time.

Observe the closing session on your watchlist stocks regularly. A stock that drifts lower throughout the day but sees a strong surge of buying volume in the final 30 minutes is sending an important signal: institutions are accumulating the stock at the close, which many technical analysts view as bullish. The reverse is also true. A stock that surges during the day but sells off heavily into the close suggests distribution by larger players.

🖥 PLATFORM FEATURE: Market Hours Indicator on stocktradesapp.com

The top navigation bar of StockTradesApp.com displays a market status indicator that shows whether the market is currently in a Pre-Market, Regular Session, After-Hours, or Closed state.

During the regular session, a green dot and the label "Market Open" are displayed. During pre-market and after-hours, an amber dot and the applicable session label appear. When the market is fully closed, a gray dot and "Market Closed" are displayed along with the time remaining until the next open.

All paper trades placed during market hours on StockTradesApp.com will execute at the real-time market price. Paper trades placed outside of market hours are queued and executed at the opening price of the next regular session, unless you specify a pre-market or after-hours order type.

4.4 Volume: The Conviction Behind the Price Move

Price tells you what happened. Volume tells you how much the market cared. Of all the secondary data points on a stock quote, volume is the one that professionals treat most seriously as a confirmation or contradiction of price movements. Learning to read volume alongside price is one of the most powerful analytical habits you can develop.

KEY TERM: Volume

The total number of shares of a stock that have been bought and sold during a specified time period, typically a single trading day. Volume is a measure of trading activity and market interest. High volume on a price move suggests strong conviction behind the move. Low volume on a price move suggests the move may lack broad participation and could reverse.

The Four Volume Scenarios Every Trader Knows

Every price move exists in one of four contexts when combined with volume. Reading these combinations correctly gives you a significant analytical edge.

Price Direction	Volume Context + Interpretation
Price Rising	HIGH VOLUME: Strong bullish signal. Many participants are buying enthusiastically. The move has conviction and is likely to continue.
Price Rising	LOW VOLUME: Weak signal. The rise lacks broad participation. Could be a short-lived bounce or manipulation by a small number of traders. Treat with caution.
Price Falling	HIGH VOLUME: Strong bearish signal. Many participants are selling aggressively. The decline has conviction. Avoid trying to "catch the falling knife."
Price Falling	LOW VOLUME: Potentially bullish signal. The decline is not well-supported. Sellers are exhausted. This type of low-volume pullback in an otherwise uptrending stock can represent a buying opportunity for experienced traders.

Average Daily Volume: Your Baseline

Because a stock's absolute volume number varies based on its size and how widely it is held, a single day's volume is only meaningful when compared to that stock's average daily volume (ADV). Apple trades roughly 55 to 60 million shares per day on average. A day with 80 million shares traded is significantly above average and signals heightened market interest. A day with 30 million shares is below average and suggests lower conviction in whatever price direction the stock is moving.

On StockTradesApp.com, the Quote Page displays both today's volume and the 30-day average daily volume side by side, making this comparison effortless. Develop the habit of checking this comparison every time you evaluate a trade. Before entering any position based on a price breakout, confirm that the volume supporting that breakout is at least 1.5 times the average daily volume. This is one of the fundamental rules of technical analysis that you will revisit in Chapter 6.

1.5x ADV

The minimum volume confirmation professional traders look for when evaluating a price breakout. A breakout on volume below average daily volume is considered unconfirmed and unreliable.

Source: Technical Analysis of the Financial Markets, John J. Murphy (1999), and the standard reference text for technical analysis

Volume Spikes: When Something Has Changed

A volume spike is a day when a stock trades at two, three, or even ten times its average daily volume. Volume spikes are among the most important signals in the market because they indicate that something significant has happened to attract dramatically elevated attention to the stock. Common causes of volume spikes include earnings reports, merger and acquisition announcements, FDA approvals or rejections (for pharmaceutical stocks), major product launches, analyst upgrades, or downgrades, and broad market events.

When you see a volume spike on StockTradesApp.com, the first step is always to check the News Tab on the Quote Page. There is almost always a story behind an unusually high-volume day. Understanding that story is essential before making any trading decision based on the price move that accompanied the spike.

🖥 PLATFORM FEATURE: Volume Display and Volume Bars on stocktradesapp.com

StockTradesApp.com displays volume in two places on each stock's page. The current day's volume appears in the Key Statistics Bar on the Quote Page. Historical volume is displayed as a bar chart beneath the price chart in the charting module, where each bar represents the total volume for one time period (one day, one week, etc.).

Volume bars that are taller than the surrounding bars represent above-average activity. The platform color-codes volume bars to match the price action for that period: green volume bars accompany up-price periods, and red volume bars accompany down-price periods. This color coding makes it easy to quickly identify whether high-volume periods were driven by buying or selling pressure.

In Chapter 6, you will learn to overlay a Volume Moving Average line on the volume chart, giving you an even cleaner visual comparison between current volume and historical norms.

4.5 The 52-Week Range: A Map of Psychological Extremes

The 52-week high and 52-week low are among the most psychologically powerful reference points in all of trading, far more so than their simple definitions would suggest. Understanding why investors care so intensely about these levels will help you use them intelligently rather than mechanically.

KEY TERM: 52-Week Range
The highest and lowest prices at which a stock has traded during the past 52 weeks (approximately one year). The 52-week high represents the peak price memory of the market over the past year; the 52-week low represents the trough. These levels frequently act as areas of psychological resistance (near the 52-week high) or support (near the 52-week low), because many investors use them as reference points for buying and selling decisions.

Why the 52-Week High Matters

When a stock approaches or breaks through its 52-week high, it enters territory where there are no remaining investors who bought within the past year and are still sitting at a loss. This is significant because one of the most powerful forces driving selling pressure in a stock is the desire of investors to "get out even" after a period of paper losses. Once a stock pushes above its 52-week high, that overhead supply of loss-averse sellers has been exhausted.

Research by Thomas George and Chuan-Yang Hwang, published in the Journal of Finance (2004), demonstrated that stocks trading near their 52-week high consistently outperform stocks trading near their 52-week low over the following six to twelve months. Their explanation aligns with prospect theory: investors systematically underreact to positive news about a stock that is already near its high, creating a persistent upward momentum effect as the market gradually catches up to the fundamental reality.

> *"Buy high and sell higher. The old Wall Street adage to buy low and sell high sounds wise, but in practice it leads investors to buy weak stocks rather than strong ones."*
> — **William J. O'Neil**, *How to Make Money in Stocks (1988): foundational text of the CANSLIM investing methodology*

Why the 52-Week Low Matters

A stock near its 52-week low is in a very different psychological environment. It is surrounded by investors who bought at higher prices and are experiencing paper losses, many of whom are waiting to sell the moment the stock recovers enough to reduce their pain. This creates what technical analysts call "overhead resistance": layers of potential sellers waiting at successively higher prices.

At the same time, a stock at its 52-week low may also attract value investors who believe the decline has created a bargain. The key question is always: why is the stock at its 52-week low? Is the business fundamentally impaired, or has the stock been dragged down by temporary market or sector-wide selling pressure despite solid underlying performance? This distinction between a value opportunity and a "value trap" is one of the most important judgment calls in investing, and it requires the fundamental analysis skills you will develop in Chapter 5.

The 52-Week Range on stocktradesapp.com

On the Quote Page, the 52-week high and low are displayed in the Key Statistics Bar as two numbers with a range indicator showing where the current price sits within that range. A stock trading at $85 with a 52-week range of $60 to $100 is positioned in the upper portion of its annual range, closer to its high than its low. This positioning, while simple, is one of the first contextual observations you should make about any stock you are considering for a trade.

PLATFORM FEATURE: 52-Week Range Visual Indicator

StockTradesApp.com displays the 52-week range as a horizontal bar between the low and high values, with a marker showing exactly where the current price sits within that range.

A marker positioned in the right third of the bar (near the 52-week high) indicates the stock is in a strong trend and trading near recent highs. A marker in the left third (near the 52-week low) indicates the stock is near its weakest point of the past year.

Hover over the range bar to see the exact percentage distance between the current price and both the 52-week high and low. This percentage gives you a quick sense of how much room the stock has to run before hitting technical resistance at the prior high, or how deeply discounted it is from where it was trading twelve months ago.

4.6 Pre-Market and After-Hours Trading: Opportunity and Danger

Extended-hours trading refers to buying and selling that occurs outside the standard 9:30 AM to 4:00 PM Eastern session. Pre-market trading runs from 4:00 AM to 9:30 AM. After-hours trading runs from 4:00 PM to 8:00 PM. Many significant market-moving events occur during these windows: earnings reports are almost always released either before the market opens or after it closes, and major company announcements often follow the same pattern.

Why Extended Hours Are Different

Extended-hours trading operates with fundamentally different characteristics than the regular session, and those differences create meaningful risks for inexperienced traders.

- **Lower Liquidity:** Far fewer participants are active in extended hours. The same stock that trades 50 million shares during the regular session might trade only 500,000 shares in after-hours. This dramatically reduces the pool of buyers and sellers.
- **Wider Spreads:** Because market makers scale back their activity in extended hours, bid-ask spreads widen significantly. A stock with a $0.02 spread during regular hours might carry a $0.30 or $0.50 spread in after-hours, making execution much more costly.
- **Increased Volatility:** With fewer participants, individual large orders can move prices dramatically. A single institutional buy or sell order that would barely affect price during regular hours can cause a 3 to 5 percent price swing in thin after-hours trading.
- **Earnings Exaggeration:** After an earnings announcement, a stock might surge 10 percent in after-hours trading on an initial positive reaction, only to give back half those gains when the regular session opens and more investors digest the full report. The after-hours price is often not the price that sticks.

A REAL-WORLD EXTENDED-HOURS EXAMPLE

In February 2023, Meta Platforms (parent company of Facebook) reported quarterly earnings after the market closed. The stock immediately surged more than 18 percent in after-hours trading as investors reacted to stronger-than-expected revenue and an aggressive share buyback announcement.

By the time the regular session opened the next morning, the after-hours surge held and actually extended further, with Meta ultimately closing up more than 23 percent on the day. In this case, the after-hours signal proved accurate.

However, this outcome is not always guaranteed. Earnings surprises frequently see large after-hours moves that partially or fully reverse during regular trading as more investors analyze the full earnings report, listen to the management conference call, and weigh analyst commentary. For beginning traders, observing earnings reactions without participating in extended hours is the safer and more educational approach.

The "Gap" Effect: Extended Hours Into the Open

One of the most important ways extended-hours trading affects regular-session traders is through what is called a price gap. A gap occurs when a stock opens at a meaningfully different price than it closed at the previous day, creating a literal gap in the price chart where no trading occurred.

KEY TERM: Price Gap

A space on a price chart where no trading occurred between one session's close and the next session's open. A gap up occurs when a stock opens higher than its previous close; a gap down occurs when it opens lower. Gaps are almost always driven by news or events that occurred while the market was closed. They represent a sudden, abrupt repricing of the stock by the collective market.

Gaps are extremely common and are some of the most meaningful price events a trader encounters. The direction of a gap tells you the market's initial reaction to overnight news. Whether the stock continues to move in the direction of the gap or reverses (called "filling the gap") reveals important information about the strength of that initial reaction. Chapter 6 covers gap analysis as part of technical analysis.

4.7 Price Change vs. Percentage Change: Always Think in Percentages

When you see a stock is up $5 today, your first question should not be "is that good?" Your first question should be "what is the stock's price?" A $5 gain on a $20 stock is a 25 percent move, an extraordinary day. A $5 gain on a $500 stock is a 1 percent move, barely noteworthy. The absolute dollar change is meaningless without the percentage context.

This principle extends in every direction. When comparing the performance of two stocks, always use percentage change. When calculating your gain or loss on a trade, always express it as a percentage of the capital invested. When setting price targets, think in percentages above your entry price. When setting stop-losses, think in percentages below your entry price.

Professional traders think almost exclusively in percentages. It normalizes comparisons across stocks of different prices and portfolio positions of different sizes, and it directly translates into the risk-reward calculations you will master in Chapter 8.

THE PERCENTAGE MINDSET IN PRACTICE

Consider two traders, each with a $10,000 paper trading position. Trader A holds 500 shares of a $20 stock. Trader B holds 20 shares of a $500 stock.

Both stocks declined $5 in a single day. Trader A has lost $2,500 (25% of position value). Trader B has lost $100 (1% of position value). The same dollar move represents wildly different outcomes.

Now reverse the scenario: both stocks gain $5. Trader A is up 25%, Trader B is up 1%. The same nominal gain tells very different stories. This is why percentage change is the universal language of professional traders, and it is the language you will use throughout this book.

Calculating Percentage Change

The formula for percentage change is straightforward:

$$\text{Percentage Change} = ((\text{Current Price} - \text{Previous Price}) \div \text{Previous Price}) \times 100$$

Example: A stock closes at $45.00 today after closing at $42.00 yesterday. The percentage change is: ((45.00 minus 42.00) divided by 42.00) times 100 = 7.14 percent. The stock gained 7.14 percent in a single day, which is a significant move for a large-cap stock.

StockTradesApp.com calculates and displays this percentage automatically for every stock across every time frame. You will not need to do this math manually in the platform. However, understanding the underlying calculation ensures you know exactly what you are looking at and can verify the number independently when needed.

4.8 Ticker Symbols, Exchanges, and What Listing Tells You

Every publicly traded company has a ticker symbol: a unique one-to-five-letter abbreviation used to identify it on exchanges and trading platforms. Ticker symbols are the shorthand language of the stock market, and fluency in the most commonly traded ones is a basic mark of market literacy.

How Ticker Symbols Work

Ticker symbols of one to three letters are almost always listed on the New York Stock Exchange (NYSE). Ticker symbols of four or five letters are almost always listed on the NASDAQ. This is not a hard rule, but it holds for the vast majority of stocks. Examples: IBM (NYSE), GE (NYSE), AAPL (NASDAQ), MSFT (NASDAQ), GOOGL (NASDAQ).

Some special characters and suffixes in ticker symbols carry specific meanings. A fifth letter added to a NASDAQ ticker indicates a special status. Common examples include: ".A" or ".B" for Class A or Class B shares, ".W" for warrants, ".U" for units of a SPAC (Special Purpose Acquisition Company), and ".Q" indicating the company is in bankruptcy proceedings. When you encounter an unfamiliar ticker suffix on StockTradesApp.com, the platform's Interactive Glossary explains its meaning.

Ticker	Company	Exchange	Sector	Notes
AAPL	Apple Inc.	NASDAQ	Technology	Largest company by market cap in the U.S. as of 2024
MSFT	Microsoft Corp.	NASDAQ	Technology	Second largest; dominant in cloud computing (Azure)
AMZN	Amazon.com Inc.	NASDAQ	Consumer Disc. / Tech	E-commerce and cloud leader (AWS)
GOOGL	Alphabet Inc.	NASDAQ	Technology	Parent of Google; Class A voting shares
META	Meta Platforms	NASDAQ	Technology	Parent of Facebook, Instagram, WhatsApp
TSLA	Tesla Inc.	NASDAQ	Consumer Disc.	High-beta, high-volatility growth stock

Ticker	Company	Exchange	Sector	Notes
BRK.B	Berkshire Hathaway	NYSE	Financials	Warren Buffett's conglomerate; B = affordable share class
JPM	JPMorgan Chase	NYSE	Financials	Largest U.S. bank by assets
JNJ	Johnson & Johnson	NYSE	Healthcare	Dividend Aristocrat with 60+ consecutive years of increases
XOM	ExxonMobil	NYSE	Energy	Largest U.S. oil and gas company by market cap
SPY	SPDR S&P 500 ETF	NYSE	ETF	Not a stock; tracks the S&P 500. Introduced in Chapter 12

This reference table represents eleven of the most actively traded and widely studied tickers in the U.S. market. As a paper trader, you will encounter these names frequently in financial news, earnings season discussions, and market commentary. Familiarity with this core group of companies is the starting vocabulary of any literate market participant.

4.9 Dividends and Dividend Yield: When Stocks Pay You

Some stocks not only appreciate in price over time but also pay their shareholders a regular cash distribution called a dividend. Understanding dividends is important even if you are primarily a growth-oriented trader, because dividend payment policies reveal important information about a company's financial health and management philosophy.

> **KEY TERM: Dividend**
> *A distribution of a portion of a company's earnings to its shareholders, typically paid quarterly (four times per year). Not all stocks pay dividends. Companies that do pay dividends are often mature, profitable businesses with predictable cash flows. The dividend yield expresses the annual dividend as a percentage of the current stock price, making it comparable across stocks of different prices.*

How Dividend Yield Works

If a company pays an annual dividend of $2.00 per share and its stock is currently trading at $50.00, the dividend yield is 4.0 percent ($2.00 divided by $50.00). If the stock price rises to $100.00 and the company maintains the same $2.00 annual dividend, the yield drops to 2.0 percent. Conversely, if the stock price falls to $25.00, the yield rises to 8.0 percent.

This inverse relationship between stock price and yield creates an important dynamic: a very high dividend yield can sometimes be a warning signal rather than an opportunity. If a stock's yield is unusually high (above 8 to 10 percent), it often means the stock price has fallen sharply, possibly because investors believe the company will cut or eliminate the dividend due to financial stress. This situation is called a "yield trap." Always investigate the underlying reason for an abnormally high yield before treating it as an attractive income opportunity.

Growth Stocks (Low or No Dividend)	Dividend / Income Stocks (Regular Payer)
Reinvest profits into expanding the business	Return profits to shareholders as regular cash
Examples: Amazon, Alphabet, Berkshire Hathaway	Examples: Johnson & Johnson, Coca-Cola, JPMorgan
Total return comes almost entirely from price appreciation	Total return is a combination of price appreciation and dividend income
Attract growth-oriented investors with longer horizons	Attract income-oriented and conservative investors
Often higher volatility during market downturns	Dividend payments provide a cushion during price declines
Higher growth potential in bull markets	More defensive performance in bear markets

Dividend Dates You Need to Know

Dividends involve four important dates that determine whether you are entitled to receive a payment:

- **Declaration Date:** The day the company's board of directors officially announces the upcoming dividend, including the amount and the payment schedule.
- **Ex-Dividend Date:** The most important date for traders. You must own the stock BEFORE this date to receive the upcoming dividend. If you buy on the ex-dividend date or after, you will not receive the payment. Stocks typically drop in price by

approximately the dividend amount on the ex-dividend date, as buyers from that date forward are not entitled to the payment.

- **Record Date:** The date on which the company checks its records to determine which shareholders will receive the dividend. This is typically one business day after the ex-dividend date.
- **Payment Date:** The date on which the dividend is actually deposited into shareholders' accounts. This typically occurs two to four weeks after the record date.

PLATFORM FEATURE: Dividend Information on stocktradesapp.com

On any stock's Quote Page, the Fundamentals Tab includes a Dividend section displaying the annual dividend per share, the dividend yield, the most recent quarterly dividend amount, and the upcoming ex-dividend date if one has been announced.

Your paper trading portfolio on StockTradesApp.com automatically credits dividend payments to your virtual cash balance when you hold a position through the ex-dividend date. This allows you to experience the full return profile of dividend-paying stocks in your simulated portfolio, including reinvestment decisions.

Stocks in the S&P 500 Dividend Aristocrats index have raised their dividends for 25 or more consecutive years. These companies represent some of the most financially disciplined and reliable businesses in the U.S. market, and they appear frequently in conservative long-term investment portfolios.

4.10 Putting It All Together: Reading a Live Quote in Real Time

The best way to consolidate everything in this chapter is to read a live stock quote on StockTradesApp.com right now, during a regular trading session, and work through it systematically. The following exercise walks you through that process step by step. Complete it during market hours (9:30 AM to 4:00 PM Eastern) for the most dynamic, real-time experience.

Reading a Full Live Quote: Chapter 4 Exercise

Step 1: Open StockTradesApp.com and search for a company you added to your watchlist in Chapter 3. Navigate to its Quote Page.

Step 2: READ THE PRICE HEADER. Record the last price, the dollar change, and the percentage change. Is the stock up or down today? By how much in percentage terms?

Step 3: CHECK THE BID-ASK SPREAD. Record the bid price and the ask price. Calculate the spread (ask minus bid). Is this a tight or wide spread? What does that tell you about the stock's liquidity?

Step 4: EXAMINE THE DAY'S RANGE. Compare the current price to today's high and low. Is the stock trading in the upper, middle, or lower portion of its intraday range? What does that suggest about whether buyers or sellers are in control right now?

Step 5: CHECK THE 52-WEEK RANGE. Where does the current price sit within the 52-week high and low? Calculate the percentage distance from the current price to both extremes.

Step 6: EXAMINE VOLUME. What is today's volume? What is the 30-day average daily volume? Is today's volume above or below average? If it is significantly above average, check the News Tab to find out why.

Step 7: LOOK AT THE DIVIDEND YIELD (if applicable). Is this a dividend-paying stock? If so, what is the current yield? Does that yield seem sustainable given what you know about the company?

Step 8: WRITE A ONE-PARAGRAPH QUOTE INTERPRETATION in your Trading Journal. Describe what the quote is telling you about this stock's current behavior. You do not need to make a trading decision. Simply narrate what the data is saying.

Complete this exercise for at least three different stocks on your watchlist. Variety matters: choose at least one large-cap tech stock, one defensive/dividend-paying stock, and one mid-cap stock you have been curious about. Each will show you a different profile of liquidity, volatility, and quote characteristics.

HOW LONG SHOULD THIS EXERCISE TAKE?

Plan to spend 15 to 20 minutes per stock for this exercise in the early stages. As you repeat this process over days and weeks, your reading speed will increase dramatically. Professional traders scan a quote in under 10 seconds and extract the same information this exercise walks you through in 20 minutes.

Speed in quote reading, like speed in any skill, comes from repetition rather than rushing. Do the exercise thoroughly now, and the fluency will develop naturally. By the time you reach Chapter 7, scanning a stock quote will feel as natural as reading a headline.

4.11 Common Beginner Mistakes When Reading Stock Quotes

Before closing this chapter, it is worth addressing the most frequent errors that beginning traders make when interpreting stock quote data. Awareness of these mistakes now will save you from making them in your paper trading.

- **Confusing Price with Value:** A stock priced at $5 is not "cheaper" than a stock priced at $500. Price per share alone tells you almost nothing about whether a stock is fairly valued, overvalued, or undervalued. A $5 stock can be wildly overpriced if the company is unprofitable and shrinking. A $500 stock can be a bargain if the company is growing rapidly and generating strong earnings. Always evaluate stocks on valuation metrics (covered in Chapter 5), not absolute price.
- **Reacting to Dollar Change Instead of Percentage Change:** A stock that moves $10 in a single day sounds dramatic. But if the stock trades at $1,000, that is a 1 percent move, nothing unusual. Always convert to percentage change before judging the significance of a price move.
- **Ignoring Volume:** Price moves without volume confirmation are among the most misleading signals in the market. A stock that surges 5 percent on half its normal daily volume is giving a very different signal than one that surges 5 percent on three times its normal volume. Never evaluate a price move without checking the volume context.
- **Treating the Last Price as the Execution Price:** If you place a market order, you will fill at approximately the ask price (for a buy) or the bid price (for a sell), not the last traded price displayed in the header. On highly liquid stocks, the difference is negligible. On illiquid stocks, the difference can be significant. Always check the bid-ask spread before placing an order.
- **Making Decisions Based on a Single Day's Quote:** A single day's price action is almost never a sufficient basis for a trading decision. Context matters enormously. A stock that falls 3 percent today might be perfectly healthy if it rose 15 percent over the prior three weeks. Always zoom out to the broader time frame before evaluating the significance of a single session's move.

> *"The single greatest edge an investor can have is a long-term orientation in a market obsessed with the short term."*
>
> — **Seth Klarman**, *Margin of Safety: Risk-Averse Value Investing Strategies for the Thoughtful Investor (1991)*

Chapter 4 Summary

Chapter 4 has equipped you with the complete vocabulary of the stock quote, from the basics of price and volume to the nuances of bid-ask spreads, market hours, and the psychological significance of the 52-week range. Here is what you now carry forward:

- **The Full Stock Quote:** Every data field on a StockTradesApp.com Quote Page has a specific meaning. The annotated quote table in Section 4.1 is your ongoing reference guide for every field you encounter.
- **The Bid-Ask Spread:** The gap between what buyers will pay and what sellers will accept represents a real, unavoidable transaction cost on every trade. Liquid large-cap stocks have tight spreads; thinly traded stocks have wide ones. Always check the spread before placing an order.
- **Market Hours:** The regular session (9:30 AM to 4:00 PM Eastern) is where beginners should focus all trading activity. The first and last 30 minutes of each session are the most volatile and require particular caution. Extended hours carry meaningful risks for inexperienced participants.
- **Volume as Confirmation:** Price moves are only meaningful in the context of volume. The four volume scenarios (price up or down, volume high or low) form a basic but powerful analytical framework. A breakout on below-average volume is an unconfirmed signal. A decline on below-average volume in an uptrending stock may be a buying opportunity.
- **The 52-Week Range:** These two reference points carry enormous psychological weight in the market. Near the 52-week high, overhead selling pressure is exhausted. Near the 52-week low, overhead resistance accumulates. Research confirms that stocks near their 52-week high tend to outperform over the following six to twelve months.
- **Extended Hours and Gaps:** Pre-market and after-hours trading are lower-liquidity, higher-spread environments. Events in these sessions create price gaps at the open that can be among the most informative signals of the trading day.
- **Percentage Always Over Dollars:** Every price move, gain, loss, and target should be expressed and evaluated in percentage terms. This normalizes comparisons across stocks of different prices and positions of different sizes.
- **Dividends and Yield:** Some stocks return cash to shareholders quarterly. The ex-dividend date determines eligibility. A very high yield can be a warning sign rather than an opportunity. Dividend-paying stocks tend to be more defensive in downturns and more attractive to income-oriented investors.

PART II

Navigating the Market

The Paper Trader

CHAPTER 5

Fundamental Analysis: Evaluating the Business Behind the Ticker

"A stock is not just a ticker symbol or an electronic blip; it is an ownership interest in an actual business, with an underlying value that does not depend on its share price."

— Benjamin Graham, Security Analysis (1934)

Everything you have learned so far has prepared you to look at the market. Chapter 5 teaches you to look through the market, past the price charts and the ticker symbols, and into the actual businesses that drive the prices you watch every day. This is the discipline of fundamental analysis, and it is the cornerstone of the most successful long-term investment approaches in history.

Fundamental analysis asks a single foundational question: what is this business actually worth? It seeks to answer that question by studying a company's financial statements, its competitive position, the quality of its management, the industry it operates in, and the broader economic environment that surrounds it. The goal is to determine a stock's intrinsic value and compare that value to its current market price. If the price is below intrinsic value, the stock may represent an opportunity. If the price significantly exceeds intrinsic value, the stock may be overvalued and carries elevated risk.

This chapter will not turn you into a certified financial analyst. That takes years of study. What it will do is give you a working framework for reading the three core financial statements, calculating and interpreting the key valuation and profitability ratios, and evaluating the qualitative factors that separate excellent businesses from merely adequate ones. You will apply each concept directly to real company data on StockTradesApp.com as you go.

> *"The secret to sound investment is a thorough understanding of financial statements."*
>
> — **Benjamin Graham**, *The Interpretation of Financial Statements (1937): the foundational text of financial statement analysis*

5.1 Fundamental vs. Technical Analysis: Two Lenses on the Same Stock

Before diving into financial statements, it is worth clearly distinguishing fundamental analysis from technical analysis, because both are covered in this book and they serve very different purposes. Understanding the distinction prevents confusion as you develop your overall analytical framework.

- **Fundamental Analysis** asks: what is this company worth? It studies financial performance, competitive position, management quality, and macroeconomic context to determine intrinsic value. It is the primary tool of long-term investors and value-oriented traders. Its time horizon is typically months to years.
- **Technical Analysis** asks: where is this stock's price going next? It studies price charts, volume patterns, and mathematical indicators to identify trends and predict short-term price direction. It is the primary tool of shorter-term traders. Its time horizon is typically days to weeks. Chapter 6 covers technical analysis in full.

The most sophisticated market participants use both. They use fundamental analysis to identify what to buy (businesses of genuine quality at reasonable prices) and technical analysis to determine when to buy (the optimal price entry point given current chart patterns and momentum). This integrated approach, sometimes called "fundamentally sound, technically timed," is the framework this book builds toward in Chapter 10.

For this chapter, the focus is exclusively on fundamentals. Close the chart. You are looking at the business.

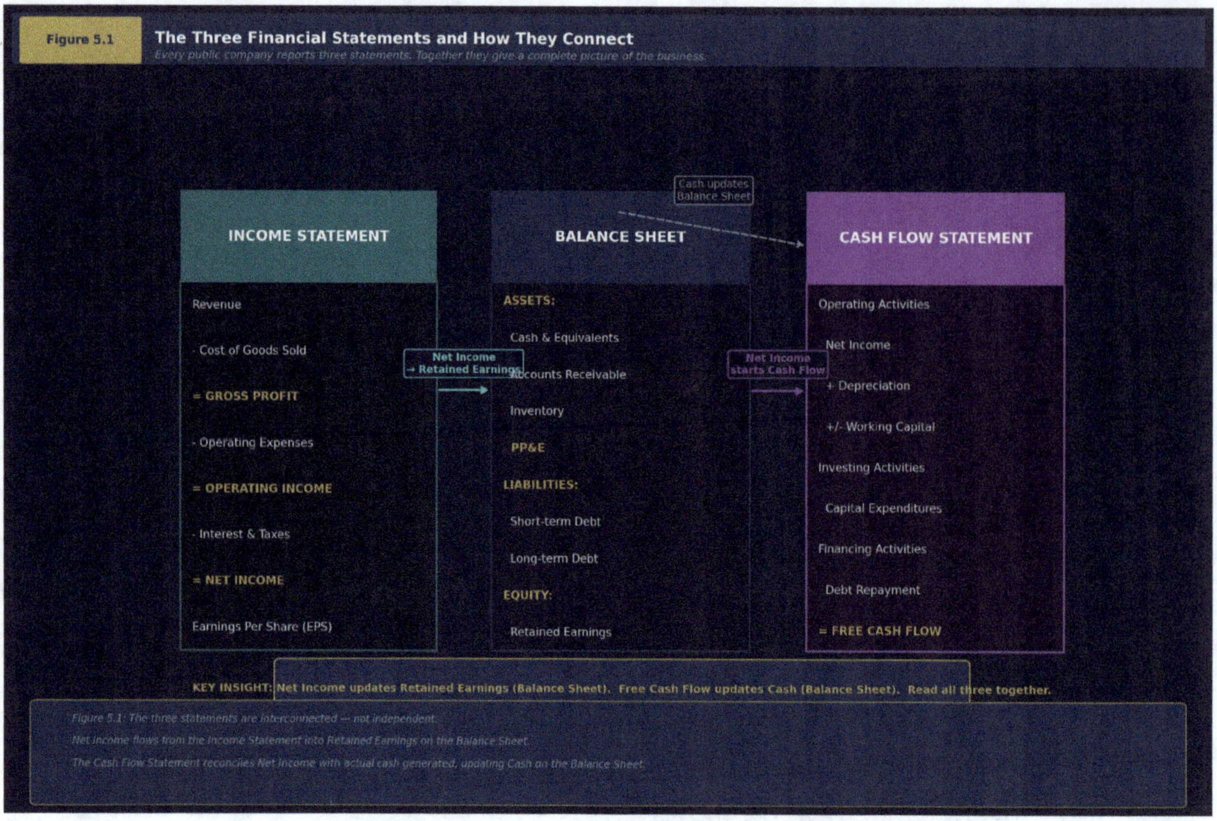

Figure 5.1 - The Three Financial Statements: The Income Statement, Balance Sheet, and Cash Flow Statement together give a complete picture of any business. Net Income connects all three.

5.2 The Three Financial Statements: The Complete Financial Picture

Every publicly traded company in the United States is required by the Securities and Exchange Commission (SEC) to file detailed financial reports on a quarterly basis (the 10-Q filing) and an annual basis (the 10-K filing). These filings contain three core financial statements that together paint a complete picture of a company's financial health. Knowing how to read each one is a foundational skill of every serious investor.

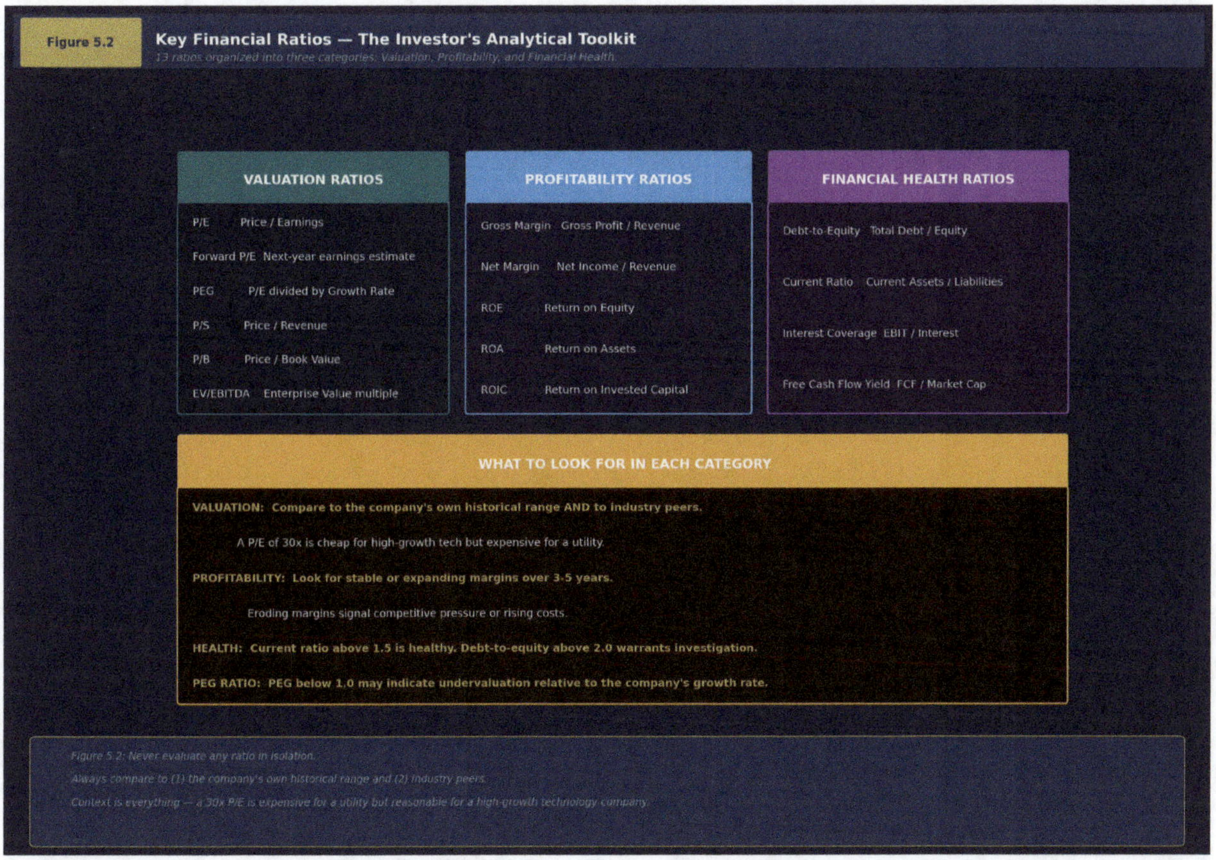

Figure 5.2 - Key Financial Ratios: 13 ratios organized into Valuation, Profitability, and Financial Health categories. Never evaluate any ratio in isolation — always compare to industry peers and historical ranges.

KEY TERM: SEC 10-K Filing

The comprehensive annual report that all publicly traded U.S. companies must file with the Securities and Exchange Commission. It contains the company's complete audited financial statements, management's discussion of performance, risk factors, business description, and executive compensation details. The 10-K is the single most authoritative source of information about a publicly traded company's financial health. It is freely available to any investor on the SEC's EDGAR database at sec.gov.

The Three Financial Statements at a Glance

- **The Income Statement** (also called the Profit and Loss Statement or P&L) shows how much money the company earned and spent over a specific period, typically one quarter or one fiscal year. It tells you whether the company is profitable and how efficiently it converts sales into earnings. Think of it as the company's report card for a specific period.
- **The Balance Sheet** (also called the Statement of Financial Position) is a snapshot of the company's financial condition on a specific date. It shows what the company

owns (assets), what it owes (liabilities), and the difference between the two (shareholders' equity). Think of it as a photograph of the company's wealth at a single moment in time.

- **The Cash Flow Statement** shows how cash actually moved in and out of the business during a period. It reconciles the accounting profit shown on the income statement with the actual cash generated by the business, because accounting rules allow for revenue to be recognized before cash is collected, and expenses to be recorded before cash is paid. Cash flow is considered the most difficult financial metric to manipulate and therefore one of the most reliable indicators of a business's true health.

WHY ALL THREE STATEMENTS MATTER TOGETHER

A company can appear profitable on its income statement while quietly running out of cash. A company can show strong cash flow while carrying a debt burden on its balance sheet that could become catastrophic in a recession. A company can have a healthy balance sheet but generate declining profits year after year.

Skilled fundamental analysts never rely on a single statement. They triangulate across all three to build a complete picture. As legendary investor and author Peter Lynch observed in One Up on Wall Street (1989): "Behind every stock is a company. Find out what it's doing." The financial statements are where you find out what it is doing.

StockTradesApp.com makes all three financial statements available for every publicly traded stock on the platform, updated every quarter after earnings reports are filed. The Fundamentals Tab on each stock's Quote Page is your gateway to this data.

5.3 The Income Statement: Reading the Company's Report Card

The income statement follows a simple logical progression: it starts with total revenue at the top (the "top line"), subtracts every category of cost and expense in sequence, and arrives at net income at the bottom (the "bottom line"). Every line in between tells you something specific about how efficiently the company converts sales into profit.

The table below shows a simplified version of Apple's income statement for fiscal years 2022 and 2023, annotated with plain-English explanations of each line item. Apple is used because it is one of the most widely studied companies in the world, its financials are publicly available, and most readers have direct experience as a customer of its products.

Line Item	FY 2023 ($B)	FY 2022 ($B)	What It Means
Revenue (Net Sales)	$383.3B	$394.3B	Total money earned from selling products and services before any deductions
Cost of Revenue (COGS)	$214.1B	$223.5B	Direct costs of producing the goods and services sold
GROSS PROFIT	**$169.1B**	**$170.8B**	**Revenue minus COGS. What's left before operating expenses**
Gross Profit Margin	**44.1%**	**43.3%**	**Gross Profit divided by Revenue. Higher = stronger pricing power**
Operating Expenses (R&D + SG&A)	$54.8B	$51.7B	Costs to run the business: research, salaries, marketing, admin
OPERATING INCOME	**$114.3B**	**$119.4B**	**Gross Profit minus Operating Expenses. Core business profitability**
Operating Margin	**29.8%**	**30.3%**	**Operating Income divided by Revenue. Key efficiency metric**
Other Income / (Expense)	$3.7B	($0.3B)	Interest earned, investment gains/losses, one-time items
Income Before Tax	$118.0B	$119.1B	Operating Income plus/minus other items
Income Tax Provision	$29.7B	$29.7B	Taxes owed on pre-tax income
NET INCOME	**$97.0B**	**$99.8B**	**The bottom line. What the company actually earned after all costs and taxes**
Net Profit Margin	**25.3%**	**25.3%**	**Net Income divided by Revenue. How many cents of profit per dollar of sales**
Earnings Per Share (EPS)	$6.13	$6.11	Net Income divided by shares outstanding. The per-share profit number

Source: Apple Inc. (AAPL) Annual Reports FY2022 and FY2023. Figures rounded. For illustration purposes only.

The Lines That Matter Most

While every line on the income statement has meaning, four in particular deserve special attention from beginning investors.

- **Revenue Growth:** Is revenue growing year over year? A business that is not growing its top line is either losing market share, operating in a declining industry, or being outmaneuvered by competitors. Notice that Apple's revenue actually declined slightly from FY2022 to FY2023 (from $394.3 billion to $383.3 billion), reflecting weaker demand in several product categories. This is important context for evaluating the stock's valuation.
- **Gross Profit Margin:** Apple's gross margin of 44.1% in FY2023 is exceptional. It means that for every dollar of revenue, Apple retains $0.44 after paying the direct costs of producing its products. This high gross margin reflects the pricing power that comes from Apple's strong brand and ecosystem. By comparison, a commodity hardware manufacturer might have a gross margin of only 10 to 15%.
- **Operating Margin:** Apple's operating margin of approximately 30% means the company keeps $0.30 of every revenue dollar after paying all operating expenses including research and development, marketing, and administrative costs. This is a world-class operating margin. The S&P 500 average operating margin has historically been approximately 15%, meaning Apple operates at roughly twice the efficiency of the average large company.
- **Earnings Per Share (EPS):** The $6.13 EPS figure represents Apple's net income divided by its total shares outstanding. This is the number that drives the P/E ratio calculation and is the most closely watched metric during every earnings season. Companies that consistently grow EPS year after year are compounding shareholder value at the per-share level, which is ultimately what drives stock price appreciation over time.

🖥 PLATFORM FEATURE: Accessing the Income Statement on stocktradesapp.com

Navigate to any stock's Quote Page and click the "Fundamentals" tab. Within that tab, select "Income Statement" from the sub-navigation.

The platform displays the income statement in both annual and quarterly formats. The annual view is better for evaluating long-term trends and business quality. The quarterly view is better for identifying near-term momentum and comparing results to analyst estimates.

Use the "Compare Period" toggle to view two years side by side, which makes it easy to identify whether key metrics like gross margin and EPS are trending in the right direction.

A red arrow next to any line item indicates year-over-year deterioration. A green arrow indicates improvement. Focus your initial attention on the direction of revenue growth, gross margin, and EPS.

5.4 The Balance Sheet: A Snapshot of Financial Health

If the income statement is a company's report card for the past year, the balance sheet is its current medical chart. It tells you the company's financial condition right now: how much it owns, how much it owes, and the net difference between those two numbers. The balance sheet is governed by a fundamental accounting equation that is always true:

Total Assets = Total Liabilities + Shareholders' Equity

This equation is always in perfect balance, which is why the document is called a balance sheet. If a company has $100 in assets and $60 in liabilities, shareholders' equity must equal $40. That $40 represents the theoretical book value of what shareholders would receive if the company sold all its assets and paid off all its debts.

The table below shows a simplified version of Apple's balance sheet as of the end of FY2023, with annotations explaining each major category.

Balance Sheet Item	FY 2023 ($B)	What It Represents
ASSETS		
Cash & Cash Equivalents	$29.9B	Liquid funds immediately available
Short-Term Investments	$31.6B	Securities that can be liquidated quickly
Accounts Receivable	$29.5B	Money owed to Apple by customers (not yet collected)
Inventories	$6.3B	Products manufactured but not yet sold
Other Current Assets	$14.7B	Prepaid expenses and other near-term assets
TOTAL CURRENT ASSETS	**$143.6B**	**Assets convertible to cash within one year**

Balance Sheet Item	FY 2023 ($B)	What It Represents
Property, Plant & Equipment (net)	$43.7B	Physical assets: buildings, equipment, machinery
Long-Term Investments	$100.5B	Securities held beyond one year
Other Long-Term Assets	$64.8B	Deferred tax assets, goodwill, intangibles
TOTAL ASSETS	**$352.6B**	**Everything the company owns**
LIABILITIES		
Accounts Payable	$62.6B	Money Apple owes to suppliers (not yet paid)
Short-Term Debt	$9.8B	Debt due within one year
Other Current Liabilities	$58.8B	Accrued expenses and deferred revenue
TOTAL CURRENT LIABILITIES	**$145.3B**	**Obligations due within one year**
Long-Term Debt	$95.3B	Bonds and loans due beyond one year
Other Long-Term Liabilities	$49.8B	Deferred taxes and other obligations
TOTAL LIABILITIES	**$290.4B**	**Everything the company owes**
SHAREHOLDERS' EQUITY		
Common Stock + Paid-In Capital	$73.8B	Capital raised through stock issuances
Retained Earnings (Deficit)	($214.0B)	Cumulative profits reinvested or returned via buybacks
Accumulated Other Comp. Income	($11.5B)	Unrealized gains/losses on investments
TOTAL SHAREHOLDERS' EQUITY	**$62.1B**	**Assets minus Liabilities. The book value of ownership**

Source: Apple Inc. (AAPL) Annual Report FY2023 (10-K filing). Figures rounded. For illustration purposes only.

Key Balance Sheet Observations for Apple FY2023

Several features of Apple's balance sheet deserve particular attention as teaching examples.

- **Massive Cash and Investment Position:** Apple holds approximately $61.5 billion in combined cash, equivalents, and short-term investments, plus an additional $100.5 billion in long-term investments. This enormous liquidity position gives Apple the financial flexibility to weather economic downturns, acquire companies, fund research and development, repurchase stock, and pay dividends without needing to borrow.

- **The Negative Retained Earnings:** Apple's retained earnings are negative ($214 billion in deficit). This unusual situation occurs because Apple has returned so much capital to shareholders through stock buybacks over the past decade that the cumulative buybacks exceed all historical retained earnings. This is not a sign of financial distress; it is a consequence of extraordinary capital returns. Apple has repurchased over $600 billion of its own stock since 2012, according to its annual reports.
- **Significant Long-Term Debt:** Apple carries $95.3 billion in long-term debt. This may seem alarming until you consider that Apple's annual operating cash flow regularly exceeds $100 billion, meaning it could theoretically pay off its entire long-term debt in approximately one year from cash generated by operations. The ratio of debt to cash generation is a far more meaningful metric than the absolute debt number.

THE DEBT QUESTION: HOW MUCH IS TOO MUCH?

One of Warren Buffett's primary balance sheet tests, as described by Mary Buffett and David Clark in Warren Buffett and the Interpretation of Financial Statements (2008), is the ability of a company to pay off its long-term debt from net earnings within three to four years.

Apple passes this test comfortably. Many other companies do not. A company carrying debt that would take 10 or 15 years of earnings to repay is financially fragile. An economic slowdown, a credit market disruption, or an industry disruption can make that debt load catastrophic.

When evaluating any company's balance sheet, ask this question: if business conditions deteriorated significantly, would this company be able to meet its debt obligations? Companies that can answer "yes" confidently are far more resilient investments than those whose survival depends on continuous access to favorable credit markets.

5.5 The Cash Flow Statement: The Truth Underneath the Numbers

If you could only read one financial statement, most sophisticated investors would choose the cash flow statement. While accounting rules give companies significant flexibility in how they recognize revenue and expenses on the income statement, cash is binary: either the company received it or it did not. The cash flow statement cuts through the accounting noise and shows you what is actually happening to real money inside the business.

KEY TERM: Free Cash Flow (FCF)
Operating Cash Flow minus Capital Expenditures (CapEx). Free Cash Flow represents the cash a business generates from its operations after paying for the investments needed to maintain and grow its asset base. It is the cash that is genuinely available to shareholders: to pay dividends, buy back stock, pay down debt, or reinvest in growth. Consistently growing FCF over multiple years is one of the strongest signals of business quality.

The Three Components of the Cash Flow Statement

- **Cash from Operating Activities** (Operating Cash Flow): The cash generated by the company's core business operations. This should be consistently positive and growing. A company whose income statement shows profits but whose operating cash flow is chronically negative is a serious red flag. Revenue is being recognized that is not actually converting to cash.
- **Cash from Investing Activities** The cash used for and generated by long-term investments. Typically negative for healthy, growing companies, because they are investing capital expenditure (CapEx) into property, equipment, and acquisitions. A mature company reducing CapEx is either efficiently managing its infrastructure or, more concerning, underinvesting in future competitiveness.
- **Cash from Financing Activities** The cash exchanged between the company and its capital providers (debt holders and equity holders). This includes borrowing money (positive cash inflow), repaying debt (negative), issuing new stock (positive), and buying back stock or paying dividends (negative).

For Apple in FY2023, operating cash flow was approximately $110 billion, capital expenditures were approximately $11 billion, producing free cash flow of roughly $99 billion. This extraordinary free cash flow generation is one of the primary reasons Apple commands such a high valuation multiple: the business is a cash-generating machine of rare power.

> *"Cash, frankly, is the oxygen of a business. Businesses that generate more cash than they consume are in a fundamentally different position than those that need to continuously access capital markets to fund their operations."*
> — **Warren Buffett**, *Berkshire Hathaway Annual Letter to Shareholders, widely paraphrased across multiple years*

🖥 PLATFORM FEATURE: Cash Flow Statement on stocktradesapp.com

Within the Fundamentals Tab on any stock's Quote Page, navigate to "Cash Flow Statement." The platform displays all three sections of the cash flow statement for the past four to five fiscal years, making it easy to identify trends.

Look for the "Free Cash Flow" row near the bottom of the operating section. StockTradesApp.com calculates this automatically as Operating Cash Flow minus CapEx.

A key check: compare Net Income (from the Income Statement) to Operating Cash Flow (from the Cash Flow Statement). They should be in reasonable alignment over time. If net income is consistently far higher than operating cash flow, the company may be using aggressive accounting to inflate reported profits.

5.6 Key Financial Ratios: The Investor's Analytical Toolkit

Financial ratios transform the raw numbers on financial statements into comparable, meaningful metrics that allow you to evaluate a company's performance in context. They let you compare a $10 stock to a $500 stock on equal terms, evaluate a small company against a large one, and benchmark any company against its industry peers or historical averages.

The table below presents the thirteen most important financial ratios for beginning investors, organized with their formulas, relevant benchmarks, and plain-English guidance on what to look for. You will find every one of these metrics in the Fundamentals Tab on StockTradesApp.com.

Metric	Formula	Benchmark / Context	What to Look For
P/E Ratio (TTM)	Price / EPS (last 12 months)	S&P 500 historical avg: ~19-20x	Compare to sector peers. High P/E = growth priced in. Low P/E = value or risk.
Forward P/E	Price / Estimated EPS (next 12 months)	Lower than TTM P/E is positive	Shows if earnings growth is expected. A stock with TTM P/E of 30x and Forward P/E

Metric	Formula	Benchmark / Context	What to Look For
			of 20x has strong expected growth.
PEG Ratio	P/E Ratio / EPS Growth Rate (%)	Under 1.0 often seen as undervalued	Developed by Peter Lynch. Adjusts P/E for growth. A P/E of 30 with 30% growth = PEG of 1.0, which Lynch considered fairly valued.
Price-to-Sales (P/S)	Market Cap / Annual Revenue	Varies widely by sector	Useful for unprofitable or early-stage growth companies where P/E is not applicable. Tech companies often carry 5-15x P/S.
Price-to-Book (P/B)	Market Cap / Total Shareholders' Equity	Under 1.0 = trading below book value	Graham favored stocks trading below book value. Buffett evolved beyond this for high-quality businesses.
Gross Profit Margin	(Revenue - COGS) / Revenue	S&P 500 average: ~44%	Higher margin = stronger pricing power and less commodity exposure. Software companies often exceed 70%.
Operating Margin	Operating Income / Revenue	S&P 500 average: ~15%	Core business profitability after R&D and SG&A. One of Buffett's primary metrics for evaluating business quality.
Net Profit Margin	Net Income / Revenue	S&P 500 average: ~11-12%	Bottom-line efficiency. Consistently above 20% is exceptional and often indicates a strong competitive moat.
Return on Equity (ROE)	Net Income / Shareholders' Equity	Above 15% considered strong	Buffett considers ROE above 15% over multiple years a hallmark of an excellent business.
Debt-to-Equity (D/E)	Total Debt / Shareholders' Equity	Below 1.0 generally preferred	Measures financial leverage. Very high D/E in a slowdown means the company may struggle to service debt.
Current Ratio	Current Assets / Current Liabilities	Above 1.5 considered healthy	Liquidity test. Can the company pay its short-term obligations? Below 1.0 is a red flag.
EPS Growth (3-5 yr)	% change in EPS per year over 3-5 years	Above 10% per year is strong	Consistent EPS growth is one of the most powerful indicators of a business

Metric	Formula	Benchmark / Context	What to Look For
			compounding value for shareholders.
Free Cash Flow (FCF)	Operating Cash Flow - Capital Expenditures	Positive and growing is ideal	Called the "oxygen of a business." A company that generates abundant FCF can self-fund growth, pay dividends, and buy back stock.

The P/E Ratio: The Most Discussed Metric in Investing

Of all the ratios in the table above, the price-to-earnings ratio (P/E) is the most widely cited and the most frequently misunderstood. It answers the question: how much are investors paying for each dollar of the company's earnings? A P/E of 20 means investors are paying $20 for every $1 of annual earnings.

~19-20x

The long-run historical average P/E ratio of the S&P 500, based on data from 1957 to present. This serves as the primary benchmark for evaluating whether the broader market is cheap or expensive relative to historical norms.

Source: us500.com / Standard & Poor's historical data series

A stock trading at a P/E well above the market average is not necessarily overvalued. High-growth companies command premium P/E ratios because investors are paying for future earnings growth, not just current earnings. A technology company growing earnings at 30% per year deserves a much higher P/E than a utility company growing earnings at 3% per year. This is why Peter Lynch developed the PEG ratio: to adjust the P/E for growth and create a more apples-to-apples comparison across companies with different growth profiles.

Conversely, a very low P/E is not automatically attractive. It can signal a value opportunity, but it can also signal a business in secular decline, a company facing legal or regulatory headwinds, or an entire industry being disrupted by technology. The market usually has a reason for pricing a stock at a deep discount. The question for the fundamental analyst is whether that reason is temporary and recoverable, or structural and permanent.

The PEG Ratio: Buffett's Favorite Refinement

> *"A P/E ratio, in and of itself, is nearly meaningless. It must be viewed in the context of earnings growth. That's why Peter Lynch's PEG ratio is so elegant: it puts the price in the context of the business's actual growth trajectory."*
> — **Peter Lynch**, *One Up on Wall Street (1989): one of the best-selling investment books of all time*

The PEG ratio is calculated by dividing a stock's P/E ratio by its annual earnings growth rate. A stock with a P/E of 30 and annual earnings growth of 30% has a PEG of 1.0. Lynch considered a PEG below 1.0 attractive and a PEG above 1.5 potentially expensive. The PEG ratio is most useful for growth stocks where the P/E alone would suggest overvaluation but the growth rate justifies the premium.

For example, a technology company with a P/E of 40 might seem expensive compared to the market average of 20. But if that company is growing earnings at 35% per year, its PEG ratio is approximately 1.14, which is actually reasonable by Lynch's standard. Meanwhile, a financial services company with a P/E of 12 might look cheap, but if it is only growing earnings at 3% per year, its PEG is 4.0, suggesting significant overvaluation relative to its growth rate.

5.7 Qualitative Analysis: What the Numbers Cannot Tell You

Numbers tell you what happened. Qualitative analysis tells you why it happened and whether it is likely to continue. The most sophisticated fundamental analysts spend at least as much time on qualitative factors as they do on financial statements, because the numbers are ultimately a lagging reflection of the business's underlying competitive dynamics.

There are four qualitative pillars that every serious fundamental analyst evaluates.

Pillar 1: The Competitive Moat

Warren Buffett popularized the concept of the economic moat: a sustainable competitive advantage that protects a company's market position and pricing power from competitors the way a medieval castle's moat protected it from invaders. Buffett has described the width and durability of a company's moat as the single most important qualitative factor in his investment decisions.

> *"The key to investing is not assessing how much an industry is going to affect society, or how much it will grow, but rather determining the competitive advantage of any given company and, above all, the durability of that advantage."*
> — **Warren Buffett**, *Fortune Magazine interview (1999)*

There are six primary types of economic moats. The table below defines each type, explains how it works, and provides real-world examples of companies that exemplify each.

Moat Type	How It Works	Real-World Example
Brand & Intangible Assets	Consumers pay premium prices because of brand loyalty, trust, or perceived quality that competitors cannot easily replicate	Apple (premium pricing power), Coca-Cola (global brand recognition), Nike (aspirational identity)
Switching Costs	Customers face significant financial, operational, or psychological costs to switch to a competing product	Microsoft (Office 365 / Azure), Salesforce (CRM systems), Oracle (enterprise database software)
Network Effects	The product becomes more valuable as more people use it, creating a self-reinforcing cycle that is nearly impossible for newcomers to break	Visa and Mastercard (more merchants and cardholders attract each other), Meta (more users = more advertisers = more users)
Cost Advantages	The company can produce goods or services at fundamentally lower costs than competitors, allowing it to undercut on price or earn superior margins	Amazon (logistics and AWS scale), Walmart (supply chain), Costco (membership model + bulk purchasing)
Efficient Scale	The company operates in a market where only a limited number of players can profitably exist, creating a natural barrier to new entrants	Utilities (water, electricity infrastructure), pipelines, major airports and seaports
Regulatory Moats	Licenses, patents, regulatory approvals, or legal protections	Pharmaceutical companies with drug patents, defense contractors with security

Moat Type	How It Works	Real-World Example
	that competitors cannot easily obtain	clearances, financial institutions with banking licenses

When evaluating any stock for a long-term investment position, ask this question directly: what would it take for a well-funded competitor to put this company out of business? If the answer is "almost nothing" (the company sells a commodity product in a competitive market with no switching costs and no brand loyalty), the moat is shallow or nonexistent. If the answer is "it would be nearly impossible because of network effects, regulatory barriers, and brand loyalty that took decades to build," the moat is wide and durable.

Pillar 2: Management Quality

The financial statements tell you what management has accomplished. Evaluating management quality requires going further and assessing whether the people running the business are honest, capable, and aligned with shareholders' long-term interests.

Key indicators of management quality include the track record of delivering on guidance (do they consistently deliver what they promise, or do they repeatedly miss their own targets?), capital allocation discipline (do they invest in high-return projects, or do they waste capital on expensive acquisitions that destroy value?), insider ownership (do executives own significant personal stakes in the company, aligning their interests with shareholders?), and compensation structure (are executives rewarded for genuine long-term value creation, or for short-term metrics that can be gamed?).

The most direct window into management's thinking is the annual letter to shareholders and the quarterly earnings conference call transcript. Both are available in the SEC filings section of StockTradesApp.com for every publicly traded company. Listen carefully to how management discusses setbacks and challenges. Leaders who take responsibility, acknowledge mistakes, and articulate credible corrective actions are far more trustworthy than those who blame external factors for every disappointment.

Pillar 3: Industry and Sector Analysis

Even an exceptional management team operating a business with a wide moat can be overwhelmed by structural headwinds in a declining industry. Kodak had superb technology, excellent margins, and a powerful brand in the film photography business right up until digital photography made film obsolete. Blockbuster Video had thousands of locations, a loyal customer base, and a recognizable brand right up until streaming made physical video rental irrelevant.

Before investing in any company, understand the long-term trajectory of the industry it operates in. Is the industry growing, stable, or contracting? Is it being disrupted by technology, regulation, or changing consumer behavior? Are the industry's pricing dynamics favorable (companies have pricing power) or unfavorable (intense competition forces constant price-cutting)?

StockTradesApp.com's Sector Performance Overview in the Analyze section provides a multi-timeframe view of how each of the eleven S&P 500 sectors is performing. This is your starting point for identifying which areas of the economy are structurally expanding and which are under pressure.

Pillar 4: Macroeconomic Context

Finally, no business operates in a vacuum. The broader economic environment affects every company, some more than others. Interest rates directly impact the cost of borrowing for businesses and consumers. Inflation affects input costs and consumer spending power. Employment levels influence consumer confidence and discretionary spending. Currency exchange rates affect the profitability of companies with significant international revenue.

Understanding the macroeconomic context does not mean trying to predict the economy, which is extraordinarily difficult even for professional economists. It means understanding which economic conditions are favorable or unfavorable for the specific businesses you are evaluating and building that context into your investment thesis.

5.8 A Five-Step Fundamental Analysis Framework

The following five-step framework synthesizes everything in this chapter into an actionable process you can apply to any stock. Use it in your paper trading research on StockTradesApp.com. As your skill develops, this process will become faster and more intuitive. For now, work through every step deliberately.

The Five-Step Fundamental Analysis Process

Step 1: UNDERSTAND THE BUSINESS FIRST. Before looking at a single number, describe in two to three sentences what the company does, how it makes money, and who its primary customers are. If you cannot explain the business clearly in plain English, you are not ready to evaluate its financials. This is the first rule Warren Buffett applies to every potential investment.

Step 2: EVALUATE THE INCOME STATEMENT. On StockTradesApp.com's Fundamentals Tab, pull up the income statement for the past three to five years. Answer these questions: Is revenue growing consistently? Is the gross profit margin stable or expanding? Is EPS growing? Are operating expenses growing faster or slower than revenue? Look for trends, not just single-year snapshots.

Step 3: EXAMINE THE BALANCE SHEET. Check the current ratio (current assets divided by current liabilities). Is it above 1.5? How much long-term debt does the company carry, and how does that compare to its annual earnings or operating cash flow? Is shareholders' equity positive and growing? Flag any major deterioration in financial position from year to year.

Step 4: ANALYZE CASH FLOW. Find the Free Cash Flow figure (Operating Cash Flow minus CapEx). Is it positive? Is it growing? Compare it to Net Income. If Net Income is consistently higher than Operating Cash Flow, investigate why. This discrepancy often signals aggressive revenue recognition or other accounting choices that may not be sustainable.

Step 5: ASSESS QUALITATIVE FACTORS AND VALUATION. Does the company have a durable competitive moat? Is management trustworthy and aligned with shareholders? Is the industry structurally sound? Then calculate the key valuation ratios: P/E, PEG, P/S, and P/B. Compare these ratios to the company's own historical averages and to its closest industry peers. Is the stock trading at a premium, discount, or in line with historical norms? Only now, after completing steps 1 through 4, does the valuation ratio become a meaningful input.

This five-step process is not quick in the early stages. A thorough fundamental analysis of a new company may take two to three hours for a beginning investor. With practice, that time shrinks to 30 to 45 minutes for most situations. Professional analysts spend days or weeks on detailed analysis of major positions. The depth of your analysis should be proportional to the size of the position you are considering and the complexity of the business.

HOW MUCH ANALYSIS IS ENOUGH?

Benjamin Graham famously wrote in The Intelligent Investor that "the investor does not need a large number of securities if he makes a thorough analysis of each one." This principle of concentrated research, going deep on fewer names rather than shallow on many, is one of the most consistently cited practices of the world's most successful long-term investors.

Warren Buffett has said that he reads 500 pages of financial and business documents every day. Charlie Munger, his longtime partner at Berkshire Hathaway, described their investment approach as "sitting quietly and reading" as the primary activity.

You do not need to read 500 pages a day to become a successful investor. But you do need to do meaningfully more research on each company you invest in than reading a headline and checking the stock's recent price performance. The five-step framework above is the minimum viable analysis for any new position.

5.9 Intrinsic Value and the Margin of Safety

The ultimate goal of fundamental analysis is to estimate a company's intrinsic value: what the business is genuinely worth, independent of what the market is currently pricing it at. This is the concept at the heart of value investing as pioneered by Benjamin Graham and refined by Warren Buffett.

KEY TERM: Intrinsic Value
The estimated true economic worth of a company, based on its financial performance, future earnings potential, competitive position, and the time value of money. Intrinsic value is calculated by analysts using methods such as discounted cash flow (DCF) analysis, comparable company analysis, and asset-based valuation. It is always an estimate rather than a precise number, and reasonable analysts applying the same methods to the same company will arrive at different values.

The concept of intrinsic value leads directly to one of the most powerful risk management principles in all of investing: the margin of safety. Graham defined the margin of safety as the difference between a stock's intrinsic value and its market price. The larger that gap (with price below value), the greater the protection against being wrong in your analysis.

> *"The three most important words in investing are margin of safety."*
> — **Warren Buffett**, *referencing the core concept of Benjamin Graham's The Intelligent Investor (1949)*

In practical terms, the margin of safety means that if you estimate a company's intrinsic value at $100 per share and require a 30% margin of safety, you would only buy the stock if it is trading at or below $70. This cushion serves two purposes: it protects you if your analysis is wrong (which it sometimes will be), and it creates the potential for above-average returns if your analysis is correct and the market eventually prices the stock closer to its intrinsic value.

Full intrinsic value calculation using discounted cash flow analysis is an advanced skill covered in depth in specialized finance curricula. For the purposes of this book and the paper trading journey on StockTradesApp.com, the most practical application of the intrinsic value concept is comparative: is this stock trading at a significant discount to both its own historical valuation averages and to the valuations of similar companies in its industry? If yes, you may have found a margin of safety opportunity worth investigating further.

🖥 PLATFORM FEATURE: Analyst Price Targets on stocktradesapp.com

StockTradesApp.com aggregates Wall Street analyst price targets for every major publicly traded stock. You will find these in the Fundamentals Tab under "Analyst Coverage."

The consensus price target represents the average of all analyst estimates for the stock's price twelve months from now, based on their individual fundamental analyses. It is not intrinsic value, but it serves as a useful reference point for how professional analysts view the stock's current valuation relative to their estimated fair value.

Use analyst price targets as one data point among many, not as a definitive answer. Analysts are frequently wrong, and their estimates are often anchored to the stock's recent price rather than derived from purely independent analysis. The most valuable information from analyst coverage is typically the reasoning and assumptions behind the target, not the target number itself.

5.10 Chapter 5 Exercise: Your First Fundamental Analysis

The following exercise asks you to apply the five-step fundamental analysis framework to a real company using StockTradesApp.com. Complete every step in writing, in your Trading Journal. Resist the temptation to skip steps or substitute general impressions for specific data. The discipline of working through the full process is more valuable than the conclusion you reach.

Chapter 5 Fundamental Analysis Exercise

Step 1: SELECT A COMPANY. Choose one stock from your watchlist that you have not yet paper traded. It should be a company whose business you understand enough to describe in plain English. Large-cap companies with abundant public information are ideal for this first exercise: Apple (AAPL), Microsoft (MSFT), Johnson & Johnson (JNJ), Coca-Cola (KO), or JPMorgan Chase (JPM) are all excellent candidates.

Step 2: STEP 1: BUSINESS DESCRIPTION. Write two to three sentences in your Trading Journal describing what the company does, how it makes money, and who its customers are. Do not look at the stock price or chart yet.

Step 3: STEP 2: INCOME STATEMENT. On StockTradesApp.com, open the company's Fundamentals Tab and navigate to the Income Statement. Record the past three years of revenue, gross profit margin, operating margin, net profit margin, and EPS. Are all three trending in the right direction?

Step 4: STEP 3: BALANCE SHEET. Record the current ratio, long-term debt, and shareholders' equity. Is the balance sheet strong enough to survive a significant economic downturn? Compare long-term debt to one year's operating cash flow.

Step 5: STEP 4: CASH FLOW. Find the Free Cash Flow figure for the past three years. Is it positive and growing? How does it compare to net income? Note any significant divergence between the two.

Step 6: STEP 5: RATIOS AND MOAT. Record the P/E ratio, PEG ratio (if available), gross margin, operating margin, ROE, and debt-to-equity ratio. Compare each to the benchmarks in Section 5.6's ratios table. Then write one paragraph evaluating the company's competitive moat. Which moat type from Section 5.7 applies, if any?

Step 7: VALUATION CONCLUSION. Based on your analysis, write a one-paragraph investment thesis. Is this a business of quality? Is it trading at a reasonable valuation? What would make you more or less confident in this business as a long-term holding? Add this analysis to your Trading Journal as the pre-trade research entry before any future paper trade in this stock.

Chapter 5 Summary

Chapter 5 has given you the foundational vocabulary and analytical framework of fundamental analysis. Here is what you now carry forward:

- **Two Complementary Disciplines:** Fundamental analysis determines what to buy by evaluating business quality and intrinsic value. Technical analysis (Chapter 6) determines when to buy by studying price and volume patterns. The most effective investors integrate both.

- **Three Financial Statements:** The income statement reports profitability over a period. The balance sheet shows financial position at a single moment. The cash flow statement reveals the actual movement of cash through the business. Together they provide a complete, triangulated picture of financial health.
- **The Income Statement Story:** Revenue is the top line; net income is the bottom line. Gross margin reveals pricing power. Operating margin reveals operational efficiency. EPS growth compounds shareholder value over time.
- **Balance Sheet Health:** The accounting equation (Assets = Liabilities + Equity) always holds. A strong current ratio, manageable long-term debt relative to cash generation, and growing shareholders' equity are hallmarks of financial resilience.
- **Free Cash Flow Is King:** FCF (Operating Cash Flow minus CapEx) is the most reliable indicator of genuine business health. It is the cash available for dividends, buybacks, debt reduction, and growth investment. Consistently growing FCF over multiple years is a powerful signal of business quality.
- **Thirteen Key Ratios:** From P/E and PEG to gross margin, ROE, and debt-to-equity, these ratios translate raw financial data into comparable, actionable metrics. Every ratio should be evaluated in the context of sector benchmarks and the company's own historical averages, never in isolation.
- **Qualitative Analysis:** Four pillars complement the quantitative ratios: the competitive moat (six types), management quality, industry trajectory, and macroeconomic context. Numbers tell you what happened; qualitative factors tell you why and whether it will continue.
- **Intrinsic Value and Margin of Safety:** The goal of fundamental analysis is to estimate what a business is genuinely worth and compare that to the current price. Buying below estimated intrinsic value (with a margin of safety) protects against analytical error and creates the potential for above-average returns.

CHAPTER 6

Technical Analysis: Reading the Story in the Charts

"The trend is your friend until the end when it bends."
— **Ed Seykota, featured in Market Wizards by Jack D. Schwager (1989)**

Every price chart is a history book. It records every battle between buyers and sellers, every surge of optimism, every wave of fear, every institutional accumulation, and every retail capitulation. Technical analysis is the discipline of reading that history accurately and using what it reveals to make more informed, better-timed trading decisions.

In Chapter 5, you learned to evaluate what a business is worth. Technical analysis answers the complementary question: what is the stock's price doing right now, and where is it likely to go next? It studies the language of price and volume directly, without requiring knowledge of earnings reports or balance sheets, because its foundational premise, as stated by Charles Dow in the early 1900s, is that price already reflects everything that is knowable about a security at any given moment.

This chapter covers the complete technical toolkit you will use on StockTradesApp.com throughout this book: candlestick charts and the patterns they form, support and resistance levels, trendlines and channels, moving averages, and the three essential indicators that every trader should understand (RSI, MACD, and Volume MA). By the end, your charting module will transform from a wall of colored lines into a readable, meaningful narrative.

> *"The market is never wrong. Opinions often are."*
> — **Jesse Livermore**, *as documented in Reminiscences of a Stock Operator by Edwin Lefevre (1923)*

6.1 The Three Premises of Technical Analysis

Technical analysis rests on three foundational premises, first articulated by Charles Dow in his editorials for The Wall Street Journal at the turn of the 20th century and later codified as Dow Theory. Every charting tool and indicator built since traces its intellectual ancestry back to these three ideas.

- **Premise 1: The Market Discounts Everything.** All available information about a stock (earnings, news, management changes, geopolitical events, investor sentiment) is already reflected in its current price. This means that studying price and volume is studying the collective knowledge of every market participant simultaneously. Technical analysts do not need to predict what will happen; they need to read what the market is already telling them.
- **Premise 2: Price Moves in Trends.** Once a trend is established, a stock is more likely to continue in that direction than to reverse. Trends persist because of momentum, the psychological tendency of buyers and sellers to continue their behavior until a significant force disrupts it. Identifying the direction and strength of a trend is the primary objective of most technical analysis.
- **Premise 3: History Repeats Itself.** Chart patterns recur because human psychology is consistent. Fear, greed, hope, and panic manifest in predictable, repeatable price formations. A head-and-shoulders pattern in 1929 looks essentially identical to one in 2024 because the underlying human behavior that creates it is the same.

DOW THEORY: THE FOUNDATION OF TECHNICAL ANALYSIS

Charles H. Dow, co-founder of Dow Jones & Company and the first editor of The Wall Street Journal, developed the foundational principles of market analysis in editorials written between 1900 and 1902. These principles were later synthesized by William Peter Hamilton and Robert Rhea into what became known as Dow Theory.

John J. Murphy, whose book Technical Analysis of the Financial Markets (1999) is the standard reference text of the field, describes Dow Theory as "the grandfather of modern technical analysis." Most of the concepts in this chapter trace their intellectual origins directly to Dow's original observations about price trends and market phases.

The most important practical implication of Dow Theory for beginning traders is the concept of the primary trend: the major, long-term direction of the market or a stock that persists for months or years. Murphy's central advice is to identify the primary trend first and then trade in the direction of that trend. Fighting the primary trend is one of the most common and costly mistakes beginning traders make.

6.2 The Four Stages of a Stock: Stan Weinstein's Framework

Before examining individual chart tools, it is worth zooming out to understand the complete life cycle of a stock's price behavior. Stan Weinstein, in his influential 1988 book Secrets for Profiting in Bull and Bear Markets, described four distinct stages that virtually every stock cycles through, which align closely with Dow Theory's three phases of accumulation, participation, and distribution.

Understanding which stage a stock is in is the single most important contextual judgment a technical analyst can make. Candlestick patterns, moving average signals, and indicator readings all carry different weight and reliability depending on whether the stock is in Stage 1, 2, 3, or 4.

Dow Theory Stage	Also Called	What It Looks Like on the Chart
Stage 1: Accumulation	Smart money phase	Price is flat or slightly rising after a prolonged decline. Volume is low. Institutional investors are quietly buying while most retail traders remain fearful from the prior downtrend. Little excitement in the media.
Stage 2: Public Participation	Markup phase	Price begins rising clearly and consistently. Moving averages trend upward. Volume increases. Financial media begins covering the stock positively. This is the longest and most profitable stage for trend followers.
Stage 3: Distribution	Smart money exit	Price reaches new highs but momentum slows. Volume surges on up-days but pullbacks also come on heavy volume. Institutions begin selling their positions to enthusiastic retail buyers. Extreme optimism in media coverage.
Stage 4: Decline	Markdown phase	Price breaks below key moving averages and prior support levels on high volume. The downtrend becomes established. Most retail investors are now holding losses and waiting for a recovery that does not come quickly.

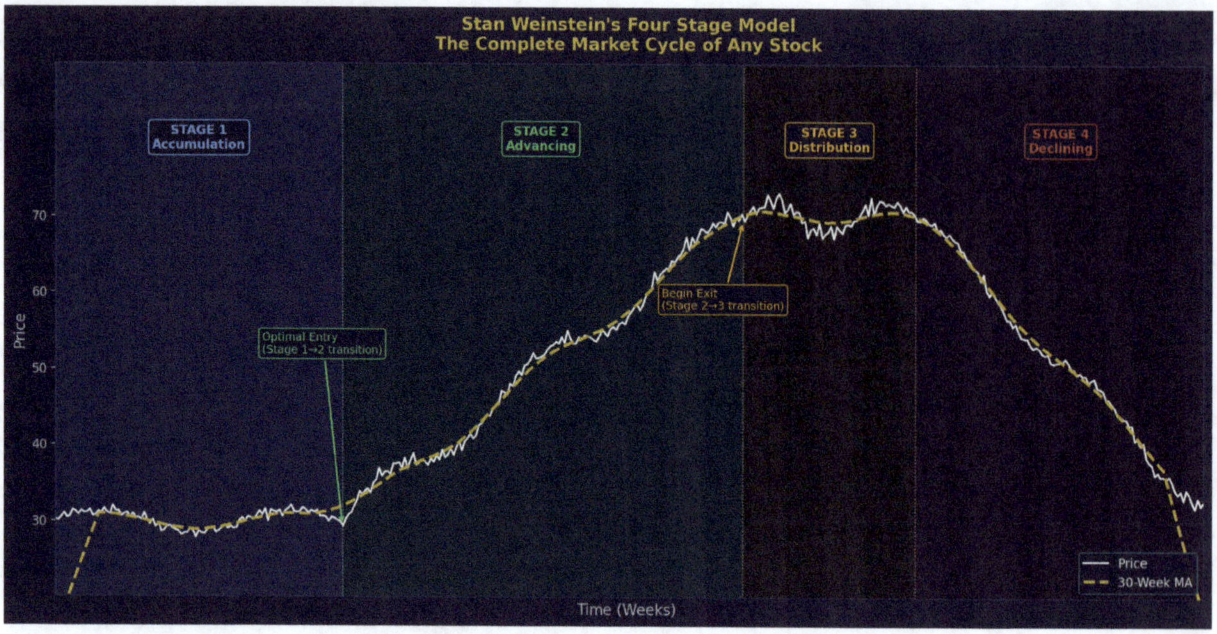

Figure 6.2 — Weinstein's Four Stage Market Cycle: Stage 2 (price above rising 30-week MA) is the only stage appropriate for new long entries.

The practical implication of this framework is direct and actionable: buy stocks in Stage 2, avoid stocks in Stage 3, do not hold stocks in Stage 4, and look for Stage 1 stocks that are showing early signs of transitioning to Stage 2. Every technical tool you learn in this chapter serves, at its core, to help you identify which stage a stock is in and when it is transitioning.

> *"There is only one side of the market, and it is not the bull side or the bear side, but the right side."*
> — **Jesse Livermore**, *Reminiscences of a Stock Operator, Edwin Lefevre (1923)*

6.3 Candlestick Charts: The Most Information-Rich Chart Type

Candlestick charting originated in Japan during the 17th century, where rice trader Munehisa Homma used price pattern analysis to trade rice futures on the Dojima Rice Exchange in Osaka. Homma is widely credited as the first person to observe that the psychological state of the market had a direct impact on price, a concept that would not be formalized in Western finance until the behavioral economics research of Kahneman and Tversky two and a half centuries later.

The technique remained essentially unknown in the Western world until 1991, when Steve Nison published Japanese Candlestick Charting Techniques, introducing these methods to Western traders for the first time. Nison's work transformed the charting landscape. Today, the candlestick chart is the standard format used by professional traders worldwide on every asset class, from equities to currencies to commodities.

> *"Candlestick charts are fascinating. Each candlestick tells a story about the emotional battle between the bulls and the bears during that time period. The body, the shadows, the color: everything carries meaning."*
>
> — **Steve Nison**, *Japanese Candlestick Charting Techniques (1991) is the book that introduced candlestick analysis to Western markets*

Reading a Single Candlestick

Every candlestick represents one time period (one day on a daily chart, one week on a weekly chart, one hour on an hourly chart). It encodes four pieces of information into a single visual element: the opening price, the closing price, the highest price reached, and the lowest price reached during that period. Understanding these four data points is the starting point for all candlestick analysis.

Candle Part	Also Called	What It Represents
Body (wide section)	Real body	The range between the opening and closing price. A TALL body means a large difference between open and close. A SHORT body means prices opened and closed near the same level.
Color: Green / White	Bullish candle	The closing price is HIGHER than the opening price. Buyers were in control during this period. Price moved up from open to close.
Color: Red / Black	Bearish candle	The closing price is LOWER than the opening price. Sellers were in control during this period. Price moved down from open to close.
Upper Wick / Shadow	Upper tail, upper shadow	The thin line above the body. Shows how high the price reached during the period before being pushed back down. A long upper wick shows sellers rejected higher prices aggressively.

Candle Part	Also Called	What It Represents
Lower Wick / Shadow	Lower tail, lower shadow	The thin line below the body. Shows how low the price fell before buyers pushed it back up. A long lower wick shows buyers rejected lower prices aggressively.
No Body (Doji)	Doji star	Open and close are at nearly the same price, creating a cross or plus-sign shape. Signals indecision and a potential reversal. The battle between buyers and sellers ended in a draw.

The most important habit to develop when reading candlesticks is examining the relationship between the body and the wicks. A large body with small wicks means one side (buyers or sellers) dominated the entire period decisively. A small body with large wicks means the period saw a battle that ended near where it started, with neither side winning clearly. These proportions reveal the intensity of market sentiment in ways that a simple line chart cannot.

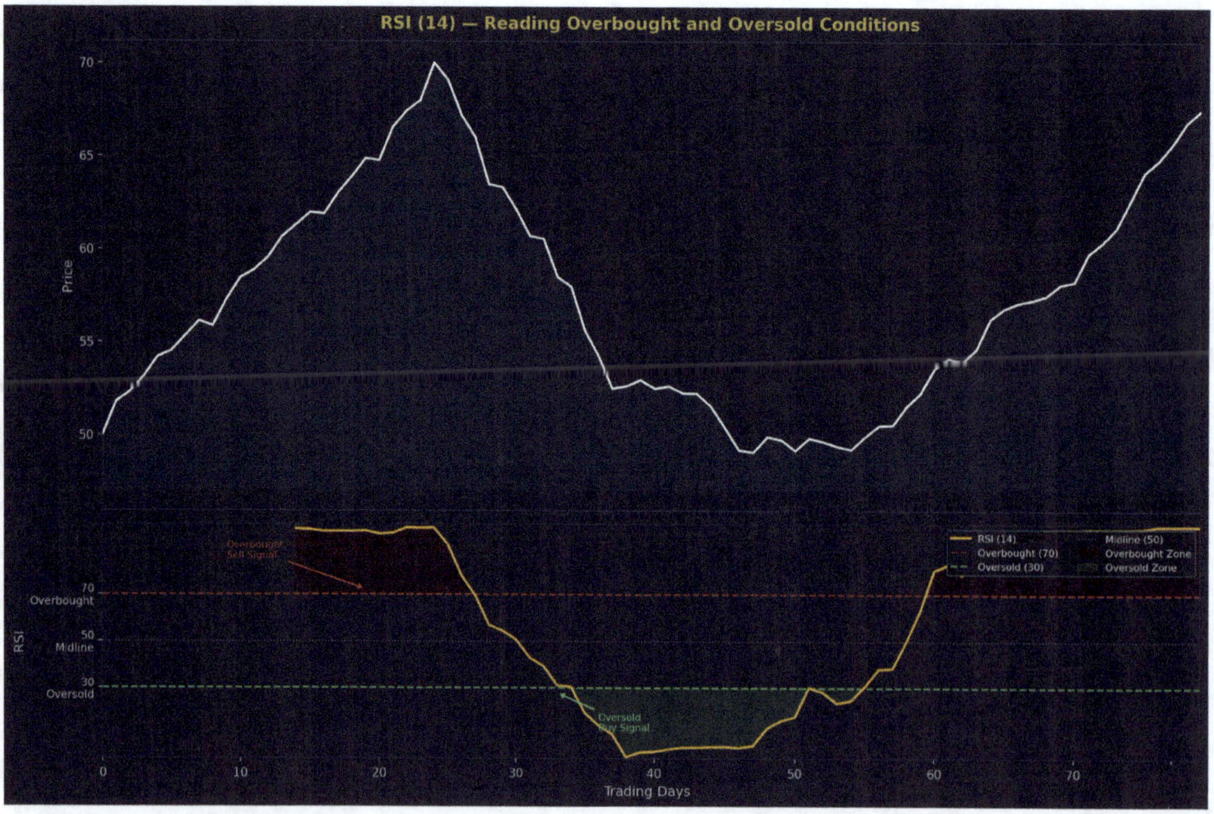

Figure 6.3 — RSI (14): Overbought and Oversold Conditions. RSI above 70 = overbought. RSI below 30 = oversold.

The Eleven Most Important Candlestick Patterns

Individual candlesticks are informative. Multi-candle patterns are even more powerful. The following table presents the eleven most important candlestick patterns that

StockTradesApp.com's charting module can help you identify. Remember that every pattern must be interpreted in the context of the trend it appears within. A bullish reversal pattern appearing after a prolonged uptrend carries very different weight than the same pattern appearing after a prolonged downtrend.

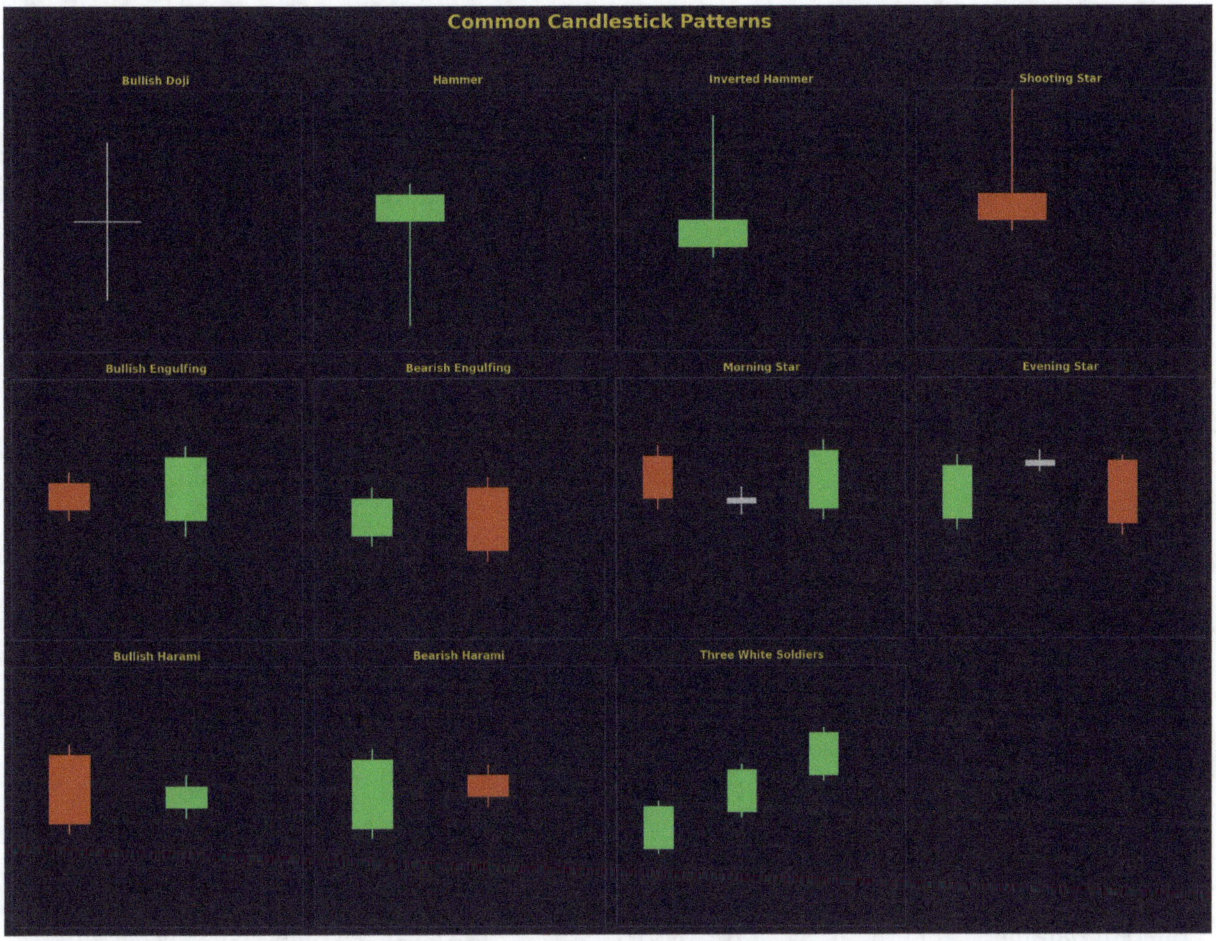

Figure 6.3.1 — The 11 Essential Candlestick Patterns: Green bodies = bullish session. Red bodies = bearish session.

Pattern Name	Type	Signal	How to Recognize It
Bullish Engulfing	Reversal	**BULLISH**	A large green candle completely engulfs the body of the preceding red candle. Signals buyers have overwhelmed sellers decisively. Most reliable after a downtrend.
Bearish Engulfing	Reversal	**BEARISH**	A large red candle completely engulfs the body of the preceding green candle. Signals sellers have overwhelmed

Pattern Name	Type	Signal	How to Recognize It
			buyers decisively. Most reliable after an uptrend.
Hammer	Reversal	**BULLISH**	Small body near the top, long lower wick at least twice the body length, little or no upper wick. Appears after a decline. Buyers rejected lower prices strongly.
Shooting Star	Reversal	**BEARISH**	Small body near the bottom, long upper wick at least twice the body length, little or no lower wick. Appears after a rally. Sellers rejected higher prices strongly.
Doji	Reversal / Indecision	**NEUTRAL**	Open and close at virtually the same level. Long wicks on both sides signal extreme indecision. A strong warning to watch for a trend change.
Morning Star	Reversal	**BULLISH**	Three-candle pattern: large red candle, followed by a small-bodied candle gapping down (the star), followed by a large green candle. Signals a bottom reversal.
Evening Star	Reversal	**BEARISH**	Three-candle pattern: large green candle, followed by a small-bodied candle gapping up (the star), followed by a large red candle. Signals a top reversal.
Bullish Harami	Reversal	**BULLISH**	A small green candle contained entirely within the body of the preceding large red candle. Signals the downward momentum may be losing force.
Bearish Harami	Reversal	**BEARISH**	A small red candle contained entirely within the body of the preceding large green candle. Signals the upward momentum may be losing force.
Marubozu	Continuation	**STRONG TREND**	A long-bodied candle with no wicks at all. Pure green Marubozu: buyers in total control from open to close. Pure red Marubozu: sellers in total control. Strong momentum signal.
Spinning Top	Indecision	**NEUTRAL**	Small body with relatively equal upper and lower wicks. Neither buyers nor sellers gained clear control. Often signals a pause within a trend rather than a reversal.

THE GOLDEN RULE OF CANDLESTICK INTERPRETATION

Steve Nison emphasized throughout Japanese Candlestick Charting Techniques that candlestick patterns are not standalone trading signals. They are most reliable when they occur at meaningful price levels (at support or resistance), are confirmed by the following session's price action, and are accompanied by above-average volume.

A bearish engulfing candle at a random price level in the middle of a chart is moderately interesting. The same bearish engulfing candle occurring precisely at the 52-week high on three times the average daily volume, after a ten-week uptrend, is one of the most powerful sell signals in technical analysis.

Context transforms patterns from interesting observations into actionable trading signals. Always ask: where on the chart did this pattern appear? What was the trend before it? What did volume say about it?

PLATFORM FEATURE: Candlestick Chart Settings on stocktradesapp.com

To switch to the Candlestick chart type on any stock's Quote Page or in the full charting module, click the chart type selector (the icon that looks like three vertical bars) and choose "Candlestick." Green candles represent periods where price closed higher than it opened; red candles represent periods where price closed lower.

For daily analysis of individual stocks, use the "1D" or "1W" time period with the candlestick view. Each candle represents one day or one week of trading, giving you the clearest picture of daily and weekly momentum.

To practice pattern recognition, look at the past 60 to 90 candlesticks on any stock's daily chart and see how many of the eleven patterns from the table above you can identify. Note where they appeared relative to prior support and resistance levels, and whether the price moved in the direction the pattern predicted over the following one to three sessions.

6.4 Support and Resistance: The Architecture of Every Chart

If you could only learn two concepts from this entire chapter, support and resistance would be the ones. They are the most universal, the most reliable, and the most practically useful concepts in all of technical analysis. Every other tool in this chapter exists, in some sense, to help you identify, confirm, and trade around support and resistance levels more effectively.

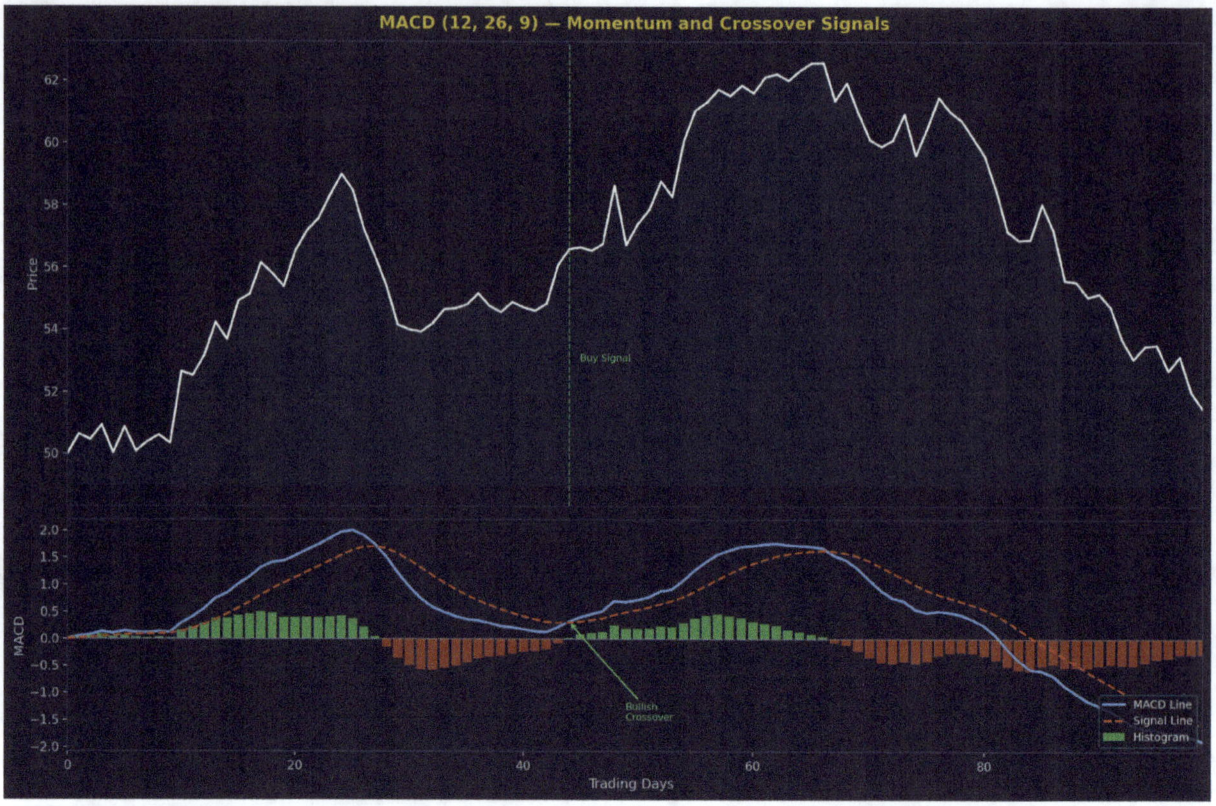

Figure 6.4 — MACD (12, 26, 9): Momentum and Crossover Signals. Bullish crossover: MACD Line crosses above Signal Line.

KEY TERM: Support

A price level where buying interest is strong enough to prevent the price from falling further. Support exists because investors who missed a previous rally decide to buy when price returns to that level, and investors holding losing positions average down at a price they consider attractive. The more times a support level has held without being broken, the stronger and more significant it becomes.

KEY TERM: Resistance

A price level where selling pressure is strong enough to prevent the price from rising further. Resistance exists because investors who bought at higher prices and are sitting on losses sell when price recovers to their entry level, and investors who profited at that level before look to sell again. Like support, resistance becomes stronger and more significant the more times it has held.

The Role Reversal Principle

One of the most powerful and counterintuitive concepts in technical analysis is the principle of polarity, or role reversal: once a support level is convincingly broken, it frequently becomes a resistance level, and once a resistance level is convincingly broken, it frequently becomes a support level.

The reason is psychological: the investors who bought at the old support level and watched it break are now sitting on losses. When price recovers to that former support level, they sell to break even, creating a new layer of overhead resistance exactly where support used to exist. The same logic applies in reverse when resistance breaks.

This principle creates one of the most reliable trading setups in technical analysis: the retest of a breakout. A stock breaks above a significant resistance level, pulls back to test that former resistance (now support), holds, and then resumes its upward move. Professional traders wait for this retest as a lower-risk entry point compared to buying the initial breakout.

Drawing Support and Resistance Lines on StockTradesApp.com

To draw a support or resistance line on the charting module, click the drawing tools icon (the pencil icon in the left sidebar) and select the horizontal line tool. Then click on a price level where you observe multiple prior highs or lows clustering together. The line represents the zone where price has repeatedly reacted.

Two important refinements. First, treat support and resistance as zones rather than precise prices. Price often overshoots these levels slightly before reversing, so a support zone of $45 to $47 is more realistic than an exact support price of $46.00. Second, the more time periods that have touched and respected a given level, the more significant it is. A level that has held on four separate occasions over two years is far more significant than one that has held twice over two weeks.

PLATFORM FEATURE: Automated Support and Resistance Detection

StockTradesApp.com's charting module includes an automated support and resistance detection feature that identifies the most significant historical price zones on any chart. Access it by clicking "Auto S/R" in the drawing tools panel.

The feature highlights the three to five most significant support and resistance zones on the current chart based on the frequency and strength of prior price reactions at each level. These automated levels are displayed as shaded horizontal bands rather than single lines, correctly representing the zone-based nature of support and resistance.

Use the automated detection as a starting point, then review each level manually. Evaluate whether the highlighted zones correspond to meaningful price history, and draw your own lines for any additional levels the automated tool may have missed.

6.5 Trendlines and Channels: Drawing the Road the Price Travels

While support and resistance are horizontal lines, trendlines are diagonal lines that capture the direction and slope of a price move. A properly drawn trendline is one of the simplest and most reliable tools in technical analysis, and it forms the foundation for identifying trend direction, measuring the strength of a move, and spotting early warning signs of a trend change.

Drawing an Uptrend Line

An uptrend line connects at least two consecutive higher lows. The logic: in an uptrend, each pullback finds buyers at a higher price than the previous pullback did, creating a series of ascending support points. The trendline connecting these higher lows represents the floor of the uptrend. Price bouncing off this trendline in an uptrend is a classic entry signal. Price breaking below this trendline is an early warning that the uptrend may be ending.

For a trendline to be valid, it must connect at least two price lows, though three or more touches significantly increase its reliability. The line should be drawn to touch the bottom of the wicks (the lowest price reached) rather than the bodies of the candles. Touch the line with precision, not approximation.

Drawing a Downtrend Line

A downtrend line connects at least two consecutive lower highs. It represents the ceiling of a downtrend, where sellers consistently emerge to push price back down after each attempted rally. A break above the downtrend line, particularly on high volume, is often the first technical signal that a downtrend is ending and a potential recovery is beginning.

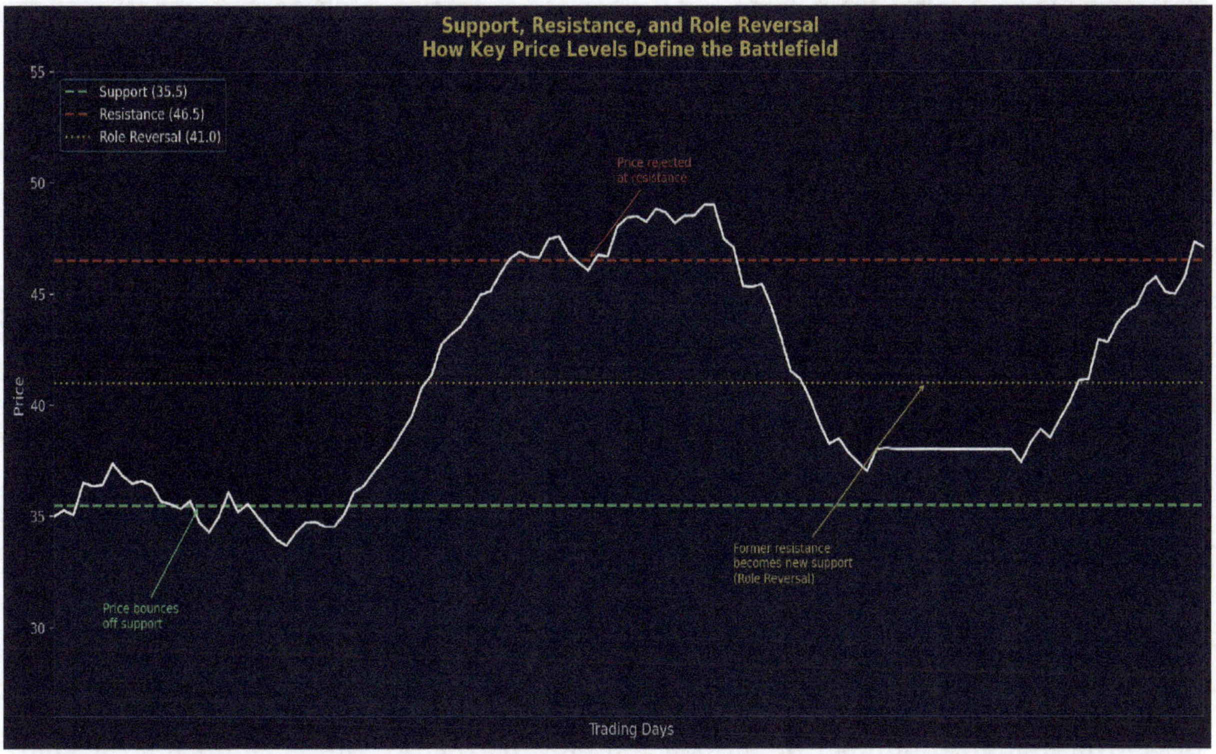

Figure 6.5 — Support, Resistance, and Role Reversal: Former resistance frequently becomes new support after a breakout.

Price Channels

A price channel is formed by drawing a second trendline parallel to the primary trendline, containing price movement between two boundaries. In an uptrending channel, the upper channel line connects the highs while the lower channel line (the trendline) connects the higher lows. Price oscillating between these two boundaries gives traders both entry signals (near the lower channel line) and profit-taking targets (near the upper channel line).

Channels are particularly useful because they quantify the expected range of price movement within a trend. A stock trading in a well-established ascending channel gives you three key pieces of information: the current trend direction is up, the current trading range within that trend is defined, and a decisive break outside either boundary of the channel is a significant signal.

THE SIGNIFICANCE OF TRENDLINE BREAKS

John J. Murphy writes in Technical Analysis of the Financial Markets that a trendline break is "one of the simplest and most effective signals available to the technical analyst." However, he is careful to emphasize that not every trendline touch that slightly penetrates the line constitutes a true break.

Murphy's guidelines for a valid trendline break require a closing price beyond the trendline (intraday penetrations that recover by the close are often false breaks), penetration of at least three percent of the stock's price, and ideally above-average volume accompanying the break.

These guidelines protect against one of the most common beginner mistakes: acting on every minor trendline penetration and generating excessive trading activity on signals that prove to be noise rather than genuine trend changes.

6.6 Moving Averages: Smoothing the Noise, Revealing the Trend

Moving averages are among the most widely used tools in technical analysis, and for good reason. They solve one of the most fundamental challenges in reading price charts: distinguishing between the signal (the underlying trend) and the noise (the random, day-to-day price fluctuations that have no trend significance). By calculating the average price over a defined number of periods and plotting that average as a line on the chart, moving averages create a smoothed representation of price that makes the underlying trend immediately visible.

KEY TERM: Simple Moving Average (SMA)
The arithmetic mean of a stock's closing prices over a specified number of periods. The 50-day SMA, for example, is calculated by adding the closing prices of the past 50 trading days and dividing by 50. The number updates each day as the newest closing price is added and the oldest is dropped. The SMA is the most widely used version of the moving average and the standard for institutional benchmarking.

KEY TERM: Exponential Moving Average (EMA)
A weighted moving average that gives greater importance to more recent price data. Unlike the SMA, which weights all periods equally, the EMA responds more quickly to recent price changes. This makes it more sensitive to new developments in the short term but also more prone to generating false signals during volatile, choppy markets.

The Six Most Important Moving Averages

The table below covers the six moving averages that appear most frequently in professional trading and that are available as standard overlays on StockTradesApp.com's charting module.

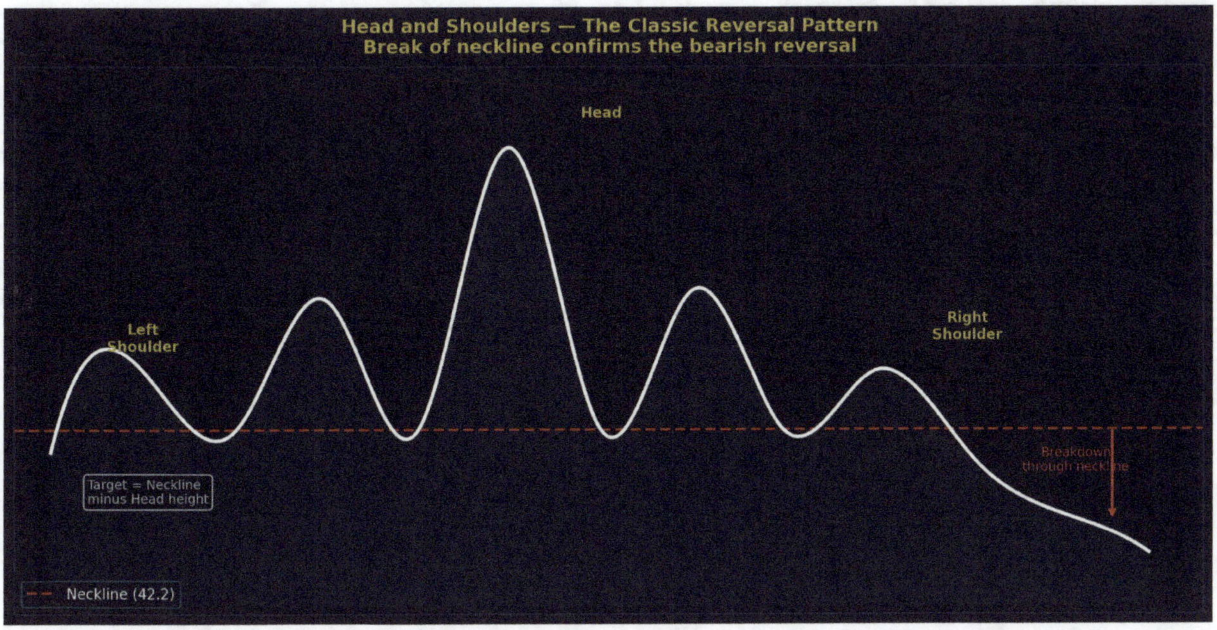

Figure 6.6 — Head and Shoulders Reversal Pattern: Neckline break confirms the bearish reversal.

MA Type	Period	Primary Use	Interpretation
SMA-20	20 days	Short-term trend	The most commonly used short-term moving average. Acts as dynamic support in uptrends and dynamic resistance in downtrends. Price bouncing off the 20-day SMA in an uptrend is a common entry signal.
SMA-50	50 days	Medium-term trend	The primary benchmark for institutional money flows. A stock trading above its 50-day SMA is generally in a medium-term uptrend; below it, a downtrend. The 50-day is the most widely watched moving average.
SMA-200	200 days	Long-term trend	The definitive trend separator. Stocks above their 200-day SMA are in long-term uptrends. Stocks below are in long-term downtrends. The 200-day crossing is one of the most significant signals in all of technical analysis.
EMA-12	12 days	MACD calculation	A faster EMA that responds more quickly to price changes. Used as the faster line in the standard MACD indicator. Also useful for very active traders who need more responsive signals.

MA Type	Period	Primary Use	Interpretation
EMA-26	26 days	MACD calculation	A slower EMA used as the slower line in the standard MACD calculation. The crossover between the EMA-12 and EMA-26 generates the primary MACD signal line.
EMA-9	9 days	Signal line	Used as the MACD signal line. When the MACD line crosses above the signal line, it generates a bullish signal. When it crosses below, a bearish signal.

The Golden Cross and Death Cross

Two of the most widely discussed signals in technical analysis involve the crossing of the 50-day and 200-day simple moving averages. These signals are named for their perceived significance and are among the most reported chart events in financial media.

- **The Golden Cross:** Occurs when the 50-day SMA crosses above the 200-day SMA. This crossing signals that shorter-term momentum has turned positive relative to the longer-term trend, and is widely interpreted as a bullish signal suggesting a potential new uptrend. Academic research has found that Golden Cross signals have historically preceded above-average equity returns over the following 6 to 12 months, though the signal is a lagging indicator and the initial entry price is often significantly above the prior low.
- **The Death Cross:** The inverse: the 50-day SMA crosses below the 200-day SMA. Signals that shorter-term momentum has turned negative and is widely interpreted as a bearish signal suggesting a potential new downtrend. Death Crosses occurred before several significant market declines including 2008 and 2020, though again they are lagging indicators that often signal the beginning of a recovery rather than the beginning of the worst decline.

USING MOVING AVERAGES AS DYNAMIC SUPPORT AND RESISTANCE

One of the most practically useful applications of moving averages is treating them as dynamic (moving) support and resistance levels. In an established uptrend, price frequently pulls back to the 20-day or 50-day SMA and then bounces, continuing the uptrend. This pullback-to-the-moving-average pattern is one of the most commonly used entry setups among professional traders.

The key to using this technique correctly is confirming that the stock is in a Stage 2 uptrend (Section 6.2) before looking for moving average pullback entries. Using moving average pullbacks as entries in a Stage 4 downtrend is one of the most expensive mistakes a beginning trader can make. The trend context must come first.

On StockTradesApp.com, you can add the 20-day, 50-day, and 200-day SMAs to any chart simultaneously by clicking "Indicators" and selecting each from the Moving Averages section. The platform displays each as a differently colored line for easy visual differentiation.

6.7 Chart Patterns: When Price Writes the Same Story Again

Chart patterns are recurring formations in price charts that have historically preceded specific types of price moves. They emerge because the same psychological dynamics between buyers and sellers play out in similar ways again and again: the same patterns of accumulation, indecision, breakout, distribution, and collapse appear across different stocks, different time periods, and different market conditions.

John J. Murphy dedicates several chapters of Technical Analysis of the Financial Markets to chart patterns, noting that "the study of price patterns is one of the most important areas in the field of technical analysis." The table below covers the nine most reliable and widely used patterns, organized by whether they signal a reversal of the prior trend or a continuation of it.

Pattern	Signal Type	Description and Trading Implication
Head and Shoulders	**Bearish Reversal**	Three successive peaks with the middle peak (head) being the highest and two lower peaks on either side (shoulders). A neckline connects the lows between the peaks. A break below the neckline confirms the reversal and projects a price target equal to the distance from the neckline to the head. Considered the most reliable reversal pattern in technical analysis by John Murphy.
Inverse Head and Shoulders	**Bullish Reversal**	The mirror image of the head and shoulders: three troughs with the middle trough (head) being the lowest. A break above the neckline confirms the reversal. Equally reliable as its bearish counterpart and frequently signals the end of a major downtrend.
Double Top	**Bearish Reversal**	Price reaches the same high level twice and fails to break through on the second attempt, forming an "M" shape. Signals that buyers could not sustain the momentum at that level and sellers are taking control. A break below the trough between the two tops confirms the pattern.

Pattern	Signal Type	Description and Trading Implication
Double Bottom	Bullish Reversal	Price reaches the same low level twice and bounces on the second test, forming a "W" shape. Signals that sellers could not push price lower on the second attempt. A break above the peak between the two bottoms confirms the pattern and suggests a new uptrend.
Ascending Triangle	Bullish Continuation	A flat upper resistance line and a rising lower trendline, creating a triangular compression. The rising lows show buyers are becoming more aggressive while sellers defend a specific price level. A breakout above the flat resistance line on high volume is the trading signal.
Descending Triangle	Bearish Continuation	A flat lower support line and a declining upper trendline. The falling highs show sellers are becoming more aggressive while buyers defend a specific support level. A breakdown below the flat support line on high volume is the trading signal.
Symmetrical Triangle	Continuation / Neutral	Both upper and lower trendlines converge symmetrically as price compresses. Neither buyers nor sellers are dominant. The price typically breaks out in the direction of the prior trend. Watch for a high-volume breakout in either direction.
Flag and Pennant	Bullish Continuation	A sharp, near-vertical price move (the flagpole) followed by a brief consolidation period that slopes slightly against the prior trend (the flag or pennant). The consolidation represents a pause before continuation. A breakout in the direction of the flagpole completes the pattern.
Cup and Handle	Bullish Continuation	Developed by William J. O'Neil. A gradual, rounded decline followed by a recovery that forms a "U" shape (the cup), then a minor pullback from the rim (the handle). A breakout above the cup's rim on high volume triggers the buy signal.

Volume Confirmation: The Non-Negotiable Requirement

For any chart pattern breakout to be considered valid and tradeable, it must be accompanied by a significant increase in volume. This rule is universal and non-negotiable. A breakout from a head-and-shoulders pattern on twice the average daily volume is a high-conviction sell signal. The identical pattern breaking down on half the average daily volume is a low-conviction signal that frequently fails and reverses.

Murphy summarizes this requirement clearly: "Volume should expand in the direction of the breakout." An ascending triangle breaking out to the upside on heavy volume is confirming that institutional buyers are participating in the move. The same breakout on thin volume suggests a lack of conviction and increases the probability of a false breakout (a price move that briefly violates the pattern's boundary before reversing back inside).

6.8 The Three Essential Indicators: RSI, MACD, and Volume MA

Technical indicators are mathematical calculations applied to price and volume data that help traders answer two fundamental questions: is the stock's momentum increasing or decreasing, and is the current trend strengthening or weakening? This section covers the three indicators that every trader should understand and that are available as standard overlays in StockTradesApp.com's charting module.

The RSI: Measuring Momentum Extremes

The Relative Strength Index (RSI) was developed by J. Welles Wilder Jr. and introduced in his 1978 book New Concepts in Technical Trading Systems. It remains, nearly five decades later, one of the most widely used momentum indicators in the world. The RSI measures the speed and magnitude of recent price changes on a scale of 0 to 100, identifying when a stock may be overbought (price has risen too far, too fast and is vulnerable to a pullback) or oversold (price has fallen too far, too fast and may be due for a recovery).

KEY TERM: Relative Strength Index (RSI)

A momentum oscillator developed by J. Welles Wilder Jr. (1978) that measures the speed and magnitude of price changes on a scale of 0 to 100. An RSI above 70 suggests the stock is potentially overbought; an RSI below 30 suggests it may be oversold. The standard calculation period is 14 days. The RSI is plotted as a line in a separate panel below the price chart.

There are three primary ways to use the RSI in your analysis:

- **Overbought and Oversold Readings:** An RSI reading above 70 signals that price has risen sharply and may be due for a pullback. An RSI below 30 signals that price has fallen sharply and may be due for a bounce. These readings are most useful in stocks trading within a defined range. In a strong trending market, the RSI can remain above 70 or below 30 for extended periods without a significant reversal.
- **RSI Divergence:** The most powerful RSI signal occurs when the price and the RSI move in opposite directions. Bearish divergence occurs when price makes a new high but the RSI makes a lower high than its previous peak. This signals that momentum is weakening even as price continues to rise, warning of a potential reversal. Bullish

divergence occurs when price makes a new low but RSI makes a higher low, signaling that selling momentum is exhausting itself.

- **The 50-Level Midpoint:** The RSI 50 level often acts as a support or resistance zone in its own right. An RSI that bounces off the 50 level during a pullback in an uptrend suggests the trend is healthy and likely to continue. An RSI that fails to reclaim the 50 level after a decline suggests the trend has shifted.

The MACD: Trend Direction and Momentum Combined

The Moving Average Convergence Divergence indicator (MACD) was developed by Gerald Appel in the late 1970s and has become one of the most popular trend-following momentum indicators used by professional traders worldwide. It works by taking the difference between two exponential moving averages (typically the 12-day EMA and the 26-day EMA) and plotting that difference as a line. A 9-day EMA of that difference (the signal line) is plotted alongside it. The difference between the MACD line and the signal line is displayed as a histogram.

> **KEY TERM: MACD (Moving Average Convergence Divergence)**
> *A trend-following momentum indicator developed by Gerald Appel that shows the relationship between two exponential moving averages of a stock's price. Standard settings: MACD line = 12-day EMA minus 26-day EMA; Signal line = 9-day EMA of the MACD line; Histogram = MACD minus Signal. The MACD is displayed in a separate panel below the price chart on StockTradesApp.com.*

The four primary MACD signals traders watch for are as follows:

- **Signal Line Crossover:** When the MACD line crosses above the signal line, it generates a bullish signal. When it crosses below, a bearish signal. This is the most commonly used MACD signal and is most reliable when it occurs near the zero line rather than at extreme distances from it.
- **Zero Line Cross:** When the MACD line crosses above the zero line, it confirms that the shorter-term trend has become positive relative to the longer-term trend (a bullish signal). When it crosses below zero, the shorter-term trend has become negative (a bearish signal). Zero line crosses are slower than signal line crossovers but carry more conviction.
- **Histogram Analysis:** The histogram (the bars shown between the MACD and signal lines) measures momentum. When the histogram bars are growing taller,

momentum is increasing in the direction of the current move. When they are shrinking, momentum is fading. A histogram that turns from growing to shrinking is an early warning that a trend may be losing strength.

- **MACD Divergence:** Like RSI divergence, MACD divergence occurs when price and the MACD move in opposite directions. Bearish MACD divergence (price makes a new high while MACD makes a lower high) is a warning of weakening momentum. It was a notable feature of charts preceding several major market peaks, including the 2000 technology bubble top.

The Volume Moving Average: Contextualizing Activity

The Volume Moving Average is the simplest of the three indicators but serves a critical role: it provides an immediate visual baseline for evaluating whether any given day's trading volume is above or below normal. It is calculated as the 20-day simple moving average of daily volume and plotted as a line through the volume bars at the bottom of the chart.

Any day on which the volume bars exceed the Volume MA line is a day of above-average activity. Any day below the line is below average. This visual comparison makes it instantly clear whether a price breakout, reversal, or continuation pattern is supported by real conviction from the market or is occurring on quiet, unconvincing volume. Refer back to Chapter 4's discussion of the four volume scenarios for a reminder of how to interpret volume in combination with price direction.

Indicator	Standard Setting	Key Levels	Primary Reading
RSI	14-period	70 = overbought, 30 = oversold	Above 70: consider taking profit or reducing position. Below 30: potential buying opportunity in an uptrend. Divergence between RSI direction and price direction is one of the most powerful signals.
MACD	12, 26, 9	Zero line, signal line	MACD line crossing above signal line: bullish. Crossing below: bearish. MACD crossing above/below zero line confirms trend direction. Histogram growing: momentum increasing. Histogram shrinking: momentum fading.
SMA-20	20 periods	Price above or below	Dynamic short-term support/resistance. Price bouncing off

Indicator	Standard Setting	Key Levels	Primary Reading
			SMA-20 in an uptrend is a common entry trigger. Price breaking below SMA-20 is a short-term warning signal.
SMA-50	50 periods	Price above or below	Medium-term trend gauge. Institutions widely follow this level. A Golden Cross (SMA-50 crossing above SMA-200) is one of the most bullish signals in technical analysis.
SMA-200	200 periods	Price above or below	Long-term trend separator. Bulls want to see price above the 200-day. A Death Cross (SMA-50 crossing below SMA-200) signals a potential long-term downtrend.
Volume MA	20 periods	Above or below average	Overlaid on the volume bars to show average activity level. Volume spikes above this line confirm price moves. Volume well below this line suggests weak conviction.

🖥 PLATFORM FEATURE: Setting Up Your Indicators on stocktradesapp.com

To add RSI, MACD, and Volume MA to any chart in the charting module, click the "Indicators" button in the top toolbar. A dropdown menu will display all available indicators organized by category.

For RSI: select "RSI" from the Momentum section. Leave the default period at 14. The RSI will appear in a separate panel below the price chart with horizontal dashed lines at 70 and 30.

For MACD: select "MACD" from the Trend/Momentum section. Leave default settings (12, 26, 9). The MACD will appear in a separate panel showing the MACD line, signal line, and histogram.

For Volume MA: select "Volume MA" from the Volume section. Leave the default at 20 periods. It will appear as a line through your existing volume bars at the bottom of the chart.

With these four elements on your chart (price candles, RSI, MACD, and Volume MA), you have the complete basic technical setup used by the majority of professional retail traders worldwide. This is your starting configuration for all paper trading analysis in the chapters ahead.

6.9 Bringing It Together: The Technical Analysis Checklist

The individual tools in this chapter are each useful on their own, but their true power emerges when used in combination. Murphy's Technical Analysis of the Financial Markets concludes with a 23-point technical checklist that professional analysts use to evaluate a chart before making any trading decision. The version below is a streamlined, beginner-focused adaptation specifically designed for use with StockTradesApp.com.

Before entering any paper trade from this point forward, work through this checklist on the stock's chart. Record your answers in your Trading Journal as part of the pre-trade thesis entry.

The Technical Analysis Pre-Trade Checklist

Step 1: STAGE IDENTIFICATION: Which of the four Weinstein stages is this stock currently in? Only enter new long positions in Stage 2 stocks. Avoid entering longs in Stage 3 or Stage 4.

Step 2: TREND DIRECTION: What is the primary trend direction on the weekly chart? What is the intermediate trend on the daily chart? Are they aligned in the same direction? (Best entries occur when both timeframes agree.)

Step 3: MOVING AVERAGE POSITION: Is price above or below the 50-day SMA and 200-day SMA? A stock trading above both is in a confirmed uptrend. Between the two is mixed. Below both is a downtrend.

Step 4: SUPPORT AND RESISTANCE: What are the nearest support level below the current price and the nearest resistance level above it? What is the distance to each? The entry should ideally be closer to support than resistance.

Step 5: CANDLESTICK CONTEXT: What do the last three to five daily candles tell you about the immediate-term battle between buyers and sellers? Is there a recognizable pattern at a meaningful price level?

Step 6: RSI READING: What is the current RSI level? Is it overbought (above 70), oversold (below 30), or neutral? Is there any divergence between the RSI direction and the price direction?

Step 7: MACD READING: Is the MACD above or below the signal line? Above or below the zero line? Is the histogram growing or shrinking? Do all three agree on the current momentum direction?

Step 8: VOLUME CONFIRMATION: Is today's volume above or below the 20-day Volume MA? On the most recent significant price move (up or down), was volume expanding or contracting?

Step 9: THE TRADE PLAN: Before entering the trade, define three things in writing: the entry price or price trigger, the stop-loss level (maximum acceptable loss), and the price target (where you plan to take profit). If you cannot define all three, do not enter the trade.

This checklist will feel slow and deliberate in the early stages. That is precisely the point. The discipline of working through each step before every trade is what separates traders who improve consistently from those who make the same mistakes repeatedly. As you complete this checklist for dozens of paper trades over the coming weeks, the process will become faster and more intuitive.

MULTIPLE TIMEFRAME ANALYSIS: A POWERFUL REFINEMENT

One of the most important advanced practices in technical analysis is confirming a signal across multiple timeframes before acting on it. The standard approach, widely practiced by professional traders, is to identify the trend on a higher timeframe (weekly chart) and then look for entry signals in the same direction on a lower timeframe (daily chart).

For example: identify that a stock is in a clear Stage 2 uptrend on the weekly chart, with the price above the rising 50-week and 200-week moving averages. Then drop to the daily chart and look for a pullback to the 20-day SMA, a bullish candlestick reversal pattern at that level, and an RSI that has returned to the 40 to 50 zone. This combination: weekly trend confirmed, daily entry signal identified, represents one of the cleanest technical setups available.

StockTradesApp.com's charting module allows you to toggle between weekly and daily views with a single click, making multiple timeframe analysis straightforward to incorporate into your pre-trade routine.

6.10 Chapter 6 Exercise: Your First Complete Technical Analysis

The following exercise walks you through a complete technical analysis of a real stock using the StockTradesApp.com charting module. You will apply every concept from this chapter and record your findings in your Trading Journal. This is your first full technical analysis, and it sets the standard for how you will approach every chart before a paper trade going forward.

Full Technical Analysis Exercise

Step 1: SELECT A STOCK from your watchlist. Choose a stock you have already researched fundamentally in Chapter 5's exercise. Use the same company so you begin building the integrated fundamental-plus-technical view that will govern your paper trading from Chapter 7 onward.

Step 2: SET UP YOUR CHART. Open the stock on StockTradesApp.com's charting module. Set the chart to Candlestick view with a 1-year time frame on the daily chart. Add the 20-day SMA, 50-day SMA, 200-day SMA, RSI (14), MACD (12,26,9), and Volume MA (20). This is your complete technical workspace.

Step 3: IDENTIFY THE STAGE. Based on the price position relative to the 200-day SMA and the general pattern of higher highs and higher lows (or lower highs and lower lows), which of the four Weinstein stages is this stock in? Record your assessment in your journal.

Step 4: DRAW SUPPORT AND RESISTANCE. Using the drawing tools, identify and draw at least two support levels below the current price and two resistance levels above it. For each level, note how many times the price has reacted to it and over what time period.

Step 5: DRAW A TRENDLINE. If the stock is in an uptrend, connect at least two higher lows with an uptrend line. If it is in a downtrend, connect at least two lower highs. If the price action is choppy and trending sideways, note that no clean trendline can be drawn and explain why.

Step 6: READ THE INDICATORS. Record the current RSI reading and note whether it is overbought, oversold, or neutral. Describe the MACD: is the MACD line above or below the signal line? Above or below zero? Is the histogram growing or shrinking? Is today's volume above or below the Volume MA?

Step 7: IDENTIFY ANY PATTERNS. Looking at the most recent 20 candles, can you identify any of the eleven candlestick patterns from Section 6.3 or any of the nine chart patterns from Section 6.7? If yes, note where it appears on the chart and what it signals.

Step 8: WORK THROUGH THE PRE-TRADE CHECKLIST from Section 6.9. Complete every point in your Trading Journal. Based on the completed checklist, write a one-paragraph technical assessment: is this stock in a position to trade right now, or do you need to wait for better conditions? What would you need to see to trigger an entry?

Chapter 6 Summary

Chapter 6 has given you the complete foundational toolkit of technical analysis. Here is what you now carry into every chart you analyze:

- **Three Core Premises:** Markets discount everything, price moves in trends, and history repeats because human psychology is consistent. These premises underpin every tool in this chapter.

- **Four Stage Framework:** Stan Weinstein's four stages (Accumulation, Markup, Distribution, Decline) provide the essential context for every other technical signal. Know the stage before reading the candles, indicators, or patterns.
- **Candlestick Charts:** Introduced to Western markets by Steve Nison in 1991, candlestick charts encode four data points (open, high, low, close) into a single visual element. Eleven key patterns ranging from the Bullish Engulfing to the Evening Star appear repeatedly across all markets and timeframes.
- **Support and Resistance:** The most universal concept in technical analysis. Support is where buyers emerge; resistance is where sellers emerge. Role reversal (broken support becomes resistance and vice versa) is one of the most reliable and exploitable phenomena in charting.
- **Trendlines and Channels:** Diagonal lines that capture the direction and slope of a price move. Valid trendlines require at least two touches. Channels quantify the expected range of price oscillation within a trend.
- **Six Moving Averages:** The 20-day, 50-day, and 200-day SMAs are the institutional benchmarks. The Golden Cross (50-day crossing above 200-day) and Death Cross (50-day crossing below 200-day) are among the most widely followed signals in technical analysis. Moving averages serve as dynamic support and resistance in trending markets.
- **Nine Chart Patterns:** From Head and Shoulders reversals to Cup and Handle continuations, these patterns recur because human psychology is consistent. Volume confirmation is required for any pattern breakout to be considered valid.
- **Three Essential Indicators:** RSI (Wilder, 1978) measures momentum extremes; MACD (Appel, late 1970s) tracks trend direction and momentum simultaneously; Volume MA provides the baseline for evaluating trading activity. Divergence between price and indicators is among the most powerful warning signals in the entire technical toolkit.
- **The Pre-Trade Checklist:** Nine structured questions that must be answered before every trade. Stage, trend, moving averages, support/resistance, candlestick context, RSI, MACD, volume, and trade plan. Discipline in completing this checklist before every entry is one of the most reliably separating habits between improving traders and stagnant ones.

PART III

Developing Strategy

Building Confidence

CHAPTER 7

Building Your Watchlist & Conducting Routine Research

"The stock market is filled with individuals who know the price of everything, but the value of nothing."

— Philip Fisher, Common Stocks and Uncommon Profits (1958)

You have now completed the foundational arc of this book. You understand what the stock market is and how it works. You know how to read a complete stock quote on StockTradesApp.com's Terminal. You have studied the income statement, balance sheet, and cash flow statement of a real company. You can read a candlestick chart, identify support and resistance, and interpret RSI, MACD, and volume signals. Those six chapters gave you a toolkit.

Chapter 7 teaches you how to use that toolkit systematically. The gap between investors who build wealth and those who merely follow financial news is almost never about who has more information. It is about who has a repeatable process for filtering that information, identifying high-quality opportunities, and building a watchlist that keeps the best candidates visible at all times. This chapter gives you that process.

You will learn how to use StockTradesApp.com's AI Screener and Compare tools to surface candidates worth studying, how to tier your Watchlist so your best opportunities are always in front of you, how to apply William O'Neil's CAN SLIM framework as a fundamental screening lens, how to read financial news objectively without being manipulated by headlines, and how to build the daily research routine that professional traders follow. Every step maps directly to tools that exist on the platform right now.

7.1 Why Most Watchlists Fail: The Difference Between a List and a System

Open the average retail trader's watchlist and you will find a graveyard of tickers collected from financial news, Reddit threads, friend recommendations, and stocks that made a dramatic move someone saw on their phone. These lists grow without discipline and shrink without logic. They contain hundreds of tickers that nobody is actually monitoring, and the genuinely great opportunities get buried under noise.

A watchlist is not a collection of interesting companies. A watchlist is a tiered, active research pipeline that sits between the raw market universe and your actual paper trading positions. Every ticker on it has earned its place through a defined research process. Every tier tells you exactly what action to take on the stocks within it. And the list is pruned regularly, removing stocks that no longer meet your criteria, to keep the signal-to-noise ratio high.

> *"The biggest winners in the stock market are not discovered by luck. They are systematically identified by investors who do their homework every week, in every market condition, with the same rigorous process applied consistently."*
> — **William J. O'Neil**, *How to Make Money in Stocks (1988): foundational text of growth stock investing, over 4 million copies sold*

The system you will build in this chapter has three components. First, a sourcing process: defined methods for identifying candidates worth adding to your watchlist in the first place. Second, a tiering system: a three-level framework that tells you exactly what to do with every stock on your list. Third, a routine: a daily and weekly research cadence that keeps your watchlist current without consuming your entire day.

2%

The percentage of stocks in a typical universe that pass all seven CAN SLIM criteria simultaneously. The market always has far more noise than signal. A disciplined screening process is the filter.

Source: American Association of Individual Investors (AAII) CAN SLIM screen research

7.2 Sourcing Candidates: Where Good Watchlist Stocks Come From

Before you can research a stock, you have to find it. Beginning traders typically discover stocks reactively: a friend mentions one, a headline catches their eye, or a social media post shows a dramatic chart. Professionals find stocks proactively, through systematic sourcing methods that are independent of the daily news cycle and immune to the emotional contagion that drives retail trading behavior.

The following five sourcing methods, used in combination, will give you a consistent pipeline of candidates worthy of deeper research. Each maps to a feature available on StockTradesApp.com or a freely available external resource.

Source 1: The AI Screener

The AI Screener (navigation menu: Screener) is your fastest sourcing tool on StockTradesApp.com. Type a plain-English description of the characteristics you are looking for and the platform returns matching candidates from its curated universe of approximately 55 popular large and mid-cap tickers.

Effective AI Screener prompts are specific and multi-criteria. Here are examples of prompts that generate high-quality candidate lists:

- **Quality growth with reasonable valuation:** "Large-cap tech with earnings growth over 20% and P/E under 30"
- **Defensive income:** "Dividend payers yielding over 3% with consistent earnings growth"
- **Momentum candidates:** "Stocks near their 52-week high with strong recent performance"
- **Recovery candidates:** "Quality companies down more than 15% this year trading near support"
- **Sector-specific:** "Mega-cap healthcare names with strong free cash flow"

Run two or three different prompts each week as part of your sourcing routine. Add any candidates that look interesting at first glance to your Watchlist for deeper evaluation.

At this stage you are casting a net, not making trading decisions. Every ticker you add from the screener is a candidate for further research, not an entry signal.

PLATFORM FEATURE: AI Screener: Running Your First Screen

Open the navigation menu and select Screener. You will see the text input field with the placeholder "DESCRIBE WHAT YOU'RE LOOKING FOR" and four preset prompt chips below it.

Try the preset chip "Defensive dividend payers yielding over 3%" first. Click "RUN SCREEN." The platform will return a list of tickers from its ~55-ticker universe that match this description.

For each result, click the ticker to open its full Terminal page. Review the Blended Signal, the chart, and the AI Signal banner. Add any that look worth monitoring to your Watchlist by clicking the SAVE button at the top of the Terminal.

Then type your own prompt in the input field. Start with something you already have a view on, such as "technology companies with strong revenue growth and low debt." Run the screen and compare the results to what you expected. The gap between your intuition and the results is itself an educational signal about the current market environment.

Source 2: The Compare Tool

The Compare tool (navigation menu: Compare) is invaluable for identifying relative strength: finding the stocks within a sector or peer group that are outperforming their competitors. Rather than evaluating stocks in isolation, the Compare tool lets you overlay multiple tickers on a normalized percentage-return chart and immediately see which are leading and which are lagging.

A practical sourcing routine with Compare: pick a sector you are interested in (Technology, Healthcare, Consumer Discretionary) and add four or five of the most prominent companies in that sector to the Compare chart. Set the time frame to 6MO or 1Y. The stock at the top of the chart (the highest percentage return line over that period) is the sector leader. Leaders tend to continue leading. This relative strength identification is one of the most time-tested principles in stock selection.

PLATFORM FEATURE: Using Compare for Relative Strength Sourcing

Open the Compare tool and add five major technology stocks: AAPL, MSFT, NVDA, GOOGL, and META.

Set the time frame to 1Y. Study the chart. Which stock has the highest percentage return over the past year? Which has the lowest? Now set the time frame to 6MO. Does the ranking change significantly?

The stock that leads across both time frames (both 6-month and 1-year) is demonstrating the most consistent relative strength. This is a candidate for your Tier 1 watchlist. The stock that lags across both periods is a candidate to either avoid or investigate for a potential turnaround.

Repeat this exercise for a different sector each week as part of your sourcing routine: healthcare, consumer, energy, financials, industrials. Over a month, you will have compared 25 to 30 stocks and identified the current relative strength leaders in every major sector.

Source 3: Earnings Season Calendars

Earnings season occurs four times per year, approximately six to eight weeks after the end of each fiscal quarter. During earnings season, companies report their quarterly financial results, and stock prices frequently make their largest single-day moves of the year in response. This volatility creates both risk and opportunity.

A disciplined sourcing practice during earnings season is to identify stocks that have just reported unexpectedly strong earnings, particularly companies showing earnings acceleration (EPS growth rate increasing from the prior quarter). These companies are often transitioning from Stage 1 to Stage 2 on the Weinstein framework (covered in Chapter 6), and the earnings report acts as the catalyst that attracts institutional attention and drives the initial momentum. Use the AI Earnings Briefing feature in the Terminal to quickly assess the quality of any company's most recent earnings report.

Source 4: Sector and Industry News

Major developments within an industry, a new regulatory framework, a technology breakthrough, a commodity price shift, an acquisition announcement, or a major product launch, can create opportunities across an entire sector simultaneously. When one airline company announces a dramatic improvement in load factor, it often signals the same dynamic is occurring across the industry. When a semiconductor company reports much stronger-than-expected demand for its AI chips, it is often a leading indicator for the broader semiconductor supply chain.

Developing a habit of reading one or two high-quality financial publications daily makes you aware of these sector-level developments before they become obvious to the broader retail trading community. This is covered in depth in Section 7.6 of this chapter on reading financial news effectively.

Source 5: Your Own Consumer and Professional Experience

Peter Lynch, the legendary manager of the Fidelity Magellan Fund who generated 29.2% average annual returns from 1977 to 1990, built his greatest investment ideas from direct observation of the world around him. He called this the most underrated edge available to ordinary investors: the knowledge you gain simply by being a consumer, an employee, or a participant in an industry.

> *"The person that turns over the most rocks wins the game. And that's always been my philosophy. You have to look at more things and find the companies where the fundamentals are improving."*
>
> — **Peter Lynch**, *One Up on Wall Street (1989): one of the most widely read investment books ever written*

If you work in healthcare and notice a particular medical device company's products dominating every procedure you observe, that is a sourcing signal. If you are a gamer and you watch one particular platform's user numbers growing dramatically among your peers, that is worth investigating. This bottom-up, observation-driven sourcing is not a replacement for rigorous analysis, but it is often what leads an investor to the right question to ask before the rest of the market has thought to ask it.

7.3 The CAN SLIM Framework: A Proven Screening Standard

Once you have a list of sourced candidates, you need a framework for evaluating whether a given stock meets the quality standard required for your watchlist. The most widely tested and academically studied growth-stock screening framework is William O'Neil's CAN SLIM methodology, developed through his analysis of the 500 biggest stock market winners from 1953 to 1993 and published in How to Make Money in Stocks (1988).

CAN SLIM is an acronym representing seven criteria that O'Neil found consistently present in the greatest-performing stocks before they made their biggest price advances.

The American Association of Individual Investors (AAII) named CAN SLIM the top-performing investment strategy from 1998 to 2009, and academic research published in the Applied Finance Letters journal (2023) confirmed that simplified versions of the model consistently outperformed major indices over multi-year test periods.

> **KEY TERM: CAN SLIM**
> *A seven-criteria growth stock screening methodology developed by William J. O'Neil and first published in How to Make Money in Stocks (1988). CAN SLIM integrates both fundamental analysis (earnings growth, new products, institutional sponsorship) and technical analysis (supply and demand dynamics, market direction) to identify high-quality growth stocks before they make their largest price advances. The American Association of Individual Investors named it the top-performing investment strategy from 1998 to 2009.*

The table below explains each letter of the CAN SLIM acronym, the minimum threshold O'Neil suggests, and how you can check each criterion using the tools available on StockTradesApp.com.

Letter	Criterion	Minimum Threshold	How to Check It on StockTradesApp.com
C	Current Quarterly Earnings Growth	EPS up at least 25% vs. same quarter prior year	Terminal > AI Earnings Briefing; Fundamentals section (where available)
A	Annual Earnings Growth	EPS up 25%+ per year for at least 3 consecutive years	Terminal > Fundamentals section; earnings history panel
N	New Product, Service, or Management	A meaningful catalyst driving the current growth	Terminal > AI News Digest; News panel; Earnings Briefing
S	Supply and Demand	Rising volume on up-days; stock near 52-week high	Terminal chart: volume bars vs. trend direction; 52-week range indicator
L	Leader vs. Laggard	Stock outperforming its sector peers on a relative basis	Compare tool: add the stock and 2-3 sector peers; check which line is highest
I	Institutional Sponsorship	Growing institutional ownership in recent quarters	Terminal > Fundamentals (where available); major fund ownership data

Lette r	Criterion	Minimum Threshold	How to Check It on StockTradesApp.com
M	Market Direction	S&P 500 and NASDAQ in a confirmed uptrend	Add ^GSPC and ^NDX to Watchlist; monitor their Blended Signals daily

Using CAN SLIM as a Watchlist Filter, Not a Buy Signal

An important clarification: CAN SLIM is a screening tool that helps you identify companies worth deeper research. It is not a mechanical buy signal. A stock that passes all seven CAN SLIM criteria is a high-quality candidate for your Tier 1 watchlist. It still requires the full technical analysis pre-trade checklist from Chapter 6 before you make any entry decision in your paper trading portfolio.

O'Neil himself emphasized that the M criterion (market direction) is perhaps the most important of all. Three out of four stocks tend to follow the general market direction, he observed repeatedly. A technically perfect CAN SLIM setup in a stock-specific chart is far less likely to succeed when the S&P 500 and NASDAQ are in a confirmed downtrend. Always check the market environment before acting on any individual stock signal.

ADAPTING CAN SLIM FOR THE AI SCREENER

The CAN SLIM criteria can be translated directly into AI Screener prompts on StockTradesApp.com. Try these adapted prompts:

"Large-cap stocks with strong recent earnings growth and accelerating revenue" (targets C and A criteria)

"Technology or healthcare companies launching new products with rising institutional interest" (targets N and I criteria)

"Stocks near 52-week highs with above-average volume on up-days" (targets S and L criteria)

Run these prompts and compare the results to your own manually researched candidates. The overlap between screener outputs and your own research is a high-conviction sourcing signal.

7.4 The Three-Tier Watchlist System

A flat, untiered watchlist is nearly useless in practice. When you open your Watchlist and see 30 tickers all displayed with equal prominence, there is no guidance about which ones require your immediate attention, which are still being researched, and which are simply on your radar. The three-tier system solves this problem by assigning every watchlist stock to a specific level of readiness and a specific action protocol.

Because StockTradesApp.com uses a single unified watchlist, you will implement the tier system through a naming convention in your personal notes and through your own research records. As you open each ticker's Terminal page from the Watchlist, you will have a clear mental model of which tier it belongs to and what you need to evaluate. Some traders maintain a separate simple document or notebook entry for each stock that records its current tier and the date it was assigned.

Tier	Status	Criteria for Inclusion
Tier 1: Ready to Trade	Actively paper trade or consider for entry	Stage 2 uptrend confirmed on weekly chart. Blended Signal is BUY or high HOLD. Strong fundamental story (earnings growth, wide moat). Clear support level for stop placement. High-conviction setup with at least 4 of the 6 technical checklist items aligned.
Tier 2: Under Study	Researching and monitoring, not yet ready	Fundamentally interesting but technically not yet in an optimal entry position. May be in Stage 1 accumulation. Needs one or two more data points before a confident entry. Return regularly to check for improvement.
Tier 3: Watch and Wait	On radar for future opportunities	An interesting company or sector story that does not yet meet your entry criteria. Flagged for re-evaluation after the next earnings report, a sector catalyst, or a change in market conditions. Low priority but worth keeping visible.

Managing Tier Transitions

Stocks move between tiers as conditions change. A Tier 2 stock becomes Tier 1 when it breaks out of a consolidation pattern on high volume, when a Blended Signal improves from HOLD to BUY, or when a fundamental catalyst (a strong earnings report, a product launch, a significant contract win) accelerates its growth story. A Tier 1 stock drops to Tier 2 when the technical setup deteriorates, or to removal entirely when the fundamental story breaks down.

Review every stock on your watchlist at least once per week against its tier criteria. This weekly audit takes 20 to 30 minutes and is one of the most valuable habits you can build as a developing trader. It forces you to constantly re-examine your assumptions and prevents you from holding stocks on your Tier 1 list out of emotional attachment rather than current evidence.

🖥 PLATFORM FEATURE: Managing Your Watchlist on stocktradesapp.com

Your Watchlist (navigation menu: Watchlist) shows every saved ticker with a date saved and an ANALYZE button. Click ANALYZE on any ticker to instantly open its full Terminal page, where you can review the Blended Signal, chart, RSI, MACD, AI News Digest, and all five analysis tabs.

To remove a stock that no longer meets your criteria, click the trash icon next to its entry. Do not hesitate to remove stocks from your list. A shorter, higher-conviction watchlist is far more useful than a long, unfocused one.

Your Watchlist Live Signals panel on the Dashboard shows all your saved tickers grouped by asset class (Bonds and Rates, Commodities, Crypto, Stocks) with their current LAST price, CHANGE, Signal (BUY/HOLD/SELL), and Score. This panel gives you a fast overview of how your entire watchlist is behaving without opening individual Terminal pages.

Use Price Alerts (navigation menu: Alerts) to set automatic notifications for key levels on your Tier 1 stocks. A "Crosses Above" alert at the breakout level and a "Crosses Below" alert at your stop-loss level creates an automated monitoring bracket so you are notified the moment a key price event occurs.

7.5 Reading and Using the Blended Signal in Your Research

The Blended Signal on StockTradesApp.com is the platform's synthesized rating for any ticker, combining a Technical score (based on RSI, MACD, momentum, and trend direction), a Fundamentals delta (adjustment from balance sheet and earnings data where available), and a News delta (sentiment adjustment from recent headline analysis) into a single composite score displayed as BUY, HOLD, or SELL.

Understanding how to use the Blended Signal correctly is essential. It is a research input, not a trading instruction. The platform's own disclaimer is explicit: "This terminal is an analytics tool, not investment advice. Technical signals reflect past price action and will fail across regime shifts. Always pair with fundamentals and paper trade first." That disclaimer deserves to be internalized, not scrolled past.

How to Read the Blended Signal Correctly

When you open a stock's Terminal page, the first thing you will see after the chart is the AI Signal banner, which gives a plain-English reason for the current signal, and the quote grid, which shows the Blended Signal with its composite score broken into Technical, Fundamentals, and News components. Scroll to the bottom and click the OVERVIEW tab for a detailed breakdown.

The OVERVIEW tab shows you five rows of information: BLENDED (the overall composite score), TECHNICAL (the raw technical score, e.g. -25), FUNDAMENTALS DELTA (the adjustment from fundamental data, shown with a triangle symbol), NEWS DELTA (the sentiment adjustment from headlines, with the number of headlines analyzed), BARS ANALYZED (the number of price bars used in the technical calculation), and RANGE (the time period analyzed, e.g. 6MO).

To go deeper, click the SIGNALS tab for a full technical breakdown of every indicator that contributed to the Technical score. Click BLEND to see how the technical, fundamental, and news components combine. Click ANALYSIS for the full AI-written briefing covering the setup, outlook, and specific risks identified for the stock.

Effective Use of the Blended Signal	Ineffective Use of the Blended Signal
Use it as one data point alongside your own technical chart analysis	Use it as the only reason to enter a trade
Check the SIGNALS tab to understand what is driving the technical score	Accept the BUY/HOLD/SELL rating without examining the inputs
Compare the signal against the broader market direction (M in CAN SLIM)	Trade individual signals when the S&P 500 is in a confirmed downtrend
Use a BUY signal on a fundamentally strong stock to confirm an entry you had already planned from your own analysis	Enter a position solely because the signal changed from HOLD to BUY
Note when the Blended Signal diverges from your own analysis and investigate why	Ignore divergences between the signal and your own chart reading
Read the full ANALYSIS tab briefing before any significant trade	Skip the AI briefing and act on the headline signal alone

The most disciplined use of the Blended Signal is as a confirmation tool. If your own fundamental and technical research leads you to a high-conviction thesis on a stock, and the Blended Signal agrees with your conclusion, that agreement strengthens your conviction. If your research produces a bullish thesis but the Blended Signal is strongly SELL, that divergence is a warning to look harder at what you might be missing.

🖥 PLATFORM FEATURE: The WALKTHROUGH Tab: Learning While You Research

The WALKTHROUGH tab in the Terminal's bottom analysis panel is specifically designed for learning. It walks you through the logic behind the current signal in a step-by-step format, explaining what each indicator is reading and why it is contributing positively or negatively to the overall score.

For every new stock you add to your watchlist, open the Terminal and read the full WALKTHROUGH tab before moving to the chart. This structured explanation will accelerate your ability to read charts independently because it connects each indicator reading to its real-world context on that specific stock at that specific moment.

Over time, you will find that your own independent chart analysis increasingly matches the platform's systematic assessment. When that happens consistently, it is a sign that your technical reading skills have matured significantly.

7.6 Reading Financial News Objectively: Signal vs. Noise

One of the most consistently destructive habits in retail trading is allowing financial news to drive trading decisions. This is not because financial news is dishonest. It is because the incentive structure of financial media is misaligned with your interests as a trader. Financial media earns attention through drama, novelty, and urgency. Markets move on expectations about the future. By the time a story is prominent enough to appear on the front page of a financial publication, it has typically already been priced into the stock by the institutional investors who were tracking the underlying data weeks or months earlier.

> *"If you spend more than 13 minutes analyzing economic and market forecasts, you've wasted 10 minutes."*
> — **Peter Lynch**, *Beating the Street (1993)*

This does not mean you should ignore financial news. It means you should read it with a specific purpose and a critical framework that separates the genuinely actionable information from the noise that masquerades as insight.

The Four Categories of Financial News

Every financial news story you read falls into one of four categories. Knowing which category a story belongs to determines how much weight it should carry in your research process.

- **Company-Specific Fundamental News:** Earnings reports, revenue guidance, new product launches, executive changes, material legal settlements, significant acquisitions, and FDA decisions. This is the category that actually moves individual stocks and deserves the most careful reading. Verify in SEC filings for accuracy.
- **Macroeconomic Data and Policy:** Federal Reserve interest rate decisions, inflation data (CPI, PCE), employment reports (non-farm payrolls), GDP growth, and Treasury yield movements. This category affects the broader market environment (the M in CAN SLIM) and your overall portfolio positioning, but rarely justifies an individual stock decision in isolation.
- **Analyst Actions:** Upgrades, downgrades, new coverage initiations, and price target changes from Wall Street research analysts. These are often lagging indicators: analysts frequently upgrade stocks after they have already risen significantly and downgrade them after they have already fallen. Read analyst commentary for the reasoning and channel checks, not the rating itself.
- **Market Commentary and Opinion:** Predictions, forecasts, expert opinions, and market narratives. This is the category with the lowest signal-to-noise ratio. The financial media ecosystem produces an enormous volume of confident-sounding market predictions, the vast majority of which have no statistically reliable track record. Consume this category with the most skepticism and never make trading decisions based on it alone.

THE PROBLEM WITH FINANCIAL MEDIA PREDICTIONS

A landmark study by Philip Tetlock, published in Expert Political Judgment: How Good Is It? How Can We Know? (Princeton University Press, 2005) and expanded in Superforecasting (2015), found that expert forecasters (including economic and market experts) performed only marginally better than random chance when making predictions more than a year into the future.

> Financial journalist and author Jason Zweig of the Wall Street Journal has repeatedly documented that the majority of market predictions made by prominent financial media commentators have no statistically significant accuracy over time.
>
> The practical implication: treat financial media commentary on where the market or a specific stock is headed as entertainment and context, not as actionable intelligence. Your own disciplined application of the tools from Chapters 5 and 6, combined with the systematic research process in this chapter, will produce more reliable decisions than any commentator's forecast.

A Framework for Reading News Objectively

When you read any financial news story, work through these four questions before allowing it to influence your thinking about a stock:

1. Is this news genuinely new information, or is it a repackaging of something the market already knows? A story headlined "Apple faces competition from Chinese smartphone makers" is describing a dynamic that has been priced into Apple's valuation for years. Genuinely new information is specific, unexpected, and material to the company's future earnings.
2. Does this news change the fundamental thesis you have built for this company through your own research? A news story is only actionable if it materially alters your assessment of the company's competitive position, revenue trajectory, or earnings power. Most stories do not.
3. Is this a signal or a narrative? A signal is a verifiable data point (EPS growth of 40% YoY, a contract win worth $2 billion in revenue). A narrative is an interpretation of conditions ("investors are losing confidence in tech valuations"). Signals deserve weight. Narratives deserve skepticism.
4. What does the price action say about how the market has already processed this news? A stock that surges on what looks like positive news may be confirming the news was genuinely new and positive. A stock that falls on what looks like positive news (the classic "sell the news" reaction) is telling you the news was already priced in and the market is now disappointed by something in the details. Always read price action alongside news, never instead of it.

The News panel on StockTradesApp.com's Terminal shows articles from Yahoo Finance and Fox Business, organized by recency. The AI News Digest button ("What Moved [Ticker]?") produces a plain-English synthesis of recent news affecting the stock, which is an excellent starting point for understanding the current news environment without reading every article. Use the AI summary to orient yourself, then click through to the two or three most significant underlying articles to verify the summary and form your own judgment.

Source Type	Examples	How to Use It
Primary Financial Press	Wall Street Journal, Financial Times, Bloomberg, Reuters, Barron's	Highest reliability. Use for macro context, earnings coverage, regulatory news, and management interviews. Prioritize over secondary sources.
SEC Filings (Primary Source)	10-K annual reports, 10-Q quarterly reports, 8-K material event filings, Proxy statements at sec.gov	The most authoritative source of company information. Earnings releases and conference call transcripts here before anywhere else.
Financial Data Aggregators	Yahoo Finance (news tab), Fox Business (news tab), Seeking Alpha, Zacks, MarketWatch	Convenient aggregators of news from multiple sources. Available in the StockTradesApp.com Terminal's News panel. Useful for speed but verify significant claims in primary sources.
Earnings Call Transcripts	Earnings call transcripts via SEC EDGAR, StockTradesApp AI Earnings Briefing	Management speaks directly. Read for guidance language, tone, and commentary on competitive dynamics. Use the Terminal's "Generate Earnings Briefing" button for an AI-synthesized plain-English summary.
AI News Digest	StockTradesApp.com "What Moved [Ticker]?" feature	A plain-English AI-written briefing of recent news affecting the stock. Excellent for a fast synthesis before your deeper research. Always verify specific claims in the underlying source articles.
Social Media / Forums	X (Twitter), Reddit (r/investing, r/stocks), StockTwits	Use only for sentiment and awareness of retail narrative, never as the basis for a trading decision. The most dangerous category for confirmation bias.

7.7 Sector Context: Understanding the Environment Your Stock Lives In

No stock exists in isolation. Every company operates within an industry, and every industry operates within a sector, and every sector is affected by the macroeconomic and interest rate environment in which the broader market operates. Building sector context into your research process is one of the most reliably differentiating practices between developing traders and fully developed ones.

The principle at work here is called top-down analysis: starting with the macro environment, narrowing to the sector, then narrowing to the industry, and finally arriving at the individual stock. Top-down analysis ensures that you are not selecting an excellent individual company in a sector that the market is actively avoiding, which is one of the most common mistakes beginning investors make.

Using Compare for Sector Rotation Analysis

The Compare tool on StockTradesApp.com is your primary instrument for sector context analysis. Here is a practical routine:

5. Add the major sector ETF proxies to a Compare chart: XLK (Technology), XLV (Healthcare), XLF (Financials), XLE (Energy), XLY (Consumer Discretionary), XLP (Consumer Staples), XLI (Industrials). Set the time frame to 3MO or 6MO.
6. The sector ETF with the highest normalized return over the period is where money is flowing. The sector at the bottom of the chart is where money is leaving. This relative sector performance is the first input to your individual stock selection.
7. Once you identify the top one or two sectors, use the AI Screener to find specific stock candidates within those sectors. You are now selecting individual stocks in sectors the market is currently favoring, dramatically improving your probability of entering stocks that will be supported by institutional money flow.
8. As a secondary check, add ^GSPC (S&P 500) and ^NDX (NASDAQ-100) to your Watchlist and monitor their Blended Signals daily. These are your market direction indicators. If both indices show SELL signals on the Terminal, exercise extreme caution about entering new positions regardless of how attractive an individual stock looks.

SECTOR ROTATION: THE MONEY ALWAYS GOES SOMEWHERE

Institutional investors managing billions of dollars do not simply hold cash when one sector falls out of favor. They rotate that capital into the sector they expect to outperform over the next cycle. This rotation creates predictable patterns: when technology stocks are under pressure from rising interest rates, defensive sectors like Consumer Staples and Healthcare tend to attract inflows. When the economy is accelerating, Financials and Industrials tend to lead.

As a beginning paper trader, you do not need to predict sector rotation. You simply need to identify where it has already begun and align your stock selection with the direction of institutional money flow, not against it.

The Compare tool makes this identification straightforward. A sector ETF that is consistently at the top of the normalized return chart on the 3-month and 6-month views is attracting capital. That is where you want to be looking for individual stock opportunities.

7.8 Building Your Daily Research Routine

One of the most consistently cited practices of successful traders is a structured daily routine that is independent of whether markets are exciting or dull. The traders who improve most consistently are not the ones who work harder when markets are moving dramatically. They are the ones who do the same disciplined work every single day, in every market condition.

The following routine is calibrated for a beginning paper trader who has limited time, typically 30 to 60 minutes per day, and wants to stay informed about their paper trading positions and watchlist without being consumed by screen time. As your skills and position sizes grow, this routine will naturally expand. For now, consistency matters more than comprehensiveness.

The Daily Pre-Market Routine (15 minutes, before 9:30 AM Eastern)

9. Open StockTradesApp.com and navigate to your Dashboard. Check your current paper trading equity, open positions, and any unrealized gain or loss on each holding.
10. Open the Watchlist. Review the Live Signals panel on the Dashboard for any significant overnight changes in signal or price for your Tier 1 stocks. If any Blended Signal has changed dramatically, open that stock's Terminal immediately.
11. Check your Alerts section. Did any price alerts trigger overnight? If a stock crossed a level you had flagged, open its Terminal and assess whether it represents an action point.
12. Read one or two brief financial news summaries. The goal is macro orientation: what is the Federal Reserve doing? Are there any major economic data releases today? Are there earnings reports due from companies on your watchlist? Keep this to five minutes maximum.

The Active Session Routine (market hours, as time permits)

13. If you have an open paper trading position, check it once per hour maximum. Compulsive price-checking is one of the most destructive habits in trading. Set alerts at your stop-loss and target levels and let the alerts do the monitoring.
14. If a stock on your Tier 1 watchlist triggers a price alert during the session, open the Terminal and work through the full pre-trade checklist from Chapter 6 before making any entry decision. Do not enter a trade under time pressure during the first 30 minutes or last 30 minutes of the session.
15. If no alerts have triggered, use active session time for Learn Hub reading, reviewing your paper trading history in the Dashboard, or researching new candidates on the Terminal.

The Evening Research Routine (15 to 30 minutes, after market close)

16. Review any paper trades you placed or closed today. Open the Dashboard and check your Trade History. For each closed trade, write a brief post-trade note in your personal journal covering what happened, whether you followed your plan, and what you learned.
17. Run one AI Screener prompt to add two or three new candidates to your Tier 2 or Tier 3 watchlist. This weekly sourcing habit ensures your watchlist pipeline never runs dry.
18. Spend 10 to 15 minutes on the Terminal researching one stock in depth. Open all five analysis tabs. Run the AI News Digest. Review the chart with your technical analysis framework. Assign the stock to a watchlist tier and note your reasoning.
19. Review your overall watchlist. Are any Tier 2 stocks ready to be promoted to Tier 1? Are any Tier 1 stocks whose conditions have deteriorated? Update your tier assignments based on current data, not on emotional attachment to prior research.

The Weekly Research Block (one session per week, 45 to 60 minutes)

20. Run the Compare tool on five to seven sector ETFs to check the current state of sector rotation. Note which sectors are gaining relative strength and which are losing it. Update your sector view accordingly.
21. Run two or three AI Screener prompts focused on the leading sectors from your Compare analysis. Add the most promising candidates to your watchlist.
22. Review your paper trading performance on the Dashboard. What is your current win rate, profit factor, and max drawdown? How do these compare to the SPY

benchmark over the same period? What patterns do you notice in your winning vs. losing trades?

23. Prepare for the coming week. Are there any earnings reports due from companies on your watchlist? Any major economic data releases (Fed meetings, jobs reports, CPI data)? Mark these dates in your awareness so you are not caught off guard.

PLATFORM FEATURE: Setting Up Your Research Workflow on stocktradesapp.com

Create a simple bookmark folder in your browser with four bookmarks: the Dashboard, the Terminal (with a default ticker you monitor frequently), the Screener, and the Compare tool. This gives you one-click access to your four primary research locations without navigating the menu each time.

Keep the Alerts section checked at the start of every session (navigation menu: Alerts). Triggered alerts stop firing until reactivated, so you will see a clean record of which levels were crossed overnight or during the previous session.

The Dashboard's Watchlist Live Signals panel, which shows all your saved tickers grouped by asset class with their current Blended Signals, is the fastest way to get an overview of your entire watchlist in one place. Make this panel the first thing you review each session.

7.9 Chapter 7 Exercise: Building Your First Systematic Watchlist

The following exercise walks you through the complete watchlist-building process from sourcing through tiering. By the end, you will have a structured, tiered watchlist of at least eight to ten stocks that you have researched using the tools and frameworks in this chapter. This watchlist will serve as the foundation for your paper trading activity in Chapters 8 and 9.

Full Watchlist-Building Exercise

Step 1: SOURCING ROUND 1: Open the AI Screener and run two different prompts. Try "Large-cap tech with strong earnings growth and below-market P/E" and "Defensive dividend payers with consistent earnings history." Add every result that has a BUY or strong HOLD Blended Signal on the Terminal to your Watchlist.

Step 2: SOURCING ROUND 2: Open the Compare tool and add five stocks from the same sector (pick any sector you find interesting). Set the time frame to 6MO. Identify the top two relative strength leaders and add them to your Watchlist. Note which stock is lagging most significantly.

Step 3: SOURCING ROUND 3: Think of three companies whose products or services you use regularly or whose industry you know well from your professional or personal life. Look each up in the Terminal. If at least two pass a quick review of the Blended Signal and chart trend, add them.

Step 4: CAN SLIM SCREEN: For each stock now on your Watchlist, open the Terminal and click the ANALYSIS tab. Read the full AI briefing. Then manually check the CAN SLIM C criterion (earnings growth) and S criterion (near 52-week high, above-average volume on up-days) using the Terminal chart and Fundamentals section. Note which stocks pass both criteria.

Step 5: TIER ASSIGNMENT: Review your full watchlist (aim for 10 to 15 stocks at this point). For each stock, work through the Chapter 6 Pre-Trade Checklist quickly (Stage, Trend, Moving Averages, Support/Resistance, RSI, MACD, Volume). Assign each stock to Tier 1, Tier 2, or Tier 3 based on your assessment. Record your tier assignments and the key reasons for each in your personal research notes.

Step 6: SET ALERTS: For every stock you have assigned to Tier 1, set two Price Alerts in the Alerts section: one "Crosses Above" at the breakout level you have identified on the chart, and one "Crosses Below" at the support level that would signal the setup has failed. This creates a monitoring bracket for each high-conviction position.

Step 7: COMPARE YOUR SECTORS: Add the sector ETFs relevant to your Tier 1 stocks to a Compare chart (1Y time frame). Confirm that the sectors your Tier 1 stocks belong to are currently showing relative strength versus the broader market. If a Tier 1 stock belongs to a clearly underperforming sector, reconsider whether it should remain at Tier 1.

Step 8: DOCUMENT YOUR WORK: Write a one-paragraph summary for each Tier 1 stock in your personal research notes, covering: the fundamental thesis (what makes this company excellent), the technical setup (where you would enter and where your stop would be), and the market context (what sector conditions and macro environment would favor this position). This document is your research foundation for the paper trading decisions you will make in Chapter 8.

Chapter 7 Summary

Chapter 7 has given you the complete system for building and maintaining a professional-grade watchlist and conducting routine research. Here is what you now carry into your paper trading:

- **Watchlists Require Systems, Not Lists:** A flat list of interesting tickers is not a watchlist. A tiered, active research pipeline with defined sourcing methods, quality criteria, and a weekly audit process is a watchlist.
- **Five Sourcing Methods:** The AI Screener (natural-language queries against ~55 curated tickers), the Compare tool (relative strength identification across sector peers), earnings season calendars (identifying accelerating earnings stories), sector and industry news, and your own consumer and professional observations.
- **CAN SLIM as a Screening Standard:** William O'Neil's seven criteria (Current earnings, Annual earnings, New product/service, Supply and demand, Leader vs. laggard, Institutional sponsorship, Market direction) provide a proven, academically validated framework for identifying high-quality growth candidates. Named the top-performing investment strategy from 1998 to 2009 by the AAII.
- **The Three-Tier System:** Tier 1 (Ready to Trade): high-conviction, technically ready setups. Tier 2 (Under Study): fundamentally interesting but technically not ready. Tier 3 (Watch and Wait): on radar for future opportunities. Every stock has a clear action protocol based on its tier.
- **Reading the Blended Signal Correctly:** The Terminal's BUY/HOLD/SELL rating is a research input, not a trading instruction. Use it for confirmation of your own independent analysis. Use the SIGNALS, BLEND, and ANALYSIS tabs for the full breakdown. The WALKTHROUGH tab is a built-in learning tool for developing your own analytical skills.
- **Financial News with a Critical Framework:** Four categories of news: company-specific fundamental news (highest signal), macroeconomic data and policy, analyst actions (often lagging), and market commentary and opinion (lowest signal). Four questions to ask of every story before allowing it to influence a trading decision.
- **Sector Context via Compare:** Add sector ETFs to the Compare tool to identify where institutional money is currently flowing. Align your individual stock selection with sector strength, not against it.
- **The Daily Research Routine:** Pre-market (15 min): Dashboard, Watchlist signals, Alerts. Active session: alert-driven monitoring only. Evening (15 to 30 min): trade review, one AI Screener run, one Terminal deep-dive. Weekly (45 to 60 min): sector rotation review, screener sourcing, performance analytics, week-ahead preparation.

CHAPTER 8

Risk Management: The Art of Not Losing Money

"The key to long-term survival and prosperity has a lot to do with the money management techniques incorporated into the technical system. There are old traders and there are bold traders, but there are very few old, bold traders."

— Ed Seykota, Market Wizards by Jack D. Schwager (1989)

Every chapter in this book so far has taught you how to find better trades. This chapter teaches you something more important: how to survive the bad ones. Because bad trades are not occasional anomalies to be avoided with better analysis. They are a guaranteed, permanent feature of every trading career at every level of skill. The greatest traders in history lose on 30, 40, or even 50 percent of their trades. What separates them from the traders who fail is not their ability to avoid losses. It is their ability to keep every loss small, every winning trade larger than every losing trade, and their overall system profitable across hundreds of repetitions.

Risk management is the discipline that makes this possible. It consists of four interconnected skills: understanding how drawdowns compound mathematically and why small losses are non-negotiable, calculating the correct position size for every trade before entry, placing stop-losses at logical structural levels rather than arbitrary percentages, and building a risk-reward framework that ensures your winners systematically outpace your losers.

None of these skills require complex mathematics. They require discipline, and the willingness to apply the same rules consistently across every trade, whether you feel confident or uncertain, whether the market is calm or volatile. This chapter gives you the framework. The paper trading environment on StockTradesApp.com gives you the laboratory to practice it before real capital is at stake.

> *"Position sizing is THE number one skill. Not technical analysis. Not economic news reading. The sizing."*
>
> — **Dr. Van K. Tharp, Ph.D.**, *Trade Your Way to Financial Freedom (1998): the foundational text on position sizing and expectancy*

8.1 The Mathematics of Loss: Why Small Drawdowns Are Non-Negotiable

Before any discussion of techniques, it is essential to understand why risk management rules exist in the first place. The answer lies in a mathematical asymmetry that surprises most beginning traders: losses and gains are not symmetrical. A loss of 50 percent requires a gain of 100 percent just to return to the starting point. This asymmetry grows more severe as the loss increases, and it is the reason that preventing large drawdowns is more important than generating large gains.

Loss Suffered	Gain to Recover	At 1% Risk Per Trade	At 10% Risk Per Trade
10% drawdown	**11.1% to break even**	Needs 10 max consecutive losses	Needs only 1 max consecutive loss
20% drawdown	**25.0% to break even**	Needs 20 max consecutive losses	Needs only 2 max consecutive losses
30% drawdown	**42.9% to break even**	Needs 30 max consecutive losses	Needs only 3 max consecutive losses
50% drawdown	**100.0% to break even**	Needs 50 max consecutive losses	Needs only 5 max consecutive losses
75% drawdown	**300.0% to break even**	Needs 75 max consecutive losses	Needs only 7 max consecutive losses
90% drawdown	**900.0% to break even**	Needs 90 max consecutive losses	Needs only 9 max consecutive losses

Study that table carefully. A trader who loses 50 percent of their account needs to double the remaining money just to break even. A trader who loses 90 percent needs to generate a 900 percent return to recover. These are not theoretical scenarios. They are the documented fate of traders who risk too much per trade and experience the inevitable losing streaks that every trading strategy produces at some point.

The practical implication is direct: protecting your capital from large drawdowns is more valuable than maximizing short-term returns. A trader who never loses more than 20 percent in a drawdown will almost always outperform one who sometimes gains 100 percent but occasionally loses 60 percent, because the recovery mathematics works so strongly against large losses.

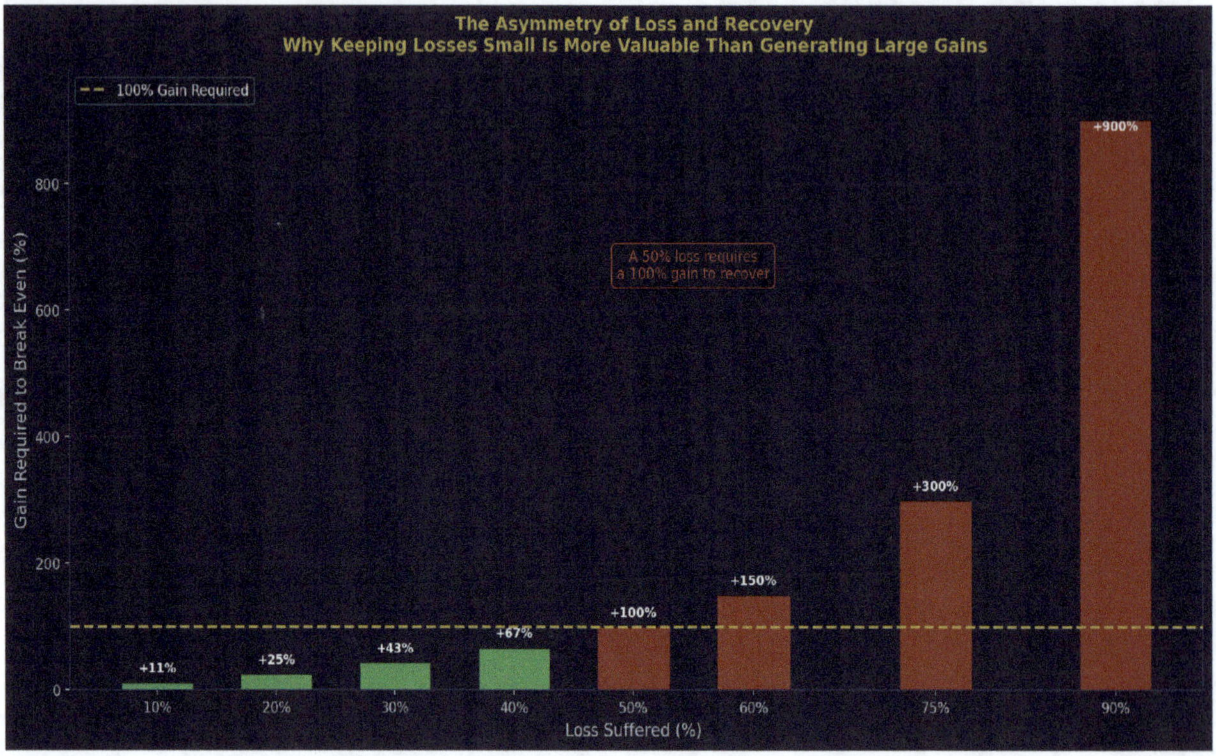

Figure 8.1 — The Asymmetry of Loss and Recovery: A 50% loss requires a 100% gain to break even. A 90% loss requires 900%.

85%

of traders who consistently apply the 1-2% risk rule per trade stay active for at least two years. Of traders who risk 10% or more per trade, 88% are wiped out within one year.

Source: QuantVPS.com quantitative trading survival research (2025)

That gap is not explained by luck or analytical skill. It is explained entirely by position sizing discipline. The traders who survive long enough for their edge to compound are the ones who make it impossible for any single trade to end their career.

8.2 The 1% Rule: The Foundation of Professional Position Sizing

The single most widely adopted risk management rule among professional traders is the 1% rule: never risk more than 1 percent of your total trading account on any single trade. This is not 1 percent of the position value. It is 1 percent of your entire account balance, applied to the maximum possible loss on the trade if your stop-loss is hit.

KEY TERM: The 1% Rule
A position sizing principle that limits the maximum risk on any single trade to 1 percent of the total trading account balance. For a $100,000 paper trading account, the maximum risk per trade is $1,000. This rule is applied to the dollar difference between the entry price and the stop-loss price, not to the total position value. A 0.5% rule is appropriate for beginning traders building their first track record. Graduating to 2% is appropriate only once a proven edge is established across 100 or more paper trades.

For a $100,000 paper trading account, the 1% rule means your maximum risk per trade is $1,000. If you buy a stock at $50 and place your stop-loss at $47.50, your risk per share is $2.50. Dividing your maximum dollar risk ($1,000) by the risk per share ($2.50) gives you a maximum position size of 400 shares. You may buy fewer shares than this, but never more.

The power of this rule becomes apparent during losing streaks. Under the 1% rule, it would take 50 consecutive maximum losses to reduce a $100,000 account by 50 percent. Under a 10% risk rule, it would take only 5 consecutive losses to reach the same point. Losing streaks of 5 to 10 trades in a row are a routine occurrence for traders with positive long-term edges. The 1% rule converts the inevitable into the manageable.

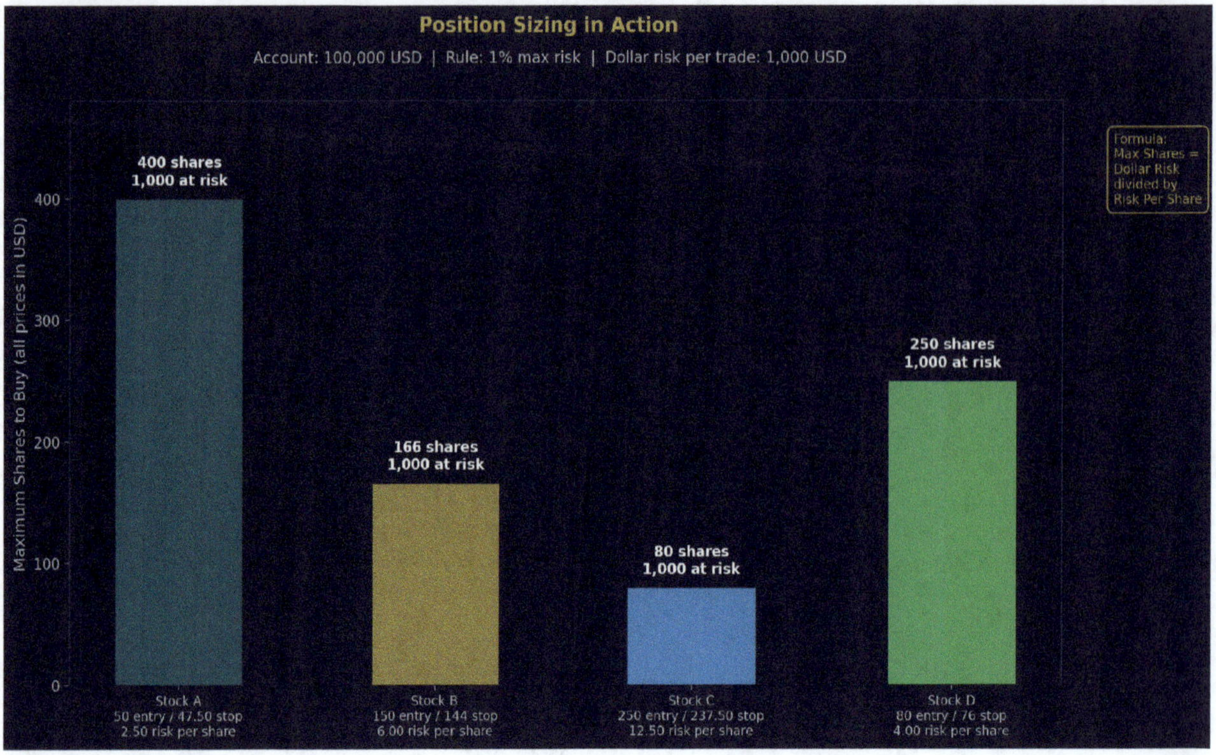

Figure 8.2 — Position Sizing in Action: The 1% Rule applied to four different stocks. Same dollar risk, different share counts.

BEGINNING TRADERS: START WITH 0.5% RISK PER TRADE

For traders in their paper trading development phase, a more conservative starting point is 0.5% risk per trade, or $500 maximum risk on a $100,000 paper account.

The reason is psychological as much as mathematical. When you begin applying risk management rules in paper trading, you are simultaneously learning position sizing mechanics and building the habit of discipline. A more conservative starting level reduces the emotional weight of any single loss and allows you to focus on whether your process is sound rather than whether this particular trade made or lost money.

As your paper trading win rate and profit factor stabilize across 30 or more trades, the minimum sample size Van Tharp considers statistically meaningful, you can graduate to the 1% rule and eventually to 2% as your proven edge justifies it.

8.3 The Position Sizing Formula: Calculating Exactly How Much to Buy

Position sizing is not a judgment call. It is a calculation. The formula is straightforward, and once you memorize it, you will never again make a position sizing decision based on gut feel, excitement, or a vague sense of confidence in a trade.

Dollar Risk = Account Size x Risk Percentage

Example: $100,000 x 1% = $1,000 maximum risk per trade

Risk Per Share = Entry Price minus Stop Loss Price

Example: Entry at $50.00, Stop at $47.50 = $2.50 risk per share

Maximum Shares = Dollar Risk divided by Risk Per Share

Example: $1,000 / $2.50 = 400 shares maximum position size

The key insight: your position size is determined by the stop-loss distance, not by the stock price or by how confident you feel. A stock at $200 with a stop $20 away requires a much smaller share count than a stock at $50 with a $2.50 stop, even though both carry exactly $1,000 of risk. Your dollars risked remain constant. Your share count varies based on where the market tells you the trade thesis is invalidated.

The table below shows worked examples across different stock prices and stop distances, all using a $100,000 paper trading account. Study these numbers until the relationship between entry price, stop distance, and maximum share count feels intuitive.

Account	Dollar Risk	Entry Price	Stop Price	Risk/Share	Max Shares
$100,000	$1,000 (1%)	$50.00	$47.50	$2.50	400 shares
$100,000	$1,000 (1%)	$150.00	$144.00	$6.00	166 shares
$100,000	$1,000 (1%)	$250.00	$237.50	$12.50	80 shares
$100,000	$1,000 (1%)	$80.00	$76.00	$4.00	250 shares
$100,000	$2,000 (2%)	$50.00	$47.50	$2.50	800 shares
$100,000	$2,000 (2%)	$150.00	$144.00	$6.00	333 shares

Formula: Max Shares = Dollar Risk / (Entry Price minus Stop Price). Rows 5-6 show 2% risk for comparison. Paper trading account starts at $100,000.

Why Stop Distance Changes Everything

A precisely placed structural stop (closer to entry) allows you to buy more shares for the same dollar risk, increasing your potential dollar profit at your price target. A loosely placed stop (further from entry) forces a smaller position size and reduces your potential return per dollar of risk taken. This is the leverage point in professional position sizing: tighter, chart-based stops are not just risk management tools. They are also return optimization tools.

PLATFORM FEATURE: Tracking Position Sizes in the Paper Trading Section

When you place a paper trade (navigation menu: Paper), the ORDER TICKET asks for a SYMBOL and a QUANTITY. Before entering any quantity, calculate your correct maximum share count using the formula above.

Your $100,000 virtual balance gives you a $1,000 maximum risk per trade at the 1% rule. Calculate your entry price and planned stop-loss level from the Terminal chart. Divide $1,000 by the difference to get your maximum shares.

After placing the trade, immediately navigate to the Alerts section (navigation menu: Alerts) and set a "Crosses Below" alert at your stop-loss level. This creates an automatic notification if the stop level is breached, removing the need to watch the price continuously.

8.4 Portfolio Heat: Managing Total Risk Across All Open Positions

The 1% rule governs how much you risk on any single trade. Portfolio heat governs how much total risk you carry across all open positions simultaneously. These are different constraints, and both are necessary. You can follow the 1% rule perfectly on every individual trade and still carry dangerous levels of total portfolio risk if you hold too many positions at once.

KEY TERM: Portfolio Heat

The total dollar risk across all open positions simultaneously, expressed as a percentage of the account. Calculated by summing the maximum loss (entry price minus stop-loss, multiplied by share count) for every open trade. Professional traders typically cap portfolio heat at 5% to 10% of total account equity, regardless of how many individual 1%-risk positions they hold.

Consider what happens without a portfolio heat limit. A trader following the 1% rule could theoretically hold 10 open positions simultaneously, each risking 1% of the account. If all 10 positions moved against them during a single-day market selloff, the combined loss would be 10% of the account in one session. A 6% portfolio heat cap prevents this scenario by limiting the trader to a maximum of six simultaneous 1%-risk positions.

THE 6% PORTFOLIO HEAT RULE IN PRACTICE

Dr. Van Tharp, in Trade Your Way to Financial Freedom (1998), recommends limiting total portfolio heat to between 6% and 10% of total equity at any time.

For a $100,000 paper trading account with a 6% heat cap: the maximum combined risk across all open positions is $6,000. If you have three open trades each risking $1,000 (1% each), your current portfolio heat is $3,000 (3%). You have room to add up to three more $1,000-risk positions before hitting the cap.

This rule forces selectivity. You cannot take every trade that looks interesting. You must choose the highest-conviction setups from your Tier 1 watchlist and let the rest remain there until a current position is closed. This constraint is one of the most powerful disciplines in professional trading.

To track your portfolio heat on StockTradesApp.com, open the Paper section and review the POSITIONS panel. For each open position, multiply the share count by the difference between your entry price and your stop-loss level. Sum these amounts across all positions. If the total exceeds 6% of your current account equity, do not open any new positions until an existing one is closed.

8.5 Stop-Loss Placement: The Logical Level, Not the Comfortable One

A stop-loss order is an instruction to close a position when the price reaches a specified level. It is the mechanism that enforces the maximum loss calculated in Section 8.3. But the location of the stop is as important as its existence. A stop placed at the wrong level will either be triggered too easily by normal price noise, stopping you out of good trades prematurely, or set too far away, allowing more loss than your risk calculation intended.

KEY TERM: Stop-Loss Order
An order that automatically closes a position when its price reaches a specified level. The stop-loss converts a potentially open-ended loss into a defined, pre-calculated maximum loss. In StockTradesApp.com paper trading, stops are managed manually by setting a "Crosses Below" Price Alert at the stop level and executing a SELL order in the Paper section when the alert fires.

The cardinal rule of professional stop placement: the stop goes where the trade thesis is invalidated, not where the loss becomes comfortable. If your reason for buying a stock is that it is bouncing off a key support level at $47, your stop-loss should be placed below that support at approximately $46.50, because if the price breaks through $47 support, your thesis is wrong. The stop should not be placed at $45 simply because a larger loss feels more manageable to hold. The loss amount is governed by position sizing. The stop location is governed by the chart.

Five Stop-Loss Types

The following table covers the five most commonly used stop-loss approaches, when to use each, and what makes each appropriate for different trade setups.

Stop Type	How It Works	Best Used When
Structural Stop	Placed just below a key support level for longs (above resistance for shorts). The stop is at the price that logically invalidates the trade thesis based on chart structure.	You have a clearly identified support level from prior lows, a moving average, or a trendline. This is the most widely used professional stop method and your default.
Percentage Stop	A fixed percentage below the entry price (e.g., 7-8% below entry, per O'Neil). Simple to calculate but ignores actual chart structure.	When no clear structural level exists near the entry, or as a maximum loss backstop. Never let a loss exceed 7-8% per William O'Neil's rule.
Moving Average Stop	Stop placed just below the 20-day or 50-day SMA. A close below the MA signals the uptrend support floor has been broken.	Trend-following swing trades where the moving average is the dynamic support floor. Useful for longer-duration positions in established Stage 2 uptrends.
Volatility Stop (ATR)	Stop distance set at a multiple of the Average True Range, the stock's average daily price movement. Wider for volatile stocks, tighter for stable ones.	When comparing stops across stocks with very different volatility profiles, or when you want the stop to account for the stock's normal daily noise range.

Stop Type	How It Works	Best Used When
Time Stop	Exit a trade if it has not moved meaningfully in your favor within a defined time period (e.g., two weeks after the catalyst you traded has passed).	When you traded a specific catalyst such as an earnings report or product launch and the catalyst has passed without producing the expected price move.

The Structural Stop: Your Default Method

For the vast majority of paper trades you will place in this book, the structural stop is your primary approach. After identifying a support level on the Terminal chart from prior lows, a moving average, or a trendline, place your stop just below that level, typically 1 to 3 percent below the support zone to account for the zone-based nature of support levels.

The structural stop has a clear logical basis: if the support level breaks convincingly, the pattern that justified your trade entry no longer exists. Exiting at that point is not defeat. It is accurate recognition that the market has changed and your original thesis no longer applies. This discipline is what prevents small thesis-invalidating losses from becoming large portfolio-threatening ones.

> *"The most important thing in making money is not letting your losses get out of hand."*
> — **Paul Tudor Jones**, *Market Wizards by Jack D. Schwager (1989)*

Where Beginners Place Stops Wrong

The two most common stop-loss errors are stops placed too tight and stops placed at round numbers. Stops too tight inside the stock's normal daily noise range are triggered repeatedly by routine price fluctuation before the stock makes its expected move. Check the stock's typical daily range on the Terminal chart and ensure your stop is outside that range, not inside it.

Stops at round numbers ($50.00, $100.00, $150.00) are one of the worst habits in retail trading. Round numbers are psychologically significant to thousands of traders simultaneously, meaning large clusters of stop orders accumulate just below these levels. Price frequently reaches these obvious levels, triggering retail stops before reversing upward. Place your stop at structurally logical levels ($47.35, $98.75) rather than at the first round number below your entry.

PLATFORM FEATURE: Managing Stops via Alerts on stocktradesapp.com

After placing any paper trade, immediately navigate to Alerts (navigation menu: Alerts). Enter the ticker, select "Crosses Below," and enter your exact stop-loss price. The platform checks prices every five minutes during market hours and notifies you when the level is crossed.

When a stop alert fires, navigate immediately to the Paper section and place a SELL order at the current market price. Honor this without exception or delay. Do not wait for news. Do not hope for a recovery. Record every triggered stop in your personal research notes and note whether the thesis invalidation proved correct.

This manual stop management process mirrors the psychological discipline required in live trading: you set the level with clear thinking before you enter the trade, and you honor it without hesitation when the market reaches it.

8.6 Risk-Reward Ratio and Expectancy: Building a Profitable System

Position sizing and stop-loss placement govern how to limit losses. The risk-reward ratio governs whether your trades are worth taking in the first place. A trade with a well-placed stop-loss is only worth entering if the potential reward justifies the defined risk. This relationship is the risk-reward ratio.

KEY TERM: Risk-Reward Ratio (R:R)
The ratio of the potential profit on a trade to the maximum risk (the stop-loss distance). A 2:1 R:R means the trade offers $2 in potential profit for every $1 at risk. Professional traders typically require a minimum 2:1 R:R for any trade entry, meaning the potential gain must be at least twice the potential loss. A trade with a 0.8:1 R:R is unprofitable as a systematic practice regardless of win rate.

The formula:

```
R:R = (Price Target minus Entry Price) divided by (Entry Price minus Stop Price)
```

Example: Entry $50, Target $56, Stop $47.50 = $6.00 / $2.50 = 2.4:1 risk-reward ratio

A 2.4:1 R:R means you stand to gain $2.40 for every $1.00 risked. This is a trade worth taking. A 0.8:1 R:R means you risk $1.00 to make $0.80. Even with a 60% win rate, a system built on sub-1:1 R:R trades will eventually struggle to produce meaningful net profits after costs.

Expectancy: The True Measure of a Trading System

The risk-reward ratio tells you the potential on any single trade. Expectancy, developed by Van Tharp in Trade Your Way to Financial Freedom (1998), tells you whether your system is profitable across a large sample of trades. It is the average amount you can expect to win or lose per dollar risked.

Expectancy = (Win Rate x Average Win) minus (Loss Rate x Average Loss)

Positive expectancy = profitable system over time. Negative expectancy = losing system regardless of how individual trades feel.

The table below illustrates how different combinations of win rate and risk-reward ratio produce dramatically different system quality. Several entries will surprise you.

Win Rate	Avg R:R	Profit Factor	Expectancy/Trade	System Verdict
40%	1:1	0.67	-$0.20 per $1 risked	**Losing system. Negative expectancy.**
50%	1:1	1.00	$0.00 per $1 risked	**Break-even. Does not cover costs.**
40%	2:1	1.33	+$0.20 per $1 risked	**Profitable. Low win rate, disciplined R:R.**
50%	2:1	2.00	+$0.50 per $1 risked	**Strong. Professional-grade edge.**
60%	1.5:1	2.25	+$0.50 per $1 risked	**Strong. High win rate with good R:R.**
35%	3:1	1.62	+$0.40 per $1 risked	**Profitable. Trend-following style.**
70%	0.5:1	1.17	+$0.05 per $1 risked	**Barely profitable. Poor R:R hidden by win rate.**

The most important insight in that table is the final row: 70% win rate with 0.5:1 R:R produces barely positive expectancy, because each loss is twice as large as each win. Many beginning traders fall into exactly this trap: cutting winners early (to lock in gains) and holding losers (hoping for recovery), producing a high win rate that masks near-zero or negative expectancy. The ideal target for a beginning paper trader is a win rate above 40% combined with a consistent R:R of at least 2:1, producing a profit factor around 1.33 and positive expectancy of approximately $0.20 per dollar risked.

THE MINIMUM SAMPLE SIZE FOR MEANINGFUL EXPECTANCY

Van Tharp recommends a minimum of 30 trades to draw statistically meaningful conclusions about a trading system's expectancy, and 100 to 200 trades for a reliable edge assessment.

This is one of the most important reasons to begin your paper trading practice as early and as systematically as possible. Every paper trade you complete adds to your sample. After 30 trades, you can begin assessing whether your system has a positive expectancy.

Your StockTradesApp.com Dashboard tracks your win rate, average win/loss, and profit factor in real time (navigation menu: Dashboard, PERFORMANCE section). These are the raw inputs for your ongoing expectancy calculation. Review them after every 10 trades and watch for trends.

8.7 Profit Targets and Active Trade Management

Risk management does not end when you enter a trade. Two skills govern the life of every open position: setting a logical profit target before entry, and managing the position actively once it is open.

Setting a Logical Profit Target

A profit target is a pre-defined price at which you plan to close a winning trade. It should satisfy three conditions. First, it must be at least 2:1 R:R from the entry to meet the minimum threshold from Section 8.6. Second, it should be placed just below the next significant resistance level on the chart, because resistance is where selling pressure typically intensifies before price can advance further. Third, it must be realistic given the stock's historical volatility. A target requiring a 25% move from a stock that typically moves 2 to 3 percent per week is unlikely to be reached.

The Trailing Stop: Letting Winners Run

One of the most persistent challenges for developing traders is taking profits too early. This is the disposition effect from Chapter 2 in action. The trailing stop manages this impulse mechanically by moving upward as the stock price rises, locking in progressively more profit while still giving the stock room to continue its trend.

- **Percentage Trailing Stop:** Always set at a fixed percentage below the current high. A 10% trailing stop on a stock that rises from $50 to $75 produces a stop at $67.50. The position closes only if the stock falls 10% from its most recent high, not from your original entry.
- **Moving Average Trailing Stop:** Use the 20-day or 50-day SMA as the dynamic exit trigger. As long as the stock closes above the moving average, the position remains open. A close below the SMA is the exit signal. This method keeps you in strong trends for longer while providing a clear, chart-based exit that is not based on emotion.

In your StockTradesApp.com paper trading, implement trailing stops manually: as the stock rises and forms a higher structural support level, update your stop alert upward to just below that new level. This ratcheting process locks in progressively more profit while keeping the position open for further upside.

8.8 The Maximum Daily Loss Rule: Your Final Safety Net

Even with the 1% rule, 6% portfolio heat cap, structural stops, and minimum R:R requirements in place, one more safeguard is essential: the maximum daily loss limit. This rule defines the largest total loss you will accept in a single trading day before stopping all activity until the next session.

The standard professional maximum daily loss limit is 2% to 3% of total account equity. For a $100,000 paper trading account, this means closing all positions and taking no new trades for the remainder of the day if cumulative losses reach $2,000 to $3,000.

- **Emotional protection:** A bad trading day activates emotional responses that impair judgment. The urgency to "make it back" leads to impulsive, oversized trades that almost universally produce larger additional losses. The daily loss limit removes the worst decision-making conditions from the equation.

- **Mathematical protection:** Even with correct position sizing, several simultaneous stop-losses on a high-volatility day can accumulate quickly. A daily cap ensures no single session produces catastrophic damage.

HOW PROFESSIONAL PROP FIRMS USE THE DAILY LOSS LIMIT

At professional proprietary trading firms, the maximum daily loss limit is not a guideline. It is an enforced hard cap embedded in the firm's risk management software. When a trader's cumulative daily loss reaches the limit, the system automatically prevents any further order entry for the remainder of the session.

Research on institutional trading performance consistently shows that the worst trading days are disproportionately responsible for overall account drawdown, and that traders who continue trading after breaching their daily loss limit almost always compound the session's losses significantly.

In your StockTradesApp.com paper trading, implement this rule manually. At the start of each session, calculate 2-3% of your current account equity. Track your combined realized and unrealized losses throughout the day. If the total approaches that limit, close all positions and step away from the platform until the next session.

8.9 Your Complete Risk Management Rule Set

The following rule set synthesizes everything in this chapter into a single, actionable framework. Write these rules down. Post them somewhere visible near your trading workspace. Apply them to every paper trade you place from this point forward without exception. These rules are most valuable precisely in the moments when you most want to break them.

The Eight Non-Negotiable Risk Management Rules

Step 1: THE 1% RULE (START AT 0.5%): Never risk more than 1% of your total paper trading account on any single trade. For a $100,000 account, the maximum risk per trade is $1,000. Begin at 0.5% ($500) until you have completed at least 30 documented paper trades.

Step 2: CALCULATE BEFORE EVERY TRADE: For every trade, calculate maximum shares using: Dollar Risk divided by (Entry Price minus Stop Price). Never enter a quantity in the Paper Trading ORDER TICKET without completing this calculation in writing first.

Step 3: THE 6% PORTFOLIO HEAT CAP: The combined maximum risk across all open positions must never exceed 6% of your account equity. Sum the potential loss on each open position. If the total reaches $6,000 on a $100,000 account, do not open any new positions until a current one is closed.

Step 4: STRUCTURAL STOPS ONLY: Place every stop-loss at a logical structural level derived from the chart, just below the nearest significant support level. Never set a stop at a round number. Never move a stop further from entry to avoid a loss.

Step 5: MINIMUM 2:1 RISK-REWARD: Before entering any trade, calculate the risk-reward ratio. If the ratio is below 2:1, the trade does not qualify for entry regardless of how attractive the setup appears.

Step 6: SET THE ALERT IMMEDIATELY: After every paper trade entry, navigate to Alerts and set a Crosses Below alert at your stop-loss level. A trade without a monitored stop is an unmanaged risk and violates the framework.

Step 7: THE 2-3% MAXIMUM DAILY LOSS LIMIT: If your total cumulative loss for the trading day (realized plus unrealized) reaches 2-3% of your account equity, close all positions and take no new trades for the remainder of the session.

Step 8: HONOR YOUR STOPS WITHOUT HESITATION: When a stop alert fires, close the position immediately at the current market price. Do not wait. Do not check for a reason to hold. Do not hope for a recovery. The stop was set with clear thinking before the trade. Honor it every time.

8.10 Chapter 8 Exercise: Applying Risk Management to Three Paper Trades

The following exercise requires you to apply the complete risk management framework to three paper trades. Each step must be completed in writing before placing any order. The goal is not to find profitable trades. The goal is to practice calculating, documenting, and applying every risk management rule with discipline before a single order is entered.

Risk Management Exercise: Three Fully Documented Paper Trades

Step 1: TRADE SELECTION: From your Tier 1 watchlist built in Chapter 7, select three stocks with a BUY or strong HOLD Blended Signal in the Terminal. Confirm each setup using the Chapter 6 pre-trade checklist. If any stock does not pass the full checklist, replace it with one that does.

Step 2: STOP PLACEMENT: For each stock, open the Terminal chart and identify the nearest significant support level below the current price. Place your stop-loss 1-3% below that level. Do not use a round number. Record the exact stop price for each of the three trades.

Step 3: POSITION SIZE CALCULATION: For each trade, calculate maximum share count: Dollar Risk ($1,000 at 1% of $100,000) divided by Risk Per Share (Entry minus Stop). Write this calculation down before touching the ORDER TICKET. Record the calculated share count.

Step 4: RISK-REWARD CALCULATION: For each trade, identify the next significant resistance level above the current price on the Terminal chart. Calculate R:R: (resistance minus entry) divided by (entry minus stop). If the R:R is below 2:1, skip this trade and select a replacement from your watchlist.

Step 5: PORTFOLIO HEAT CHECK: Before placing all three trades, sum the maximum loss across all three positions. Confirm the total is below $6,000. If it exceeds $6,000, reduce the quantity on the largest position until the combined heat is within the limit.

Step 6: PLACE THE TRADES: Enter each position using the calculated share count. After each entry, immediately set a Crosses Below alert at the stop price in the Alerts section. Do not skip this step.

Step 7: DOCUMENT EVERY TRADE: Write the complete trade record for each position: ticker, entry price, stop price, target price, risk per trade in dollars, risk-reward ratio, share count, and total position value. This documentation is what you will compare against actual outcomes in Chapter 9.

Step 8: MONITOR FOR ONE WEEK: Check the Alerts section daily. If any stop alert fires, close the position immediately in the Paper section and note the outcome. At the end of the week, proceed to Chapter 9 to learn how to formally analyze your paper trading performance.

Chapter 8 Summary

Chapter 8 has given you the complete risk management framework that protects your capital and makes your trading strategy survivable over time. Here is what you now carry forward:

- **The Mathematics of Loss:** A 50% drawdown requires a 100% gain to recover. A 90% drawdown requires 900%. These numbers make keeping individual losses small mathematically non-negotiable.
- **The 1% Rule:** Never risk more than 1% of total account equity on any single trade. Start at 0.5% while developing your track record. Research shows 85% of 1-2% rule traders stay active for at least two years; 88% of 10% risk traders are wiped out within one year.

- **The Position Sizing Formula:** Dollar Risk divided by Risk Per Share equals Maximum Shares. This calculation eliminates emotion and gut feel from position sizing. The stop distance, not confidence level, determines how many shares you buy.
- **Portfolio Heat at 6% Maximum:** The sum of all individual trade risks must not exceed 6% of account equity at any time. This prevents a single bad trading day from producing catastrophic damage regardless of how many positions are correctly sized individually.
- **Five Stop-Loss Types:** Structural (below support), Percentage (fixed percent below entry per O'Neil's 7-8% rule), Moving Average (below key SMA), Volatility-based (ATR multiple), and Time (exit if catalyst thesis fails to develop). The structural stop is your default. Never place stops at round numbers.
- **Minimum 2:1 Risk-Reward:** Every trade must offer at least $2 in potential profit for every $1 risked before it qualifies for entry. A trade with a 0.8:1 R:R is unprofitable as a systematic practice regardless of win rate.
- **Expectancy as the System Metric:** Win Rate times Average Win minus Loss Rate times Average Loss equals Expectancy. A high win rate with poor R:R produces near-zero or negative expectancy. A 40-50% win rate with consistent 2:1 R:R produces a genuinely profitable system with Profit Factor around 1.33 to 2.0.
- **The Maximum Daily Loss Limit:** 2-3% of account equity per day. When cumulative losses reach this level, close all positions and stop trading for the remainder of the session. Enforced by professional trading firms through system-level hard caps.

CHAPTER 9

Analyzing Your Paper Trading Performance: Turning Data Into Decisions

"What gets measured gets managed. What gets managed gets improved."

— Peter Drucker, The Practice of Management (1954)

Paper trading without performance analysis is practice without feedback. It builds repetitions but not improvement. The difference between a beginning paper trader who develops quickly and one who plateaus for months is almost always this: one reviews their performance data systematically and adjusts their behavior accordingly, and one does not.

This chapter teaches you to close the learning loop. You have sourced stocks with a systematic process (Chapter 7), managed risk with defined rules (Chapter 8), and accumulated a meaningful sample of paper trades. Now you will use StockTradesApp.com's Dashboard to read those results accurately, identify the specific behavioral patterns that are helping or hurting your performance, apply a diagnostic framework to determine what needs to change, and refine your strategy based on evidence rather than intuition.

By the end of this chapter, you will have conducted your first formal performance review and produced an updated strategy document that reflects what your actual trading data reveals about your decision-making. This process, repeated regularly throughout your trading career, is what converts experience into genuine, measurable improvement.

> *"An amateur practices until he gets it right. A professional practices until he cannot get it wrong."*
>
> — Traditional coaching maxim, *widely applied in performance domains from athletics to surgery to trading*

9.1 Why Most Paper Traders Do Not Improve

Before examining the metrics themselves, it is worth understanding why the paper trading phase fails to develop most traders as much as it should. The reason is not that paper trading is an insufficient simulation. It is that most traders treat paper trading as an outcome to be experienced rather than a process to be studied.

They watch trades go up and down. They feel satisfied when trades work and disappointed when they do not. But they do not examine why the winning trades worked, whether the process that led to them was repeatable, whether the losing trades reflected bad luck or flawed process, or what systematic patterns are emerging across their full trade history. Without this analytical layer, paper trading is entertainment rather than education.

Research on skill development in complex domains, from chess to surgery to sports, consistently identifies deliberate practice as the mechanism that separates rapid improvers from slow ones. Deliberate practice is characterized by specific goals, immediate feedback, repeated attempts at specific weaknesses, and expert analysis of performance. Your performance review process on StockTradesApp.com is your equivalent of this deliberate practice structure applied to trading.

30

The minimum number of paper trades Van Tharp identifies as needed before any performance metric carries statistical meaning. Below 30 trades, metrics like win rate and profit factor are dominated by randomness rather than edge. Below 10 trades, even a 100% win rate tells you nothing meaningful.

Source: Van Tharp, Trade Your Way to Financial Freedom (1998)

If you have not yet completed 30 documented paper trades with full pre-trade and post-trade notes, your priority before reading further in this chapter is to generate those trades first. The analysis framework below requires a meaningful sample to produce useful insights.

9.2 Reading the StockTradesApp.com Dashboard Performance Metrics

Navigate to the Dashboard (navigation menu: Dashboard). The PERFORMANCE section, visible immediately below the four equity tiles (Cash, Holdings Value, Total Equity, Return), is your primary performance analytics panel. It displays nine metrics across multiple time period filters: ALL, 1M, 3M, 6M, YTD, and 1Y.

The time period filter at the top of the Performance section determines which trades are included in the calculations. When analyzing your overall strategy, use ALL to see your complete paper trading history. When looking for recent trends or regime-specific performance, use the 3M or 6M filters.

The table below covers every metric displayed in the Performance section, explains its target range, and describes what each metric tells you about your trading.

Metric	Displayed On Dashboard	Target Range	What It Tells You
Win Rate	YES (WIN RATE)	Above 40% for active traders; above 50% preferred	The percentage of closed trades that were profitable. Always read alongside Profit Factor, not in isolation. A 90% win rate with 0.1:1 R:R is worse than a 40% win rate with 3:1 R:R.
Avg Win / Loss	YES (AVG WIN / LOSS)	Avg Win at least 2x Avg Loss	Shows the average dollar gain on winners versus the average dollar loss on losers. This ratio, combined with win rate, determines whether your system has positive expectancy.
Profit Factor	YES (PROFIT FACTOR)	Above 1.5 to be viable; above 2.0 is strong	Total gross profit divided by total gross loss. A Profit Factor of 1.5 means you earn $1.50 for every $1.00 lost. A Profit Factor below 1.0 means you are losing money overall.
Max Drawdown	YES (MAX DRAWDOW N)	Below 15% of account; lower is better	The largest peak-to-trough decline your account has experienced. The hardest performance number to face honestly and the most important for assessing whether you can psychologically sustain your strategy.
Sharpe-Like Score	YES (SHARPE-LI KE)	Above 1.0 is adequate; above 2.0 is strong	A risk-adjusted return metric. Measures return relative to the volatility of your results. A high return with extremely volatile results scores lower than a moderate return with consistent results.
Realized P&L	YES (REALIZED P&L)	Positive and growing over time	Total profit and loss from trades already closed. The most reliable performance number because it reflects actual completed outcomes, not open positions that could still reverse.

Metric	Displayed On Dashboard	Target Range	What It Tells You
SPY Benchmark	YES (BENCHMARK panel)	Aim to match or exceed SPY over equivalent period	Your paper trading return versus the S&P 500 ETF over the same period. The honest test: is your active trading adding value over simply buying and holding the index?
Trade Count	Via TRADE HISTORY fills count	30 minimum for initial assessment; 100+ for reliability	The number of completed trades in your sample. Small sample sizes make all other metrics unreliable. A Profit Factor of 2.0 over 10 trades is meaningless. The same number over 100 trades is significant.
Expectancy	Calculate manually	Positive value per dollar risked	(Win Rate x Avg Win) minus (Loss Rate x Avg Loss). The average amount you make or lose per dollar risked per trade. The true measure of whether your system has a sustainable edge.

The Five Numbers You Must Read Together

Each metric in the table above is meaningful on its own. But the most important analytical habit is reading five of them together as a set, because they interact with each other in ways that a single metric cannot reveal.

- **Win Rate plus Avg Win/Loss:** These two together tell you whether your system has positive expectancy. A 50% win rate with an Avg Win of $500 and Avg Loss of $500 is break-even. The same 50% win rate with Avg Win of $800 and Avg Loss of $400 is profitable. Win rate alone tells you nothing.
- **Profit Factor plus Max Drawdown:** These two together tell you whether the system is sustainable. A Profit Factor of 2.0 with a Max Drawdown of 8% is an excellent, sustainable system. The same Profit Factor with a 45% Max Drawdown suggests either inconsistent position sizing or a single catastrophic event that will eventually end the strategy.
- **Sharpe-Like Score plus Trade Count:** These two together tell you how reliable the risk-adjusted return estimate is. A Sharpe-Like Score of 1.5 over 100 trades is a meaningful signal. The same score over 8 trades could be pure luck. Always check the trade count before interpreting the Sharpe score.

🖥 PLATFORM FEATURE: Reading the Dashboard Performance Panel

Open the Dashboard (navigation menu: Dashboard) and locate the PERFORMANCE section with the green header labeled "PERFORMANCE - CLOSED TRADES." The time period filter buttons (ALL, 1M, 3M, 6M, YTD, 1Y) appear to the right of this header.

Click the ALL filter to ensure you are seeing your complete trade history. Record the values for all nine metrics in the table above in your personal research notes. This snapshot is your baseline from which all future performance comparisons will be made.

Below the performance metrics, note the BENCHMARK panel showing SPY RETURN and SPY MAX DD compared to your own figures. The comparison numbers shown in red or green indicate whether you are ahead or behind the index over the same period.

Below the benchmark, the equity curve chart shows your strategy line (green) versus SPY (gray), with green dots for winning trade closes and red dots for losing ones. Study the pattern of dots. Are wins and losses evenly distributed, or are there clusters of red dots at specific time periods that warrant investigation?

9.3 Reading the Equity Curve: What the Chart Reveals Beyond the Numbers

The equity curve, the line chart showing the growth or decline of your paper trading account over time, is one of the most informative tools in your performance review. Aggregate metrics like win rate and profit factor tell you about the average character of your trades. The equity curve tells you about the distribution and timing of those outcomes in ways that averages cannot capture.

KEY TERM: Equity Curve
A chart showing the cumulative change in a trading account's value over time. Each completed trade updates the curve. An upward-sloping equity curve indicates profitable performance. A curve that rises steadily with relatively small pullbacks indicates consistent, risk-controlled profitability. A curve that rises dramatically then falls sharply indicates high volatility and likely inconsistent position sizing or strategy application.

Four Equity Curve Patterns and What They Mean

- **Steady upward slope with small pullbacks:** This is the ideal pattern. It suggests consistent application of risk management rules, moderate and sustainable drawdowns, and a genuine positive edge being expressed across many trades. This is the equity curve a systematic, disciplined paper trader produces.

- **Irregular upward slope with large drawdowns:** The strategy has a positive expectancy but the risk management is inconsistent. Large drawdowns are almost always caused by position sizing violations or stop-loss stops being honored late or not at all. Check the five or ten largest individual losses in your trade history against the 1% rule.
- **Flat or sideways curve with low volatility:** The system is approximately break-even. Profit Factor is hovering near 1.0. This pattern often reflects a high win rate offset by poor R:R, a classic sign that winners are being cut too early. Review the average holding period of winning trades versus losing trades.
- **Volatile curve with no discernible trend:** The strategy lacks a consistent edge, or the sample size is too small to reveal one. If you have fewer than 30 trades, add more trades before drawing conclusions. If you have 50 or more trades and the curve shows no trend, the strategy itself needs to be examined and revised.

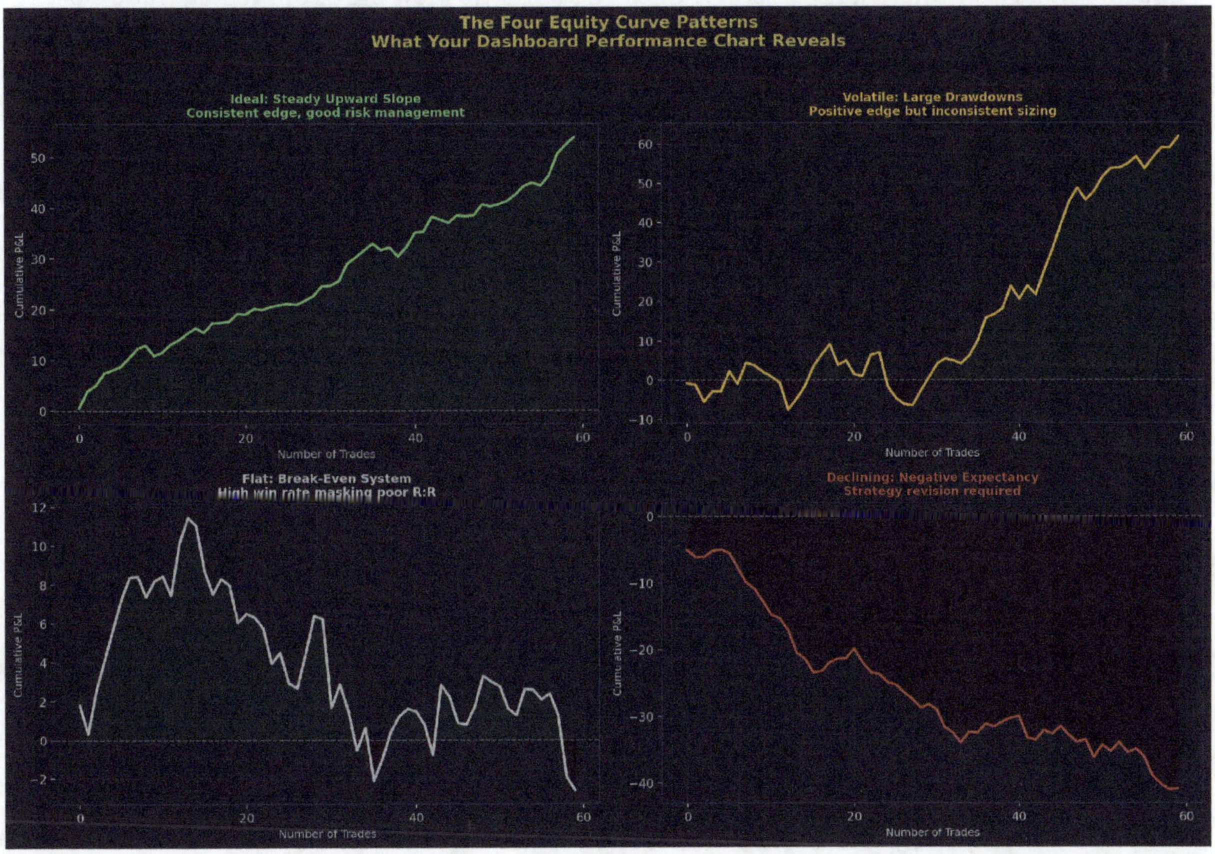

Figure 9.3 — The Four Equity Curve Patterns: Your Dashboard equity curve reveals the character of your trading system.

The equity curve also reveals something the aggregate metrics cannot: your performance in different market conditions. Use the Compare tool to overlay ^GSPC (S&P 500) with a 1Y or 6MO time frame alongside your equity curve period. Are the clusters of red dots on your equity curve correlated with S&P 500 declines? If yes, your strategy is normal: even a good strategy produces losses during broad market selloffs. If the red dot clusters are distributed randomly regardless of market conditions, the issue is in your individual trade selection or execution rather than in macro market timing.

🖥 PLATFORM FEATURE: Viewing the Equity Curve on stocktradesapp.com

The equity curve appears in the Dashboard Performance section, below the BENCHMARK panel. The green line is your paper trading strategy. The gray line is SPY. Green dots mark winning trade closes; red dots mark losing ones.

The filter above the chart (ALL, LONG, SHORT, WINS, LOSSES, SYMBOL) lets you isolate specific subsets of your trading history. Click "LOSSES" to view only your losing trade closes plotted on the equity curve. Notice whether they cluster during specific market periods or are evenly distributed. Clustering during market downturns is expected. Clustering during market uptrends is a strategy problem worth investigating.

Click "SYMBOL" and type a specific ticker to see all trades in that symbol highlighted on the curve. This lets you determine whether any single stock is disproportionately responsible for either your profits or your losses.

9.4 Identifying Behavioral Patterns in Your Trade History

The most valuable insights from a performance review are not the aggregate metrics. They are the specific behavioral patterns that the data reveals about how you actually make decisions under uncertainty, as opposed to how you intend to make decisions when writing your pre-trade plan with clear thinking.

The gap between your intended process and your actual behavior is where performance improvement lives. The following table describes the six most common behavioral patterns found in beginning traders' paper trading data, how each pattern manifests in the Dashboard metrics, and the specific correction for each.

Behavioral Pattern	What It Looks Like in Your Data	How to Correct It
Cutting Winners Too Early	Average Win is less than 1.5x your average Risk Per Trade. Win Rate is high (above 55%) but Profit Factor is below 1.5. Many trades show profits of only 1:1 R:R or less before being closed.	Review your trade journal entries for the exit reasoning on winning trades. If you closed because of anxiety or to lock in the gain rather than because the technical thesis was exhausted, you are cutting winners. Practice using trailing stops (Section 8.7) instead of taking profits at the first opportunity.
Holding Losers Too Long	Average Loss is significantly larger than your calculated stop-loss distance. Max Drawdown is disproportionately large relative to individual risk. You see occasional catastrophic single-trade losses that distort all other metrics.	Check whether your stop alerts are being honored immediately or being delayed. If you are moving stops further away when they are about to be triggered, you are holding losers too long. Implement a non-negotiable rule: when the alert fires, the position closes within five minutes, no exceptions.
Overtrading	High trade count relative to your watchlist size. Many low-conviction trades taken on setups that do not fully meet your pre-trade checklist. Win Rate declining as trade count increases.	Review your pre-trade documentation. Are you completing the full checklist on every trade, or have you started skipping steps? Reset to the Chapter 6 checklist for every entry. If you cannot fully complete the checklist in writing before entering, the trade does not qualify.
Revenge Trading	A cluster of trades placed in rapid succession after a stop-loss is triggered. Win Rate on trades placed within 30 minutes of a loss is noticeably lower than your overall win rate. Max Drawdown events are preceded by a string of quick entries.	Implement a mandatory 30-minute cooling-off period after any stop-loss. During this period, you are allowed to observe the market but not place any new orders. Write a post-trade note in your research journal immediately after the loss and before placing any new trade.
FOMO Entries (Chasing)	Entry prices are frequently at or above resistance levels rather than near support. Many trades show an immediate loss at open followed by a recovery, suggesting you entered after the move had already occurred.	For every trade entry, record the distance from your entry to the nearest support level. If you are consistently entering when the stock is already extended above support rather than near it, you are chasing. Return to the Chapter 6 checklist item requiring a close support level before entry.
Inconsistent Position Sizing	Max Drawdown events coincide with positions that were significantly larger than the 1% rule would allow. Profit Factor is acceptable but variability in	Review the position size on every trade in your TRADE HISTORY. Any trade where the maximum loss exceeded 1% of your account at the time of entry is a sizing violation. Recalculate what the correct size

Behavioral Pattern	What It Looks Like in Your Data	How to Correct It
	position size makes individual outcomes feel random.	should have been and note the discrepancy. Consistency in sizing is what allows your edge to express itself over time.

To diagnose which of these patterns applies to your trading, review your TRADE HISTORY in the Paper section. Scroll through each completed trade and look for the following:

1. For each winning trade: how many R-multiples did you capture? (Divide the actual profit by the original dollar risk). If most winning trades are below 2:1 R:R captured, you are cutting winners too early.
2. For each losing trade: how large was the loss relative to your original stop-loss distance? (Divide actual loss by the planned stop distance). If any losses exceed 1.5x the planned stop-loss distance, you either moved the stop or did not honor it when the alert fired.
3. Review entry timing: were trades entered near support (within 2-3% of the nearest structural level) or far above it (more than 5% above the nearest support)? Entries consistently far above support indicate FOMO or chasing behavior.
4. Review trade frequency: count the number of trades placed in the first 30 minutes after any previous stop-loss. If more than 25% of your trades follow within 30 minutes of a loss, revenge trading is a factor.

THE REFLECTION QUESTION THAT CHANGES EVERYTHING

After completing your behavioral pattern analysis, ask yourself this question with complete honesty: over my last 20 trades, was I following my pre-defined rules, or was I making in-the-moment discretionary decisions that deviated from my plan?

If the answer is "mostly following my rules," the performance issues are likely in the rules themselves and the correction is systematic refinement of your strategy.

If the answer is "frequently deviating from my rules," the performance issues are behavioral and the correction is not strategy change but discipline enforcement. Changing your strategy every time you have a losing streak without first confirming that your rules were actually followed is the single most common mistake that prevents paper traders from developing real skill.

The traders who improve most consistently are the ones who can honestly distinguish between these two diagnoses. Strategy problems require strategy changes. Execution problems require execution discipline. Confusing the two leads to perpetual, unproductive strategy switching.

9.5 The SPY Benchmark: Your Honest Performance Test

One of the most important performance comparisons available on the StockTradesApp.com Dashboard is the SPY benchmark comparison. SPY is the SPDR S&P 500 ETF, which tracks the performance of the S&P 500 index. It is the standard benchmark against which active traders and fund managers measure their performance.

The logic is simple and unforgiving: if you are going to spend time actively selecting, analyzing, and timing individual stock trades, the minimum bar for success is outperforming the market you are trading in. If SPY returns 15% over a period during which your paper trading returns 8%, you underperformed the benchmark. A passive investor who simply bought and held SPY would have done better than your active paper trading with no analysis, no research, and no time invested.

> *"The question is never whether you made money. The question is whether you made more money than you would have made by doing nothing more than buying the index."*
>
> — **John C. Bogle**, *Common Sense on Mutual Funds (1999): founder of Vanguard and creator of the first index fund for individual investors*

The Dashboard SPY comparison shows two sets of numbers: SPY RETURN versus your strategy return over the selected period, and SPY MAX DD versus your maximum drawdown. Both comparisons matter.

Beating the SPY return is the obvious test. But the second comparison is equally important. If your paper trading return is 20% and SPY returned 15%, you beat the benchmark. But if your maximum drawdown was 35% while SPY's maximum drawdown was 12%, you achieved your extra return by taking on dramatically more risk. A risk-adjusted comparison would likely favor the passive index investment.

Your target as a developing paper trader: match or beat SPY return with a maximum drawdown no larger than 1.5 times SPY's maximum drawdown over the same period. This is the practical minimum evidence of genuine value added through active trading.

WHAT IF SPY IS SIGNIFICANTLY OUTPERFORMING YOUR PAPER TRADING?

If SPY's cumulative return is significantly higher than your paper trading return over the same period, resist the temptation to view this as discouraging. It is genuinely useful information. It tells you that your current paper trading strategy, as executed, is not yet adding value over the passive alternative.

This is actually the ideal time to discover this, because you are trading virtual money. The diagnostic process in this chapter is designed to help you identify whether the underperformance is due to a flawed strategy, poor execution of a sound strategy, or an insufficient sample size.

Many of the world's most successful fund managers underperformed the S&P 500 index during their early years and used that experience to refine their approach before managing significant capital. Your paper trading phase exists precisely so that this refinement can happen without financial consequence.

9.6 The Strategy Refinement Framework

Performance analysis is only valuable if it leads to specific, evidence-based changes in strategy or behavior. The following diagnostic framework maps common Dashboard performance signals to their most likely causes and the recommended adjustments. Use this framework after every formal performance review.

Dashboard Signal	What It Indicates	Recommended Adjustment
Win Rate below 35% AND Profit Factor below 1.2	The strategy is generating losses too frequently and the average win is not large enough to compensate.	Review trade selection process. Are you following the Chapter 6 checklist fully? Are entries occurring near support with confirmation signals, or are you trading breakouts without volume confirmation? Tighten entry criteria before adding more trades.
Win Rate above 55% BUT Profit Factor below 1.5	You are winning frequently but winners are being cut too small relative to losses.	Focus on trailing stop implementation (Chapter 8 Section 8.7). Set your profit target at least 2:1 before entering. Review whether you are exiting winners due to anxiety rather than a chart-based signal that the move is exhausted.
Profit Factor above 2.0 but Max Drawdown above 20%	The system is profitable but individual losses are too large, possibly due to inconsistent position sizing or stops being moved away from their original levels.	Audit every trade with a loss exceeding 1% of the account. In each case, was the stop at the pre-defined structural level, or was it moved? Was the position correctly sized? Identify the pattern behind the

Dashboard Signal	What It Indicates	Recommended Adjustment
		oversized losses and enforce the 1% rule strictly.
SPY Benchmark is significantly outperforming your paper trading return	Your paper trading return is lagging the market, meaning you would have been better served by a passive index investment.	This is actually valuable data. It suggests either that your stock selection is not identifying genuine outperformers (return to Chapter 7 CAN SLIM screening) or that your timing is poor (return to Chapter 6 technical entry analysis). Both are fixable with deliberate practice.
Sharpe-Like Score below 0.5	Returns are being generated inconsistently, with high volatility in individual outcomes.	High variability in results usually indicates inconsistent position sizing or inconsistent strategy application. Identify whether large wins and large losses are alternating. If so, the issue is likely emotional decision-making overriding systematic rules.
Trade count below 30 after several weeks	Insufficient data for any metric to be statistically meaningful.	This is the most common early-stage problem. Focus on generating more paper trades by working through your Tier 1 watchlist more aggressively. Set a target of completing at least one documented paper trade per week, with all pre-trade documentation completed beforehand.

The Golden Rule of Strategy Refinement

Change one variable at a time. This is the most frequently violated principle in performance refinement. A trader who has a 35% win rate, a 1.2 Profit Factor, and a 25% maximum drawdown is tempted to simultaneously change their entry criteria, their stop-loss placement, their position sizing, and their target selection. If they then see improved results over the next 20 trades, they cannot determine which change produced the improvement. If results do not improve, they cannot determine which change was counterproductive.

The disciplined refinement process: identify the single most impactful variable based on your behavioral pattern analysis. Change only that variable. Trade at least 20 more positions under the new rule. Measure the before-and-after comparison across your full set of metrics. Only then consider whether a second variable requires adjustment.

> *"The main purpose of the trading journal is to give you feedback so you can learn to improve. If you do not have a journal and do not review it, you will not improve nearly as fast."*
> — **Dr. Van K. Tharp, Ph.D.**, *Trade Your Way to Financial Freedom (1998)*

9.7 Building Your Weekly Performance Review Habit

Performance analysis is not a one-time activity. It is a weekly practice that compounds in value over time, just as your paper trading results themselves compound. The following review process takes 20 to 30 minutes per week and produces the most improvement per unit of time of any activity in your paper trading development.

The Weekly Performance Review Process

Step 1: OPEN THE DASHBOARD and set the time filter to ALL. Record the current values for all nine performance metrics in your personal research notes. Compare them to your values from the previous week. Are the trends in the right direction (Win Rate stable or rising, Profit Factor stable or rising, Max Drawdown stable or declining)?

Step 2: REVIEW THE EQUITY CURVE. Set the filter to show ALL trades. Look at the pattern of green and red dots over the past two weeks. Are there any clusters of red dots? If yes, open the corresponding dates in your TRADE HISTORY and review what happened on those days.

Step 3: AUDIT LAST WEEK'S TRADES. Open the Paper section (navigation menu: Paper) and scroll the TRADE HISTORY to the trades placed in the past week. For each completed trade, verify: Was the position size within the 1% rule? Was the stop alert set immediately after entry? Was the stop honored immediately when triggered? Was the entry within 3% of a structural support level?

Step 4: DIAGNOSE ONE BEHAVIORAL PATTERN. Based on your audit in Step 3, identify the single behavioral pattern from Section 9.4 that was most evident in last week's trades. Write one sentence in your research notes describing the pattern and one sentence describing the specific corrective action you will take in the coming week.

Step 5: CHECK THE SPY COMPARISON. Review the SPY RETURN versus your paper trading return in the BENCHMARK panel. Is the gap widening or narrowing? If you are significantly underperforming SPY, apply the refinement framework from Section 9.6 to identify the most likely cause.

Step 6: SET ONE PROCESS GOAL FOR THE COMING WEEK. This is not a return target. It is a process goal: a specific behavior you will execute on every trade in the coming week. Examples: complete the full Chapter 6 checklist before every entry; honor every stop alert within five minutes of it firing; hold every winning trade until either the target or the trailing stop is reached. Process goals are more actionable and more effective than outcome goals in the early stages of development.

Step 7: UPDATE YOUR STRATEGY DOCUMENT. If your performance data suggests a strategy adjustment, note it in your research document with the specific metric that prompted the change and the specific variable being adjusted. This creates an accountable record that prevents the trap of changing strategies impulsively based on recent outcomes rather than on a meaningful sample of evidence.

🖥 PLATFORM FEATURE: Trade History and Performance Analytics on stocktradesapp.com

The TRADE HISTORY section at the bottom of the Paper Trading page (navigation menu: Paper) shows every completed paper trade with its timestamp, ticker, action (BUY or SELL), quantity, price, and total value. The count of fills is displayed as "X FILLS" next to the TRADE HISTORY label.

Use the timestamp and ticker information in TRADE HISTORY alongside the Dashboard's equity curve to correlate individual trades with specific points on the performance chart. This lets you investigate exactly which trades contributed to any notable equity curve movement.

The Dashboard filter buttons (ALL, LONG, SHORT, WINS, LOSSES, SYMBOL) provide the analytical segmentation you need for your weekly review. The WINS filter isolates only profitable close events. The LOSSES filter isolates only losing closes. Comparing the equity curve in WINS view versus LOSSES view reveals whether your losses are evenly distributed or concentrated in specific patterns.

9.8 Reading the Trade History for Hidden Insights

The TRADE HISTORY in the Paper section is more than a log of what happened. Analyzed carefully, it is a behavioral record of how you make decisions under real-time market conditions versus how you planned to make them with clear thinking before the session began. The gap between these two often produces the most valuable insights of the entire paper trading phase.

Three specific patterns are worth looking for when reviewing trade history:

Pattern 1: Time-of-Day Clustering

Sort your trades mentally by the time of day they were placed. Do a disproportionate number of losing trades occur in the first 30 minutes of the session (9:30 to 10:00 AM), a period the book identified in Chapter 4 as the most volatile and least predictable of the trading day? Do your worst trades tend to happen in the final 30 minutes (3:30 to 4:00 PM), often driven by urgency to capitalize on intraday momentum before the close? If so, implementing a simple rule (no new entries in the first or last 30 minutes of the session) may produce measurable improvement at zero cost to your strategy logic.

Pattern 2: Single-Stock Concentration

Use the SYMBOL filter on the Dashboard equity curve to check whether any single ticker accounts for a disproportionate share of either your profits or your losses. If 40% of your paper trading losses come from a single stock, you either have a genuine blind spot in how you analyze that sector, or you are repeatedly trying to trade a stock whose behavior does not match your strategy's assumptions. Identify it and either improve your analysis of that stock type or remove it from your active trading universe.

Pattern 3: Entry-to-Exit Timing Asymmetry

Compare the average holding period of your winning trades versus your losing trades. If your losing trades are closed after an average of 1.2 days (stop-losses being honored quickly) and your winning trades are closed after an average of 1.8 days (profits being taken relatively quickly), the R:R ratio of your closed trades is approximately 1.5:1 and your system is generating moderate positive expectancy. If the pattern is reversed, with losing trades held for 5 days on average and winning trades for 1 day, you have a classic case of letting losers run and cutting winners short. The timing data in your TRADE HISTORY is the most objective evidence of which behavior pattern dominates your trading.

THE READINESS INDICATORS FOR LIVE TRADING

Chapter 10 will begin the transition from paper trading to live trading preparation. But before that transition is appropriate, three specific performance thresholds provide meaningful evidence that your paper trading development has reached a foundational level of readiness.

First, a minimum of 50 completed paper trades with full pre-trade and post-trade documentation. This is the statistical baseline for any meaningful performance assessment.

Second, a Profit Factor of 1.3 or above over your most recent 30 trades, held consistently for at least 4 weeks. This suggests the system has a genuine edge that is being consistently applied, not a lucky run of outcomes.

Third, no stop-loss violations in your most recent 20 trades: every stop alert was honored within five minutes of firing without exception. Stop discipline is the single most predictive behavioral indicator of live trading readiness, because it is the rule that emotion most aggressively tests when real money is at stake.

If you have not yet met these three thresholds, the appropriate action is to continue paper trading with the performance review process in this chapter until you do. There is no benefit to transitioning to live trading before establishing consistent, evidence-based performance in the simulator.

9.9 Chapter 9 Exercise: Your First Formal Performance Review

The following exercise walks you through a complete formal performance review of your paper trading to date. Complete every step in your personal research notes. If you have completed fewer than 30 documented trades, complete Steps 1 through 4 now and return to complete the full review once you have 30 or more completed trades.

Full Paper Trading Performance Review Exercise

Step 1: RECORD YOUR BASELINE METRICS. Open the Dashboard (navigation menu: Dashboard) and set the time filter to ALL. Write down the current values for all nine metrics: Win Rate, Avg Win / Loss, Profit Factor, Max Drawdown, Sharpe-Like Score, Realized P&L, Return percentage, SPY Return comparison, and Trade Count. This baseline is your reference point for all future performance reviews.

Step 2: ASSESS THE FIVE-METRIC CLUSTER. Using the framework from Section 9.2, analyze Win Rate plus Avg Win/Loss together. Does your expectancy calculation (Win Rate x Avg Win) minus (Loss Rate x Avg Loss) produce a positive or negative number? Write this calculation down with your actual numbers.

Step 3: READ THE EQUITY CURVE. Set the Dashboard chart filter to ALL. Describe the shape of your equity curve in one sentence. Is it upward sloping, flat, downward, or erratic? Now set the filter to LOSSES and identify whether losing trades cluster at any specific time periods or seem evenly distributed.

Step 4: DIAGNOSE YOUR BEHAVIORAL PATTERN. Review your TRADE HISTORY in the Paper section. For each of the last 10 closed trades, record: the planned stop-loss, the actual exit price on losses, and the actual profit on winners expressed as a multiple of the original risk. Apply the behavioral patterns table from Section 9.4 and identify the single pattern most evident in your last 10 trades.

Step 5: CHECK THE SPY BENCHMARK. Record your paper trading return versus SPY return for the ALL period. If you are significantly underperforming SPY, apply the refinement framework from Section 9.6 to identify the most likely cause and the recommended adjustment.

Step 6: IDENTIFY ONE STRATEGY REFINEMENT. Based on Steps 1 through 5, write one specific, evidence-based refinement to your strategy or execution process. Be precise: not "trade better" but "extend my profit target from 1.5:1 to 2:1 R:R on all new entries" or "implement a mandatory 30-minute cooling off period after every stop-loss." This is the single change you will implement over the next 20 trades.

Step 7: SET YOUR READINESS ASSESSMENT. Review the three live trading readiness thresholds from Section 9.8. Check each one: 50 completed trades with documentation, Profit Factor above 1.3 over last 30 trades for 4 consecutive weeks, and no stop-loss violations in the last 20 trades. Write which thresholds you currently meet and which you are still working toward.

Step 8: SCHEDULE YOUR NEXT REVIEW. Set a reminder for one week from today to complete Steps 1 through 7 again with your updated data. Weekly reviews are the engine of improvement. A single review produces a single insight. Weekly reviews over three months produce compounding insight and measurable performance improvement.

Chapter 9 Summary

Chapter 9 has given you the analytical framework that closes the learning loop of your paper trading practice. Here is what you now carry forward:

- **Practice Without Feedback Does Not Improve Performance:** Paper trading without systematic performance analysis builds repetitions, not skill. Deliberate practice, defined by specific goals, immediate feedback, and analysis of weaknesses, is what converts paper trading experience into genuine trading competence.
- **Nine Dashboard Metrics to Track:** Win Rate, Avg Win/Loss, Profit Factor, Max Drawdown, Sharpe-Like Score, Realized P&L, SPY Benchmark comparison, Trade Count, and Expectancy. Always read Win Rate alongside Avg Win/Loss, and Profit Factor alongside Max Drawdown. No single metric tells the full story.
- **The Equity Curve Tells What Aggregates Cannot:** The distribution and timing of wins and losses reveals information that average metrics hide. Clustering of losses during specific market conditions indicates a macro sensitivity. Clustering during the first or last 30 minutes indicates a timing issue. A volatile, directionless curve with 50 or more trades indicates the strategy needs refinement.
- **Six Behavioral Patterns to Diagnose:** Cutting winners too early (high win rate, low profit factor), holding losers too long (average loss exceeds stop-loss distance), overtrading (win rate declining as trade count rises), revenge trading (trades clustering within 30 minutes of a loss), FOMO entries (entries consistently far above

support), and inconsistent position sizing (drawdown events associated with oversized positions).

- **The SPY Benchmark Is Your Honest Test:** Beating SPY return with a maximum drawdown no larger than 1.5 times SPY's maximum drawdown over the same period is the minimum evidence of genuine value added through active trading. Underperforming SPY is not discouraging. It is valuable diagnostic data that this chapter's framework helps you act on.
- **Change One Variable at a Time:** The most common refinement mistake is changing multiple strategy elements simultaneously after a losing period. Identify the single most impactful variable, change only that, trade 20 more positions under the new rule, and measure before-and-after results before considering a second adjustment.
- **Three Readiness Thresholds for Live Trading:** 50 completed paper trades with documentation, Profit Factor above 1.3 over the last 30 trades held for 4 consecutive weeks, and no stop-loss violations in the last 20 trades. Meeting all three does not guarantee live trading success, but failing any one of them is a reliable indicator that the paper trading phase is not yet complete.
- **The Weekly Review Is Your Engine of Improvement:** Seven steps, 20 to 30 minutes per week, producing compounding improvement through consistent measurement, diagnosis, and deliberate adjustment. The traders who improve most consistently are the ones who do this process every week without exception.

PART IV

The Transition to Mastery

Going Live

CHAPTER 10

The Psychology of Live Trading: Managing Emotion When Money Is Real

"The goal of a successful trader is to make the best trades. Money is secondary."
— Alexander Elder, Trading for a Living (1993)

Everything in this book up to this point has been preparation. The fundamental analysis of Chapter 5, the technical analysis of Chapter 6, the systematic watchlist process of Chapter 7, the risk management framework of Chapter 8, the performance review discipline of Chapter 9: all of it has been preparation for the moment you place your first trade with real money in a real brokerage account.

Chapter 10 addresses the single most underestimated challenge in the entire trader development journey: the psychological shift from paper trading to live trading. This shift is not about strategy. Your analytical tools do not change. Your risk rules do not change. Your pre-trade checklist does not change. What changes is everything happening inside your nervous system when the numbers on the screen represent money you earned through real work, money that has real consequences, money whose loss would feel genuinely painful.

The traders who successfully navigate this transition are not the ones who feel no emotion. They are the ones who have built sufficient structural distance between emotional impulse and trade execution that their rules, not their feelings, govern their decisions. This chapter teaches you to build that structure before your first live trade, so that the emotional environment of live trading does not catch you unprepared.

70-80%

of retail traders incur losses, with trading psychology identified as a primary factor by research. Traders who received structured psychological training showed 30% higher account survivability after one year compared to those who did not.

Source: BIS Behavioural Finance Review, cited by EBC Financial Group (2025)

10.1 The Neuroscience of Why Live Trading Feels Different

The difference between paper trading and live trading is not merely psychological in the casual sense of the word. It is neurological. When real money is at stake, the brain processes trading decisions through fundamentally different neural pathways than when virtual money is involved.

Research in neuroeconomics, the study of how the brain makes economic decisions, has consistently shown that financial loss activates the same neural regions (particularly the amygdala, the brain's threat-detection center) as physical pain. The anticipation of a real financial loss triggers a fight-or-flight stress response that releases cortisol, constricts executive thinking, accelerates decision speed, and narrows attention to the immediate threat rather than the longer-term context.

This neurological reality explains a phenomenon that confuses many beginning traders: why a person who consistently follows their rules in paper trading begins violating those same rules the moment real money is involved. The rules have not changed. The strategy has not changed. But the emotional environment has shifted dramatically, and the brain under stress prioritizes survival over systematic execution.

> *"Resilience is not about eliminating negative emotions from trading. Fear and greed are hardwired responses that no amount of mindfulness eliminates entirely. The practical goal is creating enough structural distance between emotional impulse and trade execution that your rules, not your nervous system, determine your actions."*
>
> — **Trading-Setup.com Research Team**, *Mastering Trading Psychology: The Ultimate Guide (2026)*

Understanding that this neurological shift is inevitable and universal, rather than a sign of weakness or insufficient preparation, is the first step toward managing it effectively. Every successful trader has experienced the emotional intensity of their first live trades. The difference between those who survived and improved and those who did not is not that the survivors felt less. It is that they had built systems that made acting on those feelings mechanically difficult.

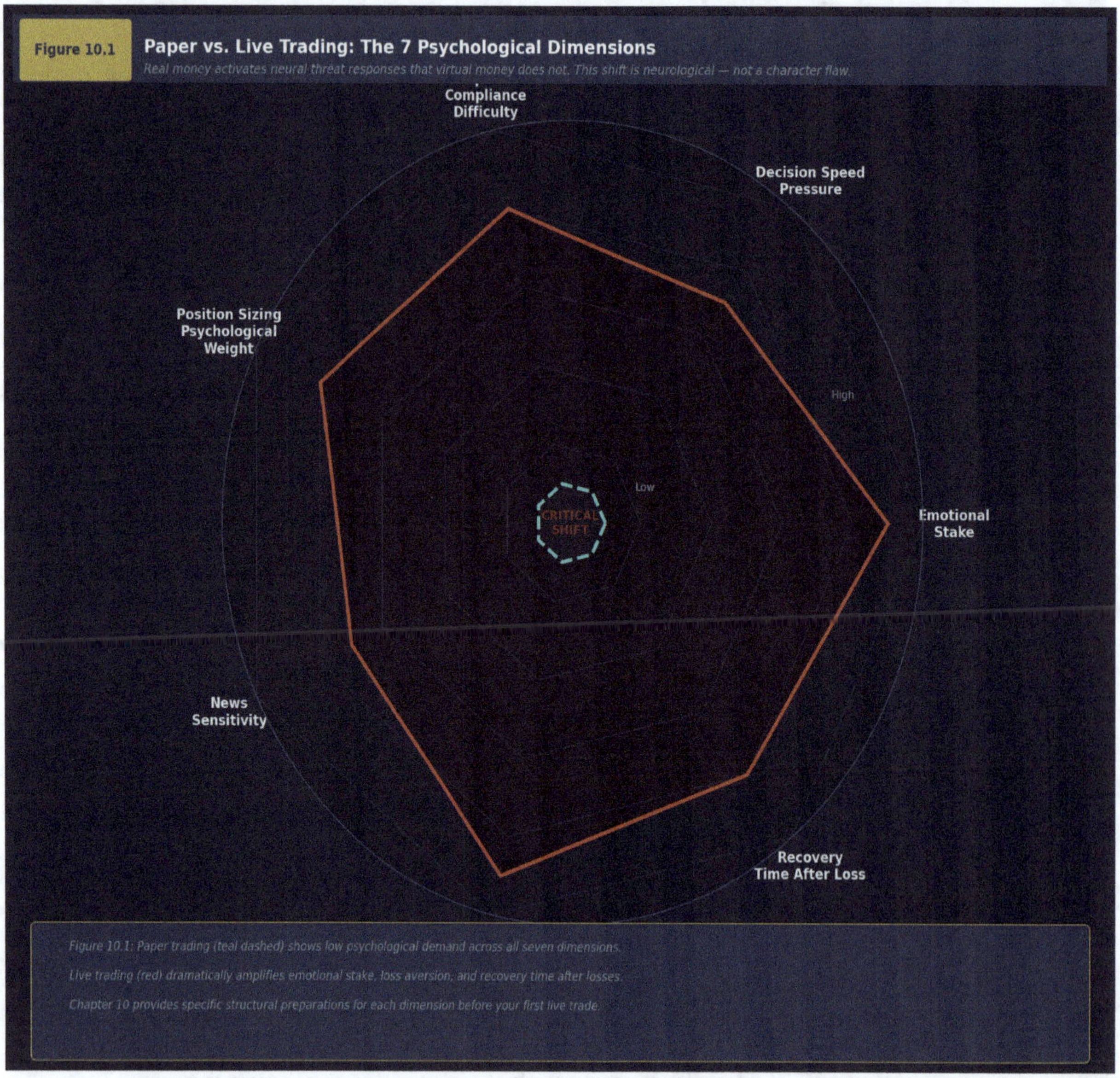

Figure 10.1 - Paper vs. Live Trading: The 7 Psychological Dimensions. Real money activates neural threat responses that virtual money does not. This shift is neurological and universal — not a character flaw.

10.2 The Seven Dimensions of the Paper-to-Live Transition

The psychological shift from paper trading to live trading is not a single moment. It is a multidimensional transition that affects every aspect of your trading decision-making. Understanding how each dimension changes helps you prepare specifically for each challenge rather than being surprised by them in the moment.

Dimension	Paper Trading	Live Trading with Real Money
Emotional stake	Zero. Virtual losses produce no lasting emotional impact.	High. Even small real losses activate the brain's pain response with the same neural pathways as physical discomfort.
Decision speed	Decisions made at a comfortable pace with no urgency.	Real-time price movement creates time pressure that triggers fight-or-flight responses in many traders.
Stop-loss compliance	Easy. Honoring a stop costs nothing. The abstract nature of virtual money makes following rules almost effortless.	Much harder. Closing a real losing position means accepting a permanent, real-money loss. The temptation to delay this moment is powerful and documented.
Position sizing	Simple calculation applied to virtual numbers.	The same calculation now applies to real money you earned through real work. The psychological weight of larger positions is significantly greater than paper trading prepares you for.
News sensitivity	Minor. Reading a negative headline about a paper position produces mild concern.	Amplified. The same headline about a real position can trigger strong anxiety responses, especially in the first weeks of live trading.
Win rate perception	Objective. Wins and losses are data points.	Subjective. Losses feel disproportionately large relative to wins of the same magnitude, consistent with Kahneman and Tversky's loss aversion research (1979).
Recovery from losses	Immediate. Virtual losses are forgotten almost instantly.	Takes time. A real loss of any size activates the brain's loss aversion circuitry and can persist as background anxiety throughout the session.

None of the challenges in this table are insurmountable. They are predictable, documented, and manageable with the right structural preparations. The purpose of laying them out explicitly is to ensure that when you encounter them in your first weeks of live trading, you recognize them for what they are: normal, expected features of the transition, not evidence that you are unsuited for trading or that your strategy is flawed.

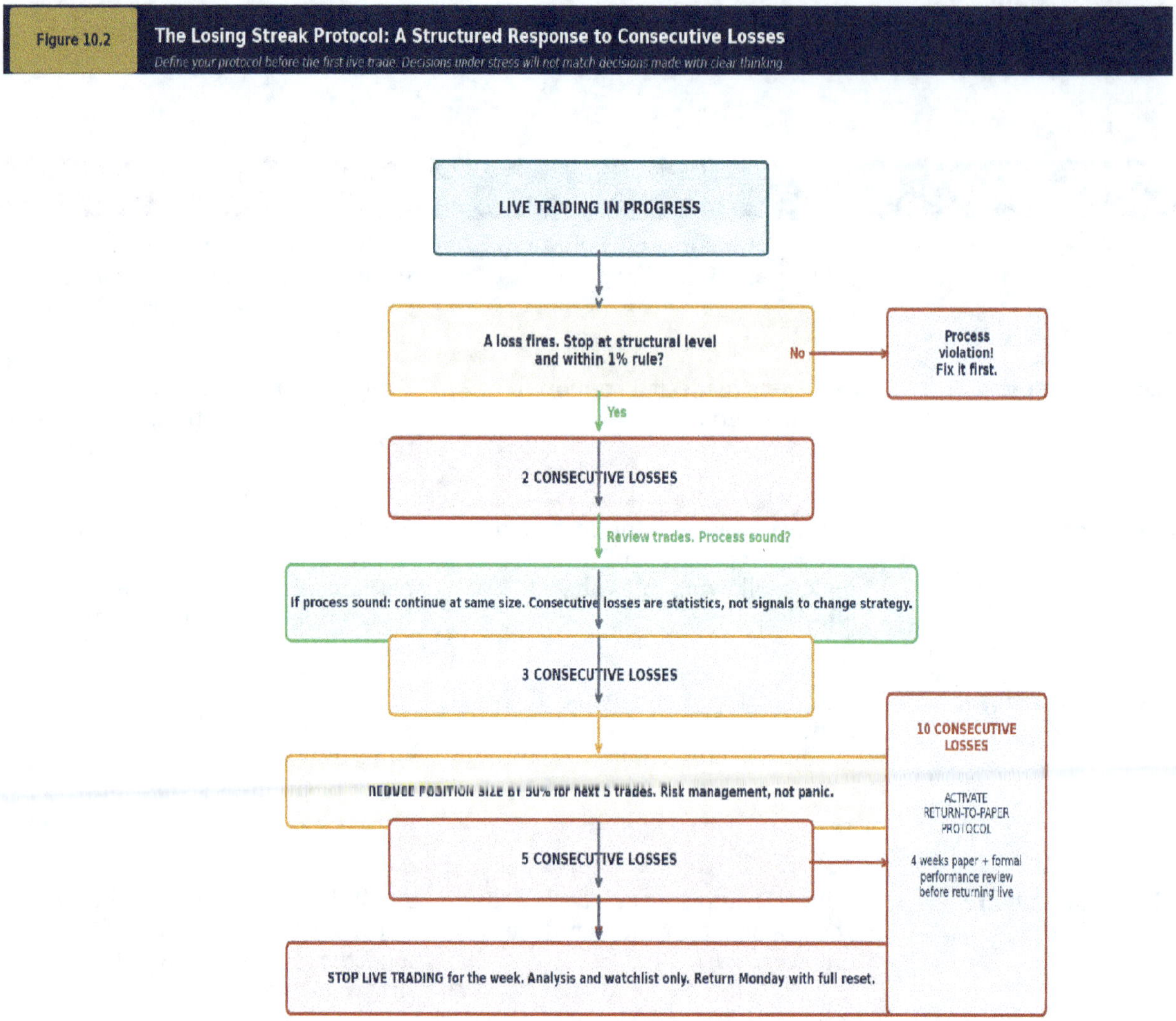

Figure 10.2 - The Losing Streak Protocol: A pre-committed, structured response to consecutive losses. Define this protocol before your first live trade, when thinking is clear.

THE NBER RESEARCH ON PAPER VS. LIVE TRADING BEHAVIOR

A working paper published by the National Bureau of Economic Research examined the correlation between hypothetical financial decisions made on paper versus real financial decisions involving live market transactions. The researchers, studying day traders in a structured training program, found scant correlation between paper trading behavior and live trading behavior across multiple psychological dimensions, particularly in areas of risk-taking and emotional decision-making.

This research underscores a critical point: paper trading builds analytical skills, pattern recognition, and systematic process habits. But it does not fully prepare you for the emotional environment of live trading, which is why this chapter exists. The transition requires specific additional preparation beyond analytical skill development.

The practical implication: do not assume that your paper trading performance is a precise predictor of your live trading performance. Your analytical edge will likely transfer. Your emotional management under real-money conditions requires its own development period with smaller position sizes than your paper trading established.

10.3 The Six Emotional States That Disrupt Live Trading

Six specific emotional states are responsible for the vast majority of live trading errors at every level of experience. Each has a recognizable pattern, a documented impact on decision quality, and a structural defense that prevents it from overriding your systematic rules. The table below covers all six, drawing on research from behavioral economics, trading psychology, and the documented experiences of professional traders.

Emotional State	How It Distorts Decision-Making	The Rule-Based Antidote
Fear of Loss	Triggers premature exit of winning positions before the target is reached. Causes hesitation at valid entry points that meet all checklist criteria. Produces paralysis during normal market fluctuations that the strategy was designed to handle.	Pre-defined profit targets set before entry. Commitment in writing to hold until either the target or the trailing stop is reached. The decision is made with clear thinking before the trade begins, not during it.
Fear of Missing Out (FOMO)	Drives entries into stocks that have already moved significantly from the ideal entry point, typically far above support and near resistance. Produces market orders at inflated prices during fast upward moves, creating immediate drawdowns when the momentum exhausts.	A written rule: no entries more than 3% above the nearest structural support level. If a stock has moved significantly without you, accept the miss and wait for the next qualified setup. There will always be another setup.
Greed	Causes holding of positions beyond defined profit targets in pursuit of additional gains. Leads	Sell at the pre-defined target without exception. If the stock continues higher after your exit, that is acceptable. You

Emotional State	How It Distorts Decision-Making	The Rule-Based Antidote
	to failure to take profits at resistance levels, resulting in watching profitable positions become losses as the stock reverses. Also drives oversized position sizes beyond the 1% rule.	captured the move you planned to capture. The alternative, holding past the target and watching it reverse, is far more costly over time.
Overconfidence After Winning Streaks	A sequence of profitable trades creates a psychological state where the trader believes their analytical skills are better than they are. This produces reduced research rigor, larger position sizes, and entries on setups that do not fully meet the checklist criteria.	After any winning streak of five or more trades, deliberately slow down. Review each winning trade and honestly assess whether the process was sound or whether luck played a significant role. Reinforce the full pre-trade checklist before the next entry.
Despair After Losing Streaks	A sequence of losing trades creates doubt about the strategy, leading to abandonment of the system at precisely the moment when the statistical distribution is most likely to produce a cluster of winning trades next. Also produces revenge trading behaviors.	Return to your performance data. Is the Profit Factor still above 1.0 over your full sample? Are the losses reflecting correct process with bad short-term outcomes, or are they reflecting process violations? If the process is sound, the strategy requires patience, not replacement.
Anchoring to Entry Price	The tendency to evaluate a position relative to the entry price rather than its current market context. A stock that was a good buy at $50 is not automatically a good buy at $40 after a fundamental deterioration simply because the price is "lower than what you paid."	Evaluate every open position daily as if you were considering it for the first time at its current price, with no knowledge of your entry. Ask: would I buy this stock today at this price given what I know now? If the answer is no, the position should be re-examined regardless of the unrealized loss.

The structural defenses in this table share a common principle: they move decision-making to a time when you have clear thinking, calm emotions, and access to your full analytical capabilities. The pre-trade plan, the written checklist, the pre-defined target and stop-loss level, these are not bureaucratic formalities. They are the specific decisions you make before the emotional environment of a live trade activates, so that those decisions can govern your behavior when emotion is at its strongest.

> *"The key to trading success is emotional discipline. If intelligence were the key, there would be a lot more people making money trading. The markets are a device for transferring wealth from the impatient to the patient."*
> — **Dr. Van K. Tharp, Ph.D.**, *Peak Performance Trading research, widely attributed*

10.4 The Five Cognitive Biases That Cost Live Traders Money

Beyond the six emotional states, five specific cognitive biases, systematic errors in thinking that affect all human beings, are particularly costly in the live trading environment. These biases are not character flaws. They are documented features of human cognition identified across decades of psychology research. Understanding them explicitly is the precondition for defending against them.

Cognitive Bias	How It Appears in Live Trading	Structural Defense
Confirmation Bias	After entering a position, you selectively seek out news and analysis that supports your bullish thesis while unconsciously dismissing or minimizing information that challenges it. The losing trade you should have exited two days ago stays open because you keep finding reasons it will recover.	During any open position, deliberately seek out the best argument against your trade. What would a thoughtful, experienced trader say to challenge your thesis right now? If you cannot honestly engage with the counter-argument, your position management is being driven by bias rather than analysis.
Recency Bias	After three consecutive winning trades, you increase your position size or loosen your entry criteria because recent success creates the feeling that you have "figured it out." After three consecutive losses, you abandon a strategy that has a positive expected value because the recent losses feel permanent.	Always evaluate strategy quality over a minimum of 30 trades, never over the most recent 3 to 5. Profit Factor and Expectancy over a meaningful sample are the truth. The last three outcomes are noise.
Sunk Cost Fallacy	Holding a losing position beyond the stop-loss level because "I have already lost $300, I might as well hold until it comes back." The original loss is a sunk cost. It has no bearing on the stock's future price direction. The only relevant question is: would I enter this position today at this price? If no, exit.	Apply the daily re-evaluation question from Chapter 10's emotional states table: would you buy this stock today at this price, knowing what you know now, without any attachment to the prior entry? If the honest answer is no, close the position. Past losses do not entitle you to future recovery from the same stock.

Cognitive Bias	How It Appears in Live Trading	Structural Defense
Availability Bias	Overweighting the most recent dramatic market event (a crash, a short squeeze, a sudden spike) when assessing the probability of future events. A trader who experienced a sharp market selloff last month may dramatically reduce position sizes for weeks afterward even when market conditions are genuinely favorable.	Before adjusting strategy parameters based on recent experience, check whether the adjustment is supported by your full performance data or only by the emotional memory of a recent event. The data over a meaningful sample is more reliable than the emotional imprint of a dramatic recent outcome.
Gambler's Fallacy	Believing that after a series of losing trades, a winning trade is "due." Trading does not work like coin flips. Each trade is an independent event. A 60% win-rate system does not owe you a win after five losses. The probability of the next trade being a winner is the same as it always was.	Never alter position size, entry criteria, or stop-loss placement based on the outcome of recent trades. Each trade stands independently on its own merit. The only criterion for entering a trade is whether it passes the full pre-trade checklist today, not whether the last three trades were winners or losers.

The behavioral defenses in this table are all variations of the same fundamental principle: replace real-time, emotion-influenced judgment with pre-committed rules designed with clear thinking. This is why the pre-trade checklist, the trading rules document from Chapter 8, and the weekly performance review from Chapter 9 are not optional add-ons. They are the specific mechanisms that defend against these five biases in the live trading environment.

10.5 Building Your Psychological Infrastructure Before Your First Live Trade

The most effective time to build psychological defenses for live trading is before the first live trade, not after the first emotional mistake. The following six structural preparations should be in place before you fund a live brokerage account with real capital. Each one creates a specific barrier between emotional impulse and trade execution.

Preparation 1: The Written Trading Rules Document

Every rule in your complete risk management framework (from Chapter 8) should exist as a written document that you can physically reference during a live session. This is not a mental checklist. It is a printed or prominently displayed document that you consult before placing any trade during your first month of live trading.

The act of reading rules from a written document during a live session creates a brief but crucial pause between the impulse to act and the execution of the action. This pause is often sufficient to prevent the most common emotional trading errors. Professional traders at institutional firms operate under written trading mandates precisely because institutional research has confirmed that written constraints produce more consistent behavior than mental commitments made under stress.

Preparation 2: A Dramatically Reduced Starting Position Size

The single most effective psychological preparation for the transition to live trading is starting with a position size so small that the emotional stakes are manageable. The recommended starting scale is 25% of your paper trading position size, or a maximum of $500 in real capital per trade, whichever is smaller.

The logic is direct: if your paper trading used $1,000 risk per trade (1% of a $100,000 paper account), your first live trades should use $250 risk per trade, equivalent to 1% of a $25,000 live account or a scaled-down version of your position size formula. This reduction is not a reflection of reduced confidence in your strategy. It is a deliberate calibration of the emotional stakes to a level you can manage while building live trading experience.

Many experienced traders recommend starting even smaller than this: position sizes so small that no single loss could produce significant emotional disturbance. The goal in the first 30 live trades is not to generate meaningful returns. The goal is to practice applying your complete process, including pre-trade analysis, risk calculation, stop-loss management, and post-trade journaling, in the live environment without the emotional disruption of significant financial stakes.

Preparation 3: The Pre-Session Routine

Establish a consistent pre-session routine that you execute before every live trading session. This routine serves two purposes: it builds a predictable psychological state before you begin trading, and it creates a structured gateway between your daily life and your trading session that reduces the probability of impulsive, unplanned trades.

A pre-session routine should include: reviewing your open positions and their current status against your defined stop-loss and target levels; checking your watchlist signals on the StockTradesApp.com Dashboard; reading the Daily Briefing or equivalent market overview; reviewing your written trading rules document; and stating your specific intentions for the session (how many trades you are looking to place, which setups you are watching, and any conditions under which you will not trade, such as a choppy market environment or a news-driven spike).

Preparation 4: The Post-Loss Cooldown Protocol

Before your first live trade, write down your specific protocol for what you will do after any losing trade. This is not a reactive decision made under emotional stress. It is a pre-committed behavioral contract with yourself, made with clear thinking.

A standard post-loss protocol: after any stop-loss is triggered, close the position immediately at market (non-negotiable), step away from all screens for a minimum of 30 minutes, write a brief post-trade note identifying whether the stop was at the original structural level and whether the loss reflected correct process or a rules violation, and only re-engage with the session after the 30-minute cooling period has elapsed. No new trades may be placed during the cooling period.

This protocol is most important in the first week of live trading, when the emotional intensity of each loss is at its peak. As you accumulate experience with real-money losses and process them within your systematic framework, the cooling period can be shortened. But in the early weeks, 30 minutes of mandatory distance after each loss is one of the highest-return psychological investments you can make.

Preparation 5: The Updated Investor Identity Statement

In Chapter 2, you wrote an Investor Identity Statement capturing your financial goals, risk tolerance, primary approach, non-negotiable rules, and identified behavioral weaknesses. Before your first live trade, revisit and update this document.

Add two specific elements to the updated version. First, your live trading parameters: the starting account size, the maximum risk per trade in dollars, the maximum daily loss limit in dollars, and the maximum drawdown percentage at which you will stop live trading and return to paper trading for further development. Second, your emotional management commitment: a written acknowledgment of the specific emotional states and biases from Sections 10.3 and 10.4 that you are most susceptible to, and the specific structural defenses you have put in place for each.

This updated document is your living agreement with yourself about how you will trade. Read it at the start of every session during your first month of live trading.

Preparation 6: The Return-to-Paper Protocol

Define in advance the specific, objective conditions under which you will voluntarily return to paper trading from live trading. Having this protocol written before you start live trading removes the emotional difficulty of making that decision in the moment, when the natural tendency is to continue trading in hopes of recovering recent losses.

A standard return-to-paper protocol: if your live trading account experiences a drawdown of 10% or more from its starting value, you will immediately stop live trading, return to paper trading for a minimum of four weeks, conduct a formal performance review using the Chapter 9 framework, identify and document the specific process failures that produced the drawdown, and only return to live trading after four consecutive profitable paper trading weeks with no stop-loss violations.

This protocol is not a prediction that you will fail. It is a structural safety net that removes the most dangerous scenario in all of trading: a new live trader who has lost money, who increases position sizes to recover those losses, who loses more, and who repeats this cycle until the account is severely damaged or depleted. The return-to-paper protocol prevents this outcome by making the decision automatic rather than emotional.

🖥 PLATFORM FEATURE: Using StockTradesApp.com During Live Trading

During live trading, StockTradesApp.com continues to serve as your research and analysis terminal. The Terminal's AI signal, Blended Score, and ANALYSIS tab remain your primary technical research tools. The Watchlist Live Signals panel on the Dashboard gives you a real-time overview of all monitored tickers with their current Buy/Hold/Sell ratings.

The key difference between paper trading and live trading on the platform: paper orders are placed in the Paper section, while real orders are executed through your separate live brokerage account. StockTradesApp.com provides the analysis; your brokerage provides the execution. Chapter 11 covers the brokerage selection and account setup process in detail.

Continue using the Alerts section (navigation menu: Alerts) during live trading exactly as you did during paper trading. Set a "Crosses Below" alert at your stop-loss level for every live position. When the alert fires, your pre-committed protocol is clear: close the position at market immediately. The alert creates the structural trigger for disciplined stop execution.

10.6 Managing the Losing Streak: The Hardest Psychological Test

No preparation for live trading is complete without directly addressing the experience of a losing streak. Every trading strategy with a genuine edge will produce clusters of consecutive losing trades as a matter of statistical probability. A strategy with a 50% win rate will produce sequences of four, five, or even six consecutive losses with meaningful frequency, simply due to random distribution. Understanding this intellectually does not fully prepare you for experiencing it emotionally.

The losing streak is the single most dangerous period in any live trader's career. Not because the losses themselves are catastrophic (if position sizing is correct, they will not be), but because the emotional environment of a losing streak systematically activates all six of the emotional states in Section 10.3 simultaneously. Fear of further losses, despair about the strategy, and the powerful temptation of revenge trading all converge in a losing streak.

> *"Every trader has a strategy that works sometimes and doesn't work other times. The great traders maintain their discipline during the periods when it doesn't work, knowing that the edge will reassert itself over time."*
>
> — **Mark Douglas**, *Trading in the Zone (2000): widely considered the definitive text on trading psychology*

The Losing Streak Protocol

Before your first live trade, write down your specific protocol for handling a losing streak. The following is the recommended structure:

1. After two consecutive losses: Conduct a brief review of both trades. Were the stops at structural levels? Were the entries near support? Were position sizes within the 1% rule? If the answer to all three is yes, the losses reflect correct process and the strategy requires patience, not modification.
2. After three consecutive losses: Reduce position size by 50% for the next five trades. This is not a prediction of continued losses. It is a risk management response to the statistical possibility that your edge is temporarily in a low-probability phase.
3. After five consecutive losses: Stop live trading for the remainder of the week. Spend the non-trading days on the StockTradesApp.com Terminal in analysis mode only, conducting research and updating your watchlist without placing orders. Return to live trading on Monday with a fresh weekly framework.
4. After ten consecutive losses: Activate your return-to-paper protocol (Section 10.5, Preparation 6). This loss sequence, while statistically possible for any

positive-expectancy strategy, suggests either a market regime change that is particularly unfavorable to your approach, a process problem in execution, or both. Four weeks of paper trading with formal performance review will clarify which.

The critical psychological insight about losing streaks: the correct response to a losing streak is almost never to change strategy, and it is never to increase position sizes. The correct response is to maintain process discipline, reduce position sizes slightly as a risk management response, and allow the statistical distribution of your edge to reassert itself over additional trades. This requires a quality that cannot be taught but can be cultivated: genuine belief in the long-term validity of your process, grounded in the evidence of your documented paper trading performance.

10.7 The Winning Streak Problem: When Success Becomes Dangerous

Most books on trading psychology focus exclusively on managing losses. This section addresses an equally important and less-discussed challenge: managing the psychological effects of a winning streak.

A sequence of profitable trades produces a psychological state that is, in many ways, more dangerous than a losing streak. Consecutive wins create a feeling of mastery and competence that is highly rewarding and that the brain seeks to reinforce. This feeling is not a reliable signal. It is the overconfidence bias described in Chapter 2 and the recency bias from Section 10.4 in operation simultaneously.

The behavioral consequences of a winning streak are predictable and well-documented. Position sizes begin to drift upward as confidence grows. The pre-trade checklist begins to be abbreviated or skipped on setups that "feel" obvious. Entry criteria loosen as the trader begins to believe their pattern recognition has improved beyond the need for systematic rules. Risk-reward requirements are relaxed for setups that "look really good."

Every one of these behaviors increases risk during a period when the probability of a reversion to the mean is elevated. This is the paradox of the winning streak: the emotional state it produces is precisely the wrong one for the risk environment it creates.

THE WINNING STREAK PROTOCOL

After any five consecutive winning paper or live trades, implement the following protocol before the next trade: review all five winning trades and assess honestly whether each one followed the complete pre-trade checklist; check whether position sizes remained at or below the 1% rule throughout the streak; verify that stop-losses were set immediately after each entry; and read your written trading rules document from beginning to end before placing the next trade.

This protocol takes 20 minutes and is designed to counteract the overconfidence that a winning streak naturally produces. The act of verifying that your process was sound (rather than assuming the wins reflect superior skill) maintains the epistemic humility that keeps disciplined traders disciplined.

If the review reveals that any trade during the winning streak involved a process violation (an oversized position, a skipped checklist item, a stop set at a round number), address the violation explicitly in your research notes before trading further. A winning outcome does not retroactively validate a flawed process.

10.8 Your Personal Trading Psychology Assessment

Before closing this chapter, complete the following self-assessment. Answer each question honestly. These questions do not have right or wrong answers. They are diagnostic prompts designed to help you identify your specific psychological profile as a live trader and the areas that require the most deliberate preparation.

Personal Trading Psychology Self-Assessment

Step 1: LOSS TOLERANCE TEST: Imagine your live account has just experienced its first real-money loss of $250. You followed all your rules: the stop was at a structural level, the position was correctly sized at 1%, and you honored the alert immediately. How long will this $250 loss occupy your thinking? A few minutes? A few hours? The rest of the day? The answer reveals your current emotional sensitivity to real-money losses and helps calibrate your starting position size.

Step 2: FOMO RESISTANCE TEST: A stock you have been watching for two weeks has just surged 8% in one day on news you did not anticipate. It is now 7% above the support level you identified as your entry point. On a scale of 1 to 10, how strong is your urge to buy it right now despite the extended entry? An honest 7 or higher means you need a written rule that prevents entries more than 3% above support, regardless of how the move feels.

Step 3: RULE COMPLIANCE UNDER PRESSURE: Think back to your paper trading history. How many times did you move a stop-loss further from entry when it was about to be triggered? How many times did you close a winning trade early because of anxiety rather than a chart-based exit signal? Your honest answers identify the specific rules you are most likely to violate under the additional pressure of real-money conditions.

Step 4: REVENGE TRADING SUSCEPTIBILITY: After your worst paper trading day, what was your first instinct? Did you want to stop trading and review what happened, or did you want to place another trade immediately to recover the loss? If the honest answer is the latter, your post-loss cooldown protocol needs to be strictly enforced in live trading from day one.

Step 5: CONCENTRATION CAPACITY: Can you place a paper trade, set the stop alert, and then genuinely not think about that position for three hours while doing other work? Or do you find yourself checking prices every 20 minutes? Your honest answer determines how aggressively you need to use the Alerts system to remove the temptation of continuous price monitoring during live trading.

Step 6: STRATEGY CONFIDENCE: Do you genuinely believe, based on your documented paper trading evidence, that your strategy has a positive expected value over a large sample of trades? Or is there lingering doubt? If there is significant doubt, the correct response is more paper trading until the evidence resolves that doubt, not more live trading in the hope that experience will replace the missing conviction.

Your honest answers to these six questions should directly inform the six psychological infrastructure preparations in Section 10.5. A high FOMO resistance score suggests stronger written entry rules are needed. A low concentration capacity score suggests more aggressive use of price alerts and deliberate screen-time boundaries. A strategy confidence rating below 7 out of 10 suggests more paper trading is needed before going live.

Chapter 10 Summary

Chapter 10 has equipped you with the psychological framework for the most significant transition in your trading journey: from consequence-free paper trading to real-money live trading. Here is what you now carry forward:

- **The Shift Is Neurological, Not Just Psychological:** Real-money trading activates the brain's threat-detection system (the amygdala) in ways that paper trading does not. Financial loss triggers the same neural pathways as physical pain. Understanding this makes the emotional intensity of live trading predictable rather than surprising.

- **Seven Dimensions of Difference:** The paper-to-live transition affects emotional stake, decision speed, stop-loss compliance, position sizing psychology, news sensitivity, loss aversion expression, and recovery time after losses. Each dimension requires specific preparation.
- **Six Emotional States to Manage:** Fear of loss, FOMO, greed, overconfidence after winning streaks, despair after losing streaks, and anchoring to entry price. Each has a rule-based structural defense that removes the decision from real-time emotional judgment.
- **Five Cognitive Biases to Defend Against:** Confirmation bias, recency bias, sunk cost fallacy, availability bias, and the gambler's fallacy. The defense for all five is the same: replace real-time emotional judgment with pre-committed, systematically derived rules.
- **Six Psychological Infrastructure Preparations:** Written trading rules document, dramatically reduced starting position size (25% of paper trading level), pre-session routine, post-loss cooldown protocol (30-minute minimum), updated Investor Identity Statement, and a written return-to-paper protocol with objective triggers.
- **The Losing Streak Protocol:** Two consecutive losses: verify process. Three consecutive losses: reduce position size by 50%. Five consecutive losses: stop trading for the week. Ten consecutive losses: activate the return-to-paper protocol. The correct response to a losing streak is never to change strategy or increase position sizes.
- **The Winning Streak Problem:** Consecutive wins produce overconfidence and loose rule compliance, which increase risk precisely when reversion to the mean is most likely. The winning streak protocol: after five consecutive wins, review all five trades for process compliance before placing the next one.

CHAPTER 11

Transitioning to a Live Brokerage Account: From Simulator to Real Capital

"Do not focus on making money; focus on protecting what you have."

— Paul Tudor Jones, widely quoted from Market Wizards by Jack D. Schwager (1989)

You have arrived at one of the most significant chapters in this book. The analytical tools, the risk management framework, the systematic research process, and the psychological infrastructure are all in place. Chapter 11 covers the practical mechanics of making the transition from StockTradesApp.com's paper trading simulator to a real brokerage account with real capital.

This chapter is deliberately practical. It covers how to evaluate and select a broker, what regulatory protections to look for, what account type to open, how to fund the account, how to navigate the differences between paper trading execution and live brokerage execution, and what the first 30 days of live trading should look like in terms of position sizing, trade frequency, and performance expectations.

One important note before proceeding: this chapter covers the general mechanics of opening and using a brokerage account. It does not constitute investment advice or a specific broker recommendation. Every broker mentioned is presented purely for educational illustration. Verify all fees, features, and regulatory information directly with any broker you are considering before opening an account, as these details change over time. Consult with a licensed financial advisor if you need personalized guidance specific to your financial situation.

11.1 The Three Readiness Checkpoints: Are You Ready to Go Live?

Before evaluating a single broker, conduct an honest final assessment against the three readiness thresholds established in Chapter 9. These are not bureaucratic gatekeeping requirements. They are the minimum evidence base that gives you a reasonable foundation for live trading. Trading real money without meeting these thresholds does not constitute ambition. It constitutes unnecessary risk.

> **KEY TERM: Live Trading Readiness**
> *The state of documented, evidence-based preparation to transition from paper trading to real-money trading. StockTradesApp.com's Dashboard provides the performance data needed to objectively assess readiness. The three minimum thresholds are: 50 completed paper trades with full pre-trade and post-trade documentation, a Profit Factor of 1.3 or above over the most recent 30 trades held for at least 4 consecutive weeks, and zero stop-loss violations in the most recent 20 trades.*

- **Threshold 1: 50 Documented Paper Trades.** Review the TRADE HISTORY in your Paper section. Count every completed paper trade (both BUY and SELL sides of each position constitute separate fills, so a round trip is typically two fills). Fifty completed positions with full pre-trade documentation provides a statistically meaningful, though not definitive, sample of your strategy's edge.
- **Threshold 2: Profit Factor of 1.3 or Above for 4 Consecutive Weeks.** Open your Dashboard and verify the Profit Factor in the PERFORMANCE section. Set the filter to 1M (one month) to assess recent performance rather than your all-time average. A Profit Factor above 1.3 sustained for four weeks suggests the edge is real and consistent, not a product of a favorable short-term sequence.
- **Threshold 3: Zero Stop-Loss Violations in the Last 20 Trades.** Review your last 20 completed trades. In every case where a stop alert fired, was the position closed within five minutes? If even one stop was moved, delayed, or not honored, this threshold is not met. Stop-loss discipline is the single behavioral indicator most predictive of live trading survival.

If you meet all three thresholds, you are ready to proceed through this chapter and fund a live account. If you do not yet meet one or more, the correct response is to continue paper trading with the specific goal of meeting the unmet threshold. Going live before meeting these thresholds adds unnecessary psychological pressure to a process that is already challenging enough.

11.2 Understanding Broker Regulation and Investor Protection

Every reputable U.S. brokerage firm operates under a framework of regulatory oversight and investor protection that is important to understand before entrusting your capital to any platform. This framework does not eliminate the risk of losing money on your investments, but it does protect your assets in the unlikely event that your broker fails as a business.

KEY TERM: SIPC (Securities Investor Protection Corporation)

A nonprofit membership organization, created by Congress in 1970, that protects customers of SIPC-member brokerage firms if the firm fails financially. SIPC protects against the loss of cash and securities held at a member firm up to $500,000 per customer, including up to $250,000 in cash. SIPC protection does NOT cover losses from market fluctuations or bad investment decisions. It protects the custody of your assets, not the performance of those assets. All reputable U.S. brokers listed in this chapter are SIPC members.

KEY TERM: FINRA (Financial Industry Regulatory Authority)

A self-regulatory organization authorized by Congress to oversee U.S. broker-dealers. FINRA licenses brokers, examines firms for compliance with financial responsibility rules, and operates BrokerCheck at brokercheck.finra.org, a free database where you can verify any broker's licensing status and review their disciplinary history. Before opening an account with any broker, verify their FINRA registration on BrokerCheck.

Every broker worth considering for your live trading account will be both SIPC-insured and FINRA-registered. These are baseline requirements, not distinguishing features. The distinguishing features are the factors covered in Section 11.3: commissions, platform quality, research tools, customer service, and alignment with your specific trading approach.

WHAT SIPC DOES AND DOES NOT COVER

SIPC covers: cash and securities missing from your account because a SIPC-member broker failed, was liquidated, or was involved in fraud involving custody of assets. This protection gives you reasonable confidence that if your broker goes out of business, your assets will be returned to you up to the coverage limit.

SIPC does not cover: any decline in the value of your securities; losses from bad trading decisions; losses from market risk; investments in commodities or futures contracts; investment advice that proved incorrect. This is a common source of confusion for new investors.

For context, no major U.S. retail broker has collapsed in a way that triggered SIPC claims for mainstream retail investors in the modern era of large, well-capitalized platforms. The SIPC protection is a regulatory safety net, not a risk that should dominate your broker selection decision. Focus instead on the practical criteria in Section 11.3.

11.3 Evaluating and Selecting Your Broker: Seven Decision Criteria

The U.S. retail brokerage industry has undergone a dramatic transformation since 2019, when Schwab, Fidelity, TD Ameritrade, and E*TRADE all eliminated stock trading commissions in rapid succession. Commission-free stock and ETF trading is now the industry standard among all major retail brokers. This means commission costs are no longer a meaningful differentiator for most beginning traders. The decision criteria that matter in 2026 are different.

Criterion 1: Regulatory Standing (Non-Negotiable)

SIPC membership and FINRA registration are the minimum requirements. Verify both on BrokerCheck at brokercheck.finra.org before opening any account. This takes less than two minutes and should be done before evaluating any other criteria.

Criterion 2: Commission Structure

For stock and ETF trades, the answer is almost universally $0 per trade at major retail brokers in 2026. Verify there are no hidden fees: account maintenance fees, inactivity fees, transfer fees, or platform access fees. The one area where commissions still vary is options contracts, where fees typically range from $0.50 to $0.65 per contract. If options are part of your strategy development (covered in Chapter 14), this comparison matters.

Criterion 3: Platform and Charting Quality

Since StockTradesApp.com serves as your primary research and analysis tool, the charting requirements for your live brokerage are actually less critical than they would be for a trader who relies on their broker's native tools for analysis. That said, your brokerage platform should offer a clean, reliable order entry interface, real-time quote data, basic charting, and a mobile application that functions well for monitoring open positions.

Traders who want to run advanced technical analysis directly within their brokerage platform (rather than using StockTradesApp.com for analysis and the broker for execution) should consider Charles Schwab's thinkorswim platform, which is widely considered the most powerful free charting and analysis tool available through any retail broker. It is available to all Schwab account holders at no additional cost.

Criterion 4: Fractional Share Availability

Fractional shares allow you to buy a portion of one share of a stock, rather than being required to purchase whole shares. For a beginning live trader starting with a small account, fractional shares are an important feature. They allow you to practice your position sizing formula even on high-priced stocks (Apple at $190, Amazon at $180, or Google at $170) without being forced to commit a disproportionate amount of capital to a single position.

Fidelity, Schwab (via Schwab Slices), Robinhood, and Interactive Brokers all offer fractional shares starting from as little as $1. E*TRADE does not offer fractional shares. This difference matters for beginning traders building small live accounts.

Criterion 5: Customer Service Quality

When you are learning to trade with real money for the first time, access to knowledgeable, responsive customer support is genuinely valuable. Technical issues, deposit delays, order entry errors, and tax form questions will all arise, and the quality of your broker's support team significantly affects how disruptive these issues are.

Fidelity and Charles Schwab consistently rank highest for customer service quality among retail brokers, with 24/7 phone and chat support, extensive educational resources, and local branch access. Robinhood and Webull are primarily digital-first platforms with more limited customer service depth, which is a meaningful trade-off for beginning traders.

Criterion 6: Interest on Uninvested Cash

When your account holds uninvested cash (the capital not currently deployed in open positions), the interest rate the broker pays on that balance varies significantly. As of 2025 to 2026, with interest rates at elevated levels, this difference can be meaningful. Fidelity and E*TRADE offer competitive rates on uninvested cash. Schwab and Robinhood have historically offered lower rates on default cash balances, though sweep programs and money market options are available. Check current rates directly with each broker, as these change with monetary policy.

Criterion 7: Alignment with Your Trading Style and Account Size

Different brokers are optimized for different trader profiles. The table below provides a simplified comparison of six major retail brokers as of June 2026, sourced from NerdWallet, Bankrate, and Motley Fool broker reviews. Use it as a starting point for your research, then verify all details directly with each broker before making a final decision.

Broker	Min. Deposit	Stock Commissions	Fractional Shares	SIPC Protected	Best For
Fidelity	$0	$0	Yes (from $1)	Yes	Beginners and long-term investors. Exceptional research tools, educational resources, and customer service. Consistently ranked highest for beginner-friendliness.
Charles Schwab	$0	$0	Yes (via Schwab Slices)	Yes	Beginners through advanced traders. Four trading platforms including thinkorswim. 24/7 customer support. Acquired TD Ameritrade's platform.
Robinhood	$0	$0	Yes (from $1)	Yes (+ Lloyd's of London excess)	Mobile-first, simplicity-focused traders. Pioneered commission-free trading. Clean interface. Limited research depth vs. Fidelity/Schwab.
Webull	$0	$0	Yes	Yes	Active traders who want advanced charting and technical analysis tools in a mobile-first environment. Strong paper trading simulator.
E*TRADE (Morgan Stanley)	$0	$0	No	Yes	Intermediate to advanced traders. Two platforms: standard E*TRADE and Power E*TRADE for active

Broker	Min. Deposit	Stock Commissions	Fractional Shares	SIPC Protected	Best For
					traders. Strong options tools.
Interactive Brokers	$0 (Lite)	$0 (Lite tier)	Yes	Yes	Experienced and cost-focused traders. Pro tier offers volume discounts. Access to 135+ markets globally. Steeper learning curve.

Sources: NerdWallet, Bankrate, Motley Fool broker reviews (June 2026). All brokers listed are SEC and FINRA registered. Verify current terms directly with each broker before opening an account. This is educational content, not a financial endorsement of any specific broker.

11.4 Account Types: Choosing the Right Structure for Your Trading Capital

Before opening a brokerage account, you must choose the account type. Each type has different tax treatment, contribution limits, and withdrawal rules. The wrong choice creates tax complications or restricts access to your capital in ways that could interfere with your active trading.

Account Type	Key Characteristics	Best For Your Trading Journey
Taxable Brokerage Account (Standard)	No contribution limits. No withdrawal restrictions. All realized gains taxed as either short-term (held under 1 year, taxed as ordinary income) or long-term capital gains (held over 1 year, taxed at 0%, 15%, or 20% depending on income). Most flexible account type.	This is the account to open for your initial live trading transition. The flexibility to trade freely without tax-advantaged restrictions matches the active, learning-focused nature of your first live trading year.
Traditional IRA	Contributions may be tax-deductible. Growth is tax-deferred until withdrawal. Withdrawals in retirement taxed as ordinary income. Annual contribution limit of $7,000 in 2025 ($8,000 if age 50+). 10% penalty for withdrawals before age 59.5.	Not recommended as your primary active trading account. The early withdrawal penalty creates a serious problem if you need to access funds. Best used for a separate, long-term, diversified portfolio alongside your active trading account.

Account Type	Key Characteristics	Best For Your Trading Journey
Roth IRA	Contributions made with after-tax dollars. Growth and qualified withdrawals are tax-free. Same annual contribution limits as Traditional IRA. Income limits apply for direct contributions. Contributions (not earnings) can be withdrawn penalty-free at any time.	An excellent long-term wealth-building vehicle, but subject to the same withdrawal restriction concerns as the Traditional IRA for active trading. Open one for retirement savings separate from your active trading account.
401(k)	Employer-sponsored. Contributions pre-tax, reducing current taxable income. Annual limit of $23,500 in 2025. Many employers offer matching contributions. Investment options typically limited to a fund menu selected by the employer.	Max your employer match first. This is an immediate 50-100% return on those dollars, unmatched by any trading strategy. Manage separately from your active trading brokerage account.

The recommendation for your first live trading account is unambiguous: open a standard taxable brokerage account. Its flexibility, absence of withdrawal restrictions, and straightforward tax treatment make it the correct vehicle for the active, developing trader. Maintain separate retirement accounts (IRA, 401k) for long-term wealth building, and keep those accounts invested in diversified, low-cost index funds rather than in the active trading strategies you are developing.

THE PATTERN DAY TRADER RULE: WHAT YOU MUST KNOW

The Pattern Day Trader (PDT) rule is a FINRA regulation that significantly affects traders with accounts below $25,000. Under the PDT rule, if you execute four or more day trades (opening and closing a position within the same trading day) within any five-business-day rolling period in a margin account, and those day trades constitute more than 6% of your total trading activity in that period, you are classified as a Pattern Day Trader.

Once classified as a PDT, your broker is required to maintain at least $25,000 in equity in your margin account. If your account falls below $25,000, you will be restricted from placing further day trades until the balance is restored above the threshold.

For beginning live traders with accounts below $25,000, the practical implication is straightforward: open a cash account (not a margin account) at the start, and plan your trading approach around swing trades held for multiple days rather than day trades. Cash accounts are not subject to the PDT rule. Alternatively, keep day trading activity below the four-trade threshold per rolling five-day period. Chapter 14 covers more sophisticated trading approaches as your account grows.

11.5 Funding Your Account and Your First Live Deposit

Once you have selected a broker and opened an account, the next step is funding it. How much capital you deposit in your first live account is one of the most consequential decisions of your early trading career. It determines the position sizes you can implement, the number of simultaneous positions you can hold within the portfolio heat limit, and the psychological stakes of each trade.

How Much to Deposit: The First Account Sizing Framework

The correct amount for your first live trading account is the smallest amount that allows you to practice your complete risk management framework with meaningful, real-money consequences without creating financial jeopardy if the account experiences a significant drawdown.

The minimum viable amount for a beginning live trader is $5,000 to $10,000, based on the following logic: at the 1% risk rule, a $5,000 account limits your maximum risk per trade to $50. At a position size consistent with $50 risk on a $50 stock with a $2.50 stop, you could buy 20 shares. This is a meaningful position that carries genuine financial stakes but poses no threat to your financial security if the account experiences the 10% maximum drawdown discussed in Chapter 10's return-to-paper protocol (a 10% drawdown on $5,000 is $500, a manageable consequence for most traders).

A $25,000 or larger first deposit is not recommended for traders in their first live trading year, regardless of their paper trading success. The psychological intensity of a 10% drawdown on $25,000 ($2,500) is significantly greater than on $5,000 ($500), and managing that intensity while simultaneously applying a full systematic framework requires a level of emotional control that typically develops over the first 6 to 12 months of live trading experience.

THE MINIMUM RECOMMENDED STARTING CAPITAL BY TRADING STYLE

Day Traders (opens and closes positions within the same day): Due to the Pattern Day Trader rule, if you plan to day trade actively, you should fund your margin account to at least $25,000 to avoid PDT restrictions. However, given the recommendation for beginning traders to avoid day trading in their first live year, this scenario should be deferred until your paper trading performance specifically demonstrates edge in intraday setups.

Swing Traders (holds positions for days to weeks): $5,000 to $15,000 is appropriate for the first live account. This range allows meaningful position sizing within the 1% rule while keeping maximum drawdown consequences financially manageable.

Long-Term Investors (holds positions for months to years): Amount is less critical from a PDT perspective, since long-term investors rarely day trade. The key criterion is investing only capital you genuinely do not need for at least 3 to 5 years, so that normal market volatility does not force premature liquidation.

Funding Methods and Settlement Times

Most U.S. brokers accept the following deposit methods: ACH (Automated Clearing House) bank transfer (free, typically 1 to 3 business days to settle), wire transfer (may carry a small fee, typically settles the same business day), check (slowest option, typically 3 to 5 business days), and transfer from another brokerage account via ACATS (the Automated Customer Account Transfer Service, typically 3 to 5 business days).

An important timing consideration: even after your deposit clears and appears in your account balance, funds from ACH transfers are typically subject to a holding period of 3 to 5 business days before they are available to purchase securities. This means that when you make your initial deposit, you should allow approximately one week before you expect to place your first live trade. Plan accordingly so that the delay does not create impatience-driven shortcuts in your preparation.

11.6 Live Order Execution: How It Differs from Paper Trading

The mechanics of placing an order in a live brokerage account are similar to placing a paper trade in StockTradesApp.com's Paper section, but with several important technical differences that every beginning live trader must understand before placing their first order.

Order Type	How It Works	When to Use It in Live Trading
Market Order	Buys or sells immediately at the best currently available price. Guarantees execution but not price.	Use for highly liquid large-cap stocks when speed of execution matters more than the exact fill price. Avoid for thinly traded stocks or during the first/last 30 minutes of the session, when bid-ask spreads are widest.

Order Type	How It Works	When to Use It in Live Trading
Limit Order	Buys at your specified price or lower (for buys) or sells at your specified price or higher (for sells). Guarantees price but not execution.	Use for all live trading entries and exits where price precision matters. A buy limit order at $49.80 on a stock trading at $50.00 ensures you will not overpay if the stock moves quickly against you. Most professional traders use limit orders for almost all entries.
Stop-Loss Order (Stop Market)	Becomes a market order when the stock price reaches your stop level. Guarantees execution once triggered but not the exact exit price.	Use to protect existing positions. Set your stop price at the structural level calculated in Chapter 8. Note: during fast market moves, the actual fill may be below your stop price (called slippage). Most liquid large-cap stocks have minimal slippage.
Stop-Limit Order	Becomes a limit order (not a market order) when the stop price is reached. Guarantees price but risks non-execution if the market moves past your limit price quickly.	Use in slower-moving markets where you want price certainty on your stop exit. Be aware that in a fast market decline, a stop-limit can fail to execute entirely if the price drops through your limit without filling, leaving you in a deteriorating position.
Trailing Stop Order	A stop-loss that automatically adjusts upward (for long positions) as the stock price rises, always maintaining a fixed percentage or dollar distance from the current high.	Use for managing winning positions where you want to let profits run while protecting against a reversal. Set as a percentage trailing stop (e.g., 8-10%) or a dollar amount trailing stop, depending on your broker's options.
Good-Till-Cancelled (GTC)	An order that remains active until it is either executed or you manually cancel it. By default most orders are "Day Orders" that expire at the close of the trading session.	Use for limit orders placed at your planned entry price that may not fill immediately. A GTC limit buy order at $47.50 will remain active across multiple trading sessions until the stock reaches that level or you cancel it.

The Professional Preference: Limit Orders Over Market Orders

One of the most significant practical differences between beginning and experienced live traders is order type preference. Beginners tend to default to market orders because they guarantee execution. Experienced traders prefer limit orders for almost all entries because they guarantee price.

For most large-cap stocks with tight bid-ask spreads (Apple, Microsoft, Amazon), the difference between a market order and a limit order placed at the ask price is negligible. But the habit of using limit orders protects you in two important situations: on less-liquid stocks where the spread is wider, and during volatile market conditions when bid-ask spreads widen even on liquid stocks.

The recommended practice for beginning live traders: use limit orders for all planned entries, placing the limit at or just above the current ask price for a buy order to ensure a high probability of execution while still controlling the exact price. Use stop-market orders for stop-loss exits, accepting the small slippage risk in exchange for the certainty of execution.

Slippage: The Gap Between Expected and Actual Fill Price

Slippage is the difference between the price you expected to pay or receive when placing an order and the price you actually received on the fill. It occurs on market orders during fast-moving markets, on stop-market orders when price gaps through the stop level, and on limit orders that are partially filled at different prices.

For the liquid large-cap stocks appropriate for beginning live traders, slippage on stop-market orders is typically minimal: a few cents per share on most normal market days. During high-volatility events (earnings reports, macro news events, market circuit breaker conditions), slippage on stop exits can be significantly larger. This is one practical reason to maintain a slightly larger cash buffer in your position sizing calculation, always erring on the side of slightly fewer shares rather than slightly more.

🖥 PLATFORM FEATURE: Using StockTradesApp.com Alongside Your Live Brokerage

During live trading, StockTradesApp.com remains your research and analysis command center. The workflow is: research in StockTradesApp.com Terminal, execute orders in your live brokerage account.

Pre-trade: Use the Terminal to run the pre-trade checklist, verify the Blended Signal, review the SIGNALS and ANALYSIS tabs, confirm the support level for your stop placement, and calculate your position size. Then switch to your brokerage account to place the order.

Post-trade: After placing a live order, set a Price Alert in StockTradesApp.com's Alerts section (navigation menu: Alerts) at your stop-loss level. When the alert fires, open your brokerage account and execute the stop. This workflow keeps your analysis in StockTradesApp.com and your execution in your brokerage, using each tool for its primary purpose.

Watchlist coordination: Keep the same tickers on your StockTradesApp.com Watchlist that you hold as live positions. The Watchlist Live Signals panel on the Dashboard gives you a real-time overview of your positions' current Blended Signal status alongside your other monitored tickers.

11.7 Tax Implications of Active Trading

Active trading in a taxable brokerage account generates taxable events with every profitable sale. Understanding the basic tax framework before you begin live trading is essential, not because you need to become a tax expert, but because tax awareness influences holding period decisions, position management, and year-end strategy. None of the information in this section constitutes tax advice. Consult a qualified CPA or tax professional for guidance specific to your situation.

Tax Event	When It Occurs	Key Rules to Know
Short-Term Capital Gain	When you sell a stock for a profit after holding it for 1 year or less	Taxed as ordinary income at your regular federal tax rate (10% to 37% depending on income bracket). This is the tax outcome for most active traders. Every short-term winning trade generates a taxable event.
Long-Term Capital Gain	When you sell a stock for a profit after holding it for more than 1 year	Taxed at preferential rates of 0%, 15%, or 20% depending on total taxable income. The significant tax advantage of holding positions longer than 12 months is one reason many active traders evolve toward longer holding periods as their skills develop.
Capital Loss	When you sell a stock for less than you paid for it	Capital losses can offset capital gains dollar-for-dollar. Up to $3,000 of net capital losses can be deducted against ordinary income per year. Excess losses carry forward to future tax years indefinitely.
Wash Sale Rule	When you sell a security at a loss and buy the same or "substantially identical" security within 30 days before or after the sale	The loss is disallowed for tax purposes in the current year and added to the cost basis of the repurchased shares. This rule prevents traders from harvesting tax losses while maintaining continuous market exposure. Important for active traders who frequently re-enter the same positions.
Dividend Income	When a dividend-paying stock in your taxable account issues a distribution	Qualified dividends (from most U.S. stocks held more than 60 days) are taxed at long-term capital gains rates. Non-qualified dividends are taxed as ordinary income. Dividends are taxable whether reinvested or taken as cash.

Tax Event	When It Occurs	Key Rules to Know
Year-End Tax-Loss Harvesting	Selling positions at a loss before December 31 to offset realized gains	A legitimate and widely used strategy to reduce your annual tax bill. Sell losing positions to generate capital losses that offset your winners. Remember the wash sale rule: do not repurchase the same or substantially identical security within 30 days.

The Practical Tax Guidance for Beginning Live Traders

Three straightforward practices minimize your tax complexity in the first year of live trading. First, keep detailed records of every trade: the date of purchase, the purchase price, the number of shares, the date of sale, and the sale price. Most brokers automatically provide this information in year-end Form 1099-B statements, but maintaining your own records provides a useful cross-reference.

Second, be aware of the 12-month holding period that separates short-term from long-term capital gains. As your strategy matures and your holding periods extend (a natural evolution for most developing traders), the tax advantage of long-term capital gains treatment becomes increasingly meaningful. A profitable trade held 367 days is taxed at 0%, 15%, or 20%. The same gain held 363 days is taxed at your ordinary income rate, which may be 22%, 24%, or higher.

Third, understand the wash sale rule before attempting any tax-loss harvesting. Selling a stock at a loss and immediately repurchasing it to generate a tax loss while maintaining market exposure is a common strategy, but the wash sale rule disallows the loss if you repurchase the same or a substantially identical security within 30 days. Plan any tax-loss harvesting with this rule explicitly in mind.

11.8 Your First 30 Days of Live Trading: A Structured Approach

The first 30 days of live trading is the most psychologically intensive period of your entire trading journey. The combination of real financial stakes, the inevitable first real-money losses, and the gap between paper trading expectations and live trading reality creates a unique stress environment that requires specific management.

The following structured approach to the first 30 days is designed to minimize unnecessary psychological pressure while generating the live trading experience and data you need to develop further.

Your First 30 Days of Live Trading: A Structured Plan

Step 1: WEEK 1: SETUP AND ORIENTATION ONLY. After funding your account, spend the first week observing and setting up, not trading. Configure your watchlist in both StockTradesApp.com and your brokerage. Set up any mobile alerts you need. Familiarize yourself with the order entry interface by placing one very small test trade (1 share of a liquid stock) and immediately closing it. Get comfortable with the mechanics of your brokerage before placing any real strategy trades.

Step 2: WEEK 2: FIRST LIVE TRADE, MINIMUM POSITION SIZE. Place your first live strategy trade at 25% of your paper trading position size (or maximum $500 at risk per the recommendations of Chapter 10). Complete the full pre-trade checklist in writing before placing the order. Use a limit order, not a market order. Immediately set a Price Alert in StockTradesApp.com at your stop level. Record everything in your research notes.

Step 3: WEEK 2-3: MAXIMUM TWO OPEN POSITIONS. Limit yourself to a maximum of two simultaneously open live positions during the first two weeks of live trading. Even if your portfolio heat limit allows more, the psychological load of managing multiple live positions simultaneously in the early weeks is more than most beginning traders can handle without letting one position affect their decision-making on another.

Step 4: WEEK 3-4: EVALUATE AND ADJUST. After completing your first two to three live trades (regardless of outcome), conduct a mini-performance review. Did you follow your pre-trade checklist completely? Were stops set immediately? Were limit orders used? Were stops honored within five minutes of alerts firing? If yes across all three, you are applying your process correctly. If no on any item, identify the specific protocol breach and reinforce it before placing more trades.

Step 5: END OF MONTH 1: FORMAL REVIEW. At the end of your first 30 days of live trading, conduct a full performance review using the Chapter 9 framework applied to your live trading data. Compare your live trading win rate, profit factor, and drawdown to your paper trading baseline. Document any significant behavioral differences. Update your written trading rules if any protocol adjustments are warranted based on what you learned about your live trading behavior versus your paper trading behavior.

WHAT TO EXPECT IN THE FIRST 30 DAYS

It is normal for your live trading performance to be weaker than your paper trading performance in the first 30 days. The psychological intensity of real money produces decision-making that is measurably different from paper trading, even for well-prepared traders. Expect this and do not use it as evidence that your strategy is flawed.

The most important outcome of your first 30 days is not a specific return. It is the identification of which specific behaviors differ between your paper trading and your live trading. Those behavioral differences are your development priorities for months two and three of live trading.

If your first 30 days produce a drawdown of more than 5% of your starting live account balance, activate the evaluation protocol from Chapter 10: reduce position size by 50%, conduct a formal trade audit, and do not add new positions until you have identified the specific behavioral cause of the drawdown.

Chapter 11 Summary

Chapter 11 has taken you through the complete practical mechanics of transitioning from paper trading to live trading. Here is what you now carry forward:

- **Three Readiness Thresholds First:** 50 documented paper trades, Profit Factor of 1.3 or above for 4 consecutive weeks, zero stop violations in the last 20 trades. Meeting all three before funding a live account is the highest-return preparation step available.
- **Regulatory Foundation:** All reputable U.S. retail brokers are SIPC-insured (up to $500,000 per customer) and FINRA-registered. Verify both on BrokerCheck at brokercheck.finra.org before opening any account. SIPC covers custody of assets, not investment performance.
- **Seven Broker Selection Criteria:** Regulatory standing (non-negotiable), commission structure (now $0 at most major brokers), platform and charting quality, fractional share availability, customer service quality, interest on uninvested cash, and alignment with your trading style and account size. Fidelity and Charles Schwab consistently rank highest for beginners.
- **Account Type: Taxable Brokerage First:** The standard taxable brokerage account is the correct first live trading account: no contribution limits, no withdrawal restrictions, and straightforward tax treatment. Keep retirement accounts (IRA, 401k) separate and invested in diversified index funds.
- **The Pattern Day Trader Rule:** Four or more day trades in a rolling 5-day period in a margin account triggers PDT classification, requiring $25,000 minimum equity. Beginning live traders should use cash accounts and swing trading approaches to avoid PDT restrictions.

- **Starting Capital: $5,000 to $10,000:** The minimum viable amount that allows meaningful real-money consequences without financial jeopardy. Start with this range, not with larger sums that create disproportionate psychological pressure before live trading experience is established.
- **Order Types Matter:** Market orders guarantee execution, not price. Limit orders guarantee price, not execution. Stop-market orders guarantee exit, not exact price. Stop-limit orders guarantee price, not exit. Use limit orders for entries and stop-market orders for stop-loss exits as your default live trading practice.
- **Tax Awareness from Day One:** Short-term gains (under 12 months) are taxed at ordinary income rates. Long-term gains (over 12 months) at preferential rates of 0%, 15%, or 20%. The wash sale rule disallows losses if you repurchase the same security within 30 days. Keep detailed trade records. Consult a CPA for tax guidance specific to your situation.
- **The First 30 Days: Structure Over Ambition:** Week 1 is setup only. Week 2 introduces the first live trade at 25% of paper trading position size. Weeks 2-3 limit exposure to two simultaneous positions. End of month 1 is a formal performance review. Underperforming your paper trading baseline in the first 30 days is normal and expected. It is information, not failure.

CHAPTER 12

Advanced Horizons: ETFs, Options, and Beyond

"Don't look for the needle in the haystack. Just buy the haystack."

— John C. Bogle, founder of Vanguard and creator of the first index fund for individual investors

By the time you reach Chapter 12, you have completed one of the most comprehensive trader development journeys available to any retail investor: from understanding what a stock is, to reading financial statements, to technical chart analysis, to systematic watchlist building, to rigorous risk management, to paper trading performance review, to the psychology and mechanics of live trading. You have built a complete, functioning framework.

This chapter expands that framework in three directions. First, it introduces exchange-traded funds (ETFs) and index funds in depth, because every serious investor needs to understand both how to trade individual stocks and how to use passive, diversified instruments alongside them. Second, it provides a meaningful introduction to options, specifically the two strategies most relevant to stock traders: the covered call and the protective put. Third, it introduces sector rotation as a portfolio construction discipline that integrates everything you have learned.

The goal of this chapter is not to make you an ETF specialist or an options expert in one sitting. The goal is to give you sufficient understanding to make informed decisions about when and whether these instruments belong in your evolving investment strategy, and to prepare you for the more detailed study that Chapter 14 covers as you continue your development.

12.1 Why Every Stock Trader Needs to Understand ETFs

Throughout this book, StockTradesApp.com has referenced SPY (the S&P 500 ETF) as the primary benchmark against which your paper and live trading performance is measured. You have added ^GSPC (the S&P 500 index) and ^NDX (the NASDAQ-100) to your watchlist as market direction indicators. You have used sector ETFs in the Compare tool to analyze sector rotation. ETFs have been woven into your analytical workflow from Chapter 3 onward.

Now it is time to understand them from the inside: what they are, how they work, why they offer compelling advantages for certain objectives, and how they fit alongside individual stock trading in a complete, mature investment strategy.

> **KEY TERM: Exchange-Traded Fund (ETF)**
> *A type of investment fund that holds a collection of securities (stocks, bonds, commodities, or other assets) and trades on a stock exchange just like an individual share. When you buy one share of SPY, you own a proportional interest in all 500 companies in the S&P 500 index. ETFs combine the diversification benefit of mutual funds with the intraday tradability of individual stocks. The first ETF, the SPDR S&P 500 ETF Trust (SPY), was launched by State Street Global Advisors in January 1993.*

> *"Nothing is simpler than owning the stock market and holding it forever, and that is essentially the idea behind the index fund."*
> — **John C. Bogle**, *The Little Book of Common Sense Investing (2007): Bogle created the first index mutual fund in 1976*

The case for ETFs and index funds is rooted in a simple mathematical reality that Bogle spent decades documenting: the average actively managed fund, after fees, underperforms its benchmark index over long periods. A landmark study by S&P Dow Jones Indices, the SPIVA (S&P Indices Versus Active) Scorecard, has tracked this underperformance for decades. According to SPIVA data, over a 15-year period ending in 2023, approximately 92% of large-cap active fund managers underperformed the S&P 500 after fees. The implication is clear: for the portion of your capital that is not being actively managed with a genuine, documented edge, a low-cost index ETF is likely to outperform the alternatives.

This finding does not mean that active trading is futile. It means that active trading requires a genuine, evidence-based edge (which is precisely what the paper trading performance framework of Chapter 9 is designed to help you build and verify) to justify the additional time, risk, and complexity compared to passive index investing.

92%

of actively managed large-cap U.S. funds underperformed the S&P 500 over a 15-year period ending in 2023, after accounting for fees. The case for low-cost index ETFs as a core portfolio holding is one of the most consistently supported findings in financial research.

Source: S&P Dow Jones Indices SPIVA U.S. Scorecard, Year-End 2023

12.2 ETFs vs. Mutual Funds: Understanding the Key Differences

ETFs and mutual funds are both pooled investment vehicles that provide diversification across many securities. But they operate differently in several important ways that affect cost, tax efficiency, trading flexibility, and minimum investment requirements. Understanding these differences helps you choose the right vehicle for each component of your financial strategy.

Feature	ETF (Exchange-Traded Fund)	Mutual Fund
Trading	Trades throughout the day like a stock. Price updates in real time during market hours.	Priced once per day at market close (NAV). Orders placed during the day all execute at that single end-of-day price.
Minimum Investment	Usually the price of one share (or as little as $1 with fractional shares at most brokers)	Often $1,000 to $3,000 minimum initial investment, though some no-minimum funds exist.
Commission	$0 at most major brokers for stock and ETF trades	Many brokers offer no-transaction-fee (NTF) mutual funds, but some charge transaction fees.
Tax Efficiency	Generally more tax-efficient than mutual funds due to the in-kind creation/redemption mechanism that avoids most capital gains distributions	May generate taxable capital gains distributions to all shareholders, even those who did not sell, due to internal portfolio rebalancing.
Transparency	Holdings disclosed daily by most ETFs	Holdings disclosed quarterly with a delay of up to 60 days for most actively managed funds.

Feature	ETF (Exchange-Traded Fund)	Mutual Fund
Expense Ratio	Ranges from 0.03% (broad index ETFs) to 0.75%+ (specialty or active ETFs)	Ranges from 0.03% (index mutual funds) to 1.5%+ (actively managed funds). Index mutual funds and ETFs have converged in cost.
Best For	Traders who want intraday liquidity, tax efficiency, and low minimums. Also excellent for long-term passive investors.	Long-term passive investors who prefer end-of-day pricing simplicity. Dollar-cost averaging with fractional investments is often easier with traditional mutual funds.

For the active trader using StockTradesApp.com, ETFs are generally the superior choice for any pooled investment in your taxable brokerage account. Their intraday tradability, generally superior tax efficiency, lower minimums, and full transparency make them better aligned with an active trading workflow. Index mutual funds remain excellent choices within tax-advantaged accounts (IRA, 401k) where intraday tradability is irrelevant and the simplicity of dollar-cost averaging at the end of each day is genuinely useful.

12.3 The Core ETF Universe: Your Reference Guide

The ETF market contains more than 3,000 products as of 2026, covering virtually every asset class, sector, geography, factor, and investment strategy imaginable. For the purposes of a stock trader building toward mastery, the relevant universe is much smaller: the handful of broad-market, sector, and thematic ETFs that appear regularly in market analysis, that are used as benchmark and hedging instruments, and that StockTradesApp.com's Terminal fully supports for analysis.

The table below presents the ten most important ETFs for a developing stock trader to understand. These are the instruments you will encounter repeatedly in market commentary, in the Compare tool, in your Watchlist monitoring, and eventually in your own portfolio construction.

Ticker	Full Name	Tracks	Expense Ratio	Best For
SPY	SPDR S&P 500 ETF Trust	S&P 500 index (500 large-cap U.S. stocks)	0.09%	Traders wanting maximum liquidity for the S&P 500. Oldest and most actively traded ETF in the world. Highest volume makes it ideal for short-term trading of broad market exposure.
VOO	Vanguard S&P 500 ETF	S&P 500 index	0.03%	Long-term investors seeking the lowest-cost S&P 500 exposure. Identical holdings to SPY but at one-third the expense ratio. Preferred by buy-and-hold investors over SPY.
QQQ	Invesco QQQ Trust	NASDAQ-100 (100 largest non-financial NASDAQ stocks)	0.20%	Investors seeking concentrated technology and growth exposure. Top 10 holdings represent about 50% of the fund. Higher volatility than SPY/VOO but stronger long-term performance history.
VTI	Vanguard Total Stock Market ETF	Entire U.S. stock market (~3,700 stocks)	0.03%	Maximum U.S. diversification. Includes large, mid, small, and micro-cap stocks. Broader than the S&P 500. Bogle's preferred vehicle for U.S. equity exposure.
IWM	iShares Russell 2000 ETF	Russell 2000 small-cap index (2,000 small-cap U.S. stocks)	0.19%	Investors seeking small-cap exposure or domestic economic growth plays. Higher volatility than SPY. Often used as a leading indicator of economic sentiment.
GLD	SPDR Gold Trust	Physical gold bullion price	0.40%	Portfolio diversification and inflation hedge. Gold frequently moves inversely to equities during risk-off periods. Note: expense ratio is higher than equity ETFs due to physical gold storage costs.
TLT	iShares 20+ Year Treasury Bond ETF	Long-duration U.S. Treasury bonds	0.15%	Fixed income exposure and equity market hedge. Long bonds typically rise when the Federal Reserve cuts rates and fall when rates rise. Important context: the StockTradesApp.com Terminal supports TLT for analysis.
XLK	Technology Select Sector SPDR Fund	Technology sector stocks within the S&P 500	0.09%	Concentrated technology sector exposure without the concentration risk of individual tech stocks. One of the most actively traded sector ETFs.
XLV	Health Care Select Sector SPDR Fund	Healthcare sector stocks within the S&P 500	0.09%	Defensive sector exposure. Healthcare tends to outperform during economic slowdowns as

Ticker	Full Name	Tracks	Expense Ratio	Best For
				spending on health is relatively inelastic.
DIA	SPDR Dow Jones Industrial Average ETF	Dow Jones Industrial Average (30 large U.S. companies)	0.16%	Exposure to the 30 blue-chip companies comprising the Dow Jones. Less diversified than SPY but widely followed as a market barometer.

Sources: ETF provider websites, Morningstar, etf.com. Expense ratios verified as of 2025-2026. Verify current rates directly with fund providers. This table is educational only and does not constitute a recommendation to buy any specific ETF.

Expense Ratios: The Silent Compound Cost

The expense ratio is the annual fee charged by an ETF to cover management and administrative costs, expressed as a percentage of assets under management and deducted automatically from the fund's value on a daily basis. While the differences between ETF expense ratios often look trivially small (0.03% versus 0.09% for S&P 500 exposure), compounding makes these differences meaningful over long time horizons.

On a $100,000 investment generating 8% annually before fees over 30 years, the difference between a 0.03% expense ratio (ending value approximately $983,000) and a 1.0% expense ratio (ending value approximately $761,000) is over $220,000. This example explains why Bogle was so passionate about low-cost investing, and why SPY at 0.09% is perfectly acceptable for traders but VOO at 0.03% is the more rational choice for long-term investors making the same S&P 500 investment.

🖥 PLATFORM FEATURE: Analyzing ETFs in the StockTradesApp.com Terminal

The StockTradesApp.com Terminal fully supports ETF analysis. Type any ETF ticker (SPY, QQQ, VOO, XLK) in the search bar and the Terminal loads the same analysis page as for individual stocks: price chart with SMA20 and SMA50 overlays, RSI (14), MACD (12,26,9), AI Signal banner, Blended Signal score, and News panel.

The Terminal also includes an ETF PROFILE section below the indicators for supported ETFs. This section displays the ETF's category, holdings count, top holdings exposure, and any available fundamental data.

Use the Compare tool (navigation menu: Compare) to overlay multiple sector ETFs (XLK, XLV, XLE, XLF, XLY, XLP, XLI) to conduct the sector rotation analysis described in Chapter

7. The normalized percentage return chart makes it immediately clear which sectors are currently leading and lagging.

12.4 The Portfolio Architecture: Combining Individual Stocks and ETFs

One of the most important strategic decisions any developing trader makes is how to divide their capital between active individual stock positions and passive ETF holdings. This is not a binary choice between being a stock trader and being an index investor. A mature, integrated strategy uses both, with each serving a distinct purpose.

The Core-Satellite Framework

The core-satellite framework is the most widely adopted portfolio architecture among sophisticated retail investors. It divides total investable capital into two components: a core of passive, diversified index ETFs that provide stable, low-cost market exposure, and a satellite of actively selected individual stock positions that seek to generate above-market returns with the analytical edge you have developed through this book.

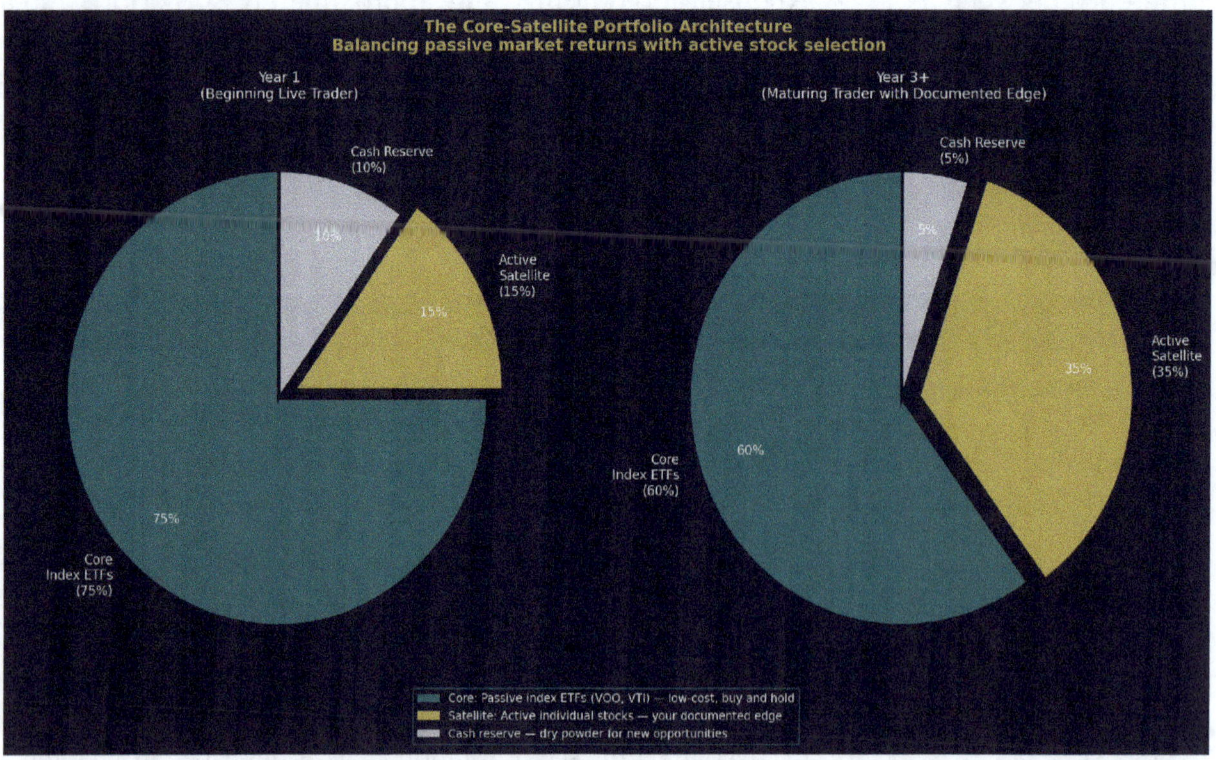

Figure 12.4 — The Core-Satellite Portfolio Architecture: Year 1 (75/15/10) vs Year 3+ (60/35/5) allocation.

- **The Core (60-80% of total capital):** Held in one to three broad index ETFs: typically a U.S. total market fund (VTI), an S&P 500 fund (VOO or SPY), and optionally an international fund. The core is managed passively: buy and hold with periodic rebalancing, not active trading. It ensures that even if the active satellite produces modest results, the portfolio as a whole participates in broad market returns.
- **The Satellite (20-40% of total capital):** The active trading portion: individual stock positions selected through the systematic fundamental and technical research process from Chapters 5 through 9, managed with the risk management framework from Chapter 8, monitored through StockTradesApp.com. The satellite is where your analytical edge expresses itself. It should generate meaningful alpha (above-market return) to justify the additional time, complexity, and risk compared to simply holding the core.

The practical benefit of this architecture is that it manages the psychological reality of active trading more effectively than an all-or-nothing approach. When the active satellite goes through a losing streak (which every strategy does), the stable core provides a psychological anchor and a performance floor. When the satellite generates strong returns, the portfolio significantly outperforms a pure passive approach.

SIZING THE SATELLITE APPROPRIATELY

The satellite portion of your portfolio should never exceed your ability to actively manage it with full attention. A satellite of 20 to 30% of total capital with three to five simultaneous stock positions represents a manageable active workload for a beginning live trader who has a full-time career outside of trading.

As your live trading experience grows and your paper-to-live performance gap closes, the satellite can expand. Experienced traders who have built a genuine, documented edge over 12 to 18 months of live trading may allocate 40% or more to their active satellite. But this expansion should follow demonstrated performance, not precede it.

Never allocate more than 20% of total investable capital to the active satellite during your first year of live trading. The core provides the performance floor that prevents a difficult first live trading year from being catastrophic to your overall wealth-building trajectory.

12.5 Sector Rotation: The Macro Layer of Stock Selection

You were introduced to sector rotation in Chapter 7 as a sourcing tool for your individual stock watchlist. This section expands that framework into a complete portfolio discipline that operates at the intersection of individual stock selection and ETF portfolio management.

Sector rotation is the systematic practice of overweighting the sectors of the market that are most likely to outperform in the current economic environment, and underweighting or avoiding sectors that are least likely to do so. It is not market timing, which requires predicting market direction with precision. It is economic cycle awareness, which requires only a reasonable understanding of which phase of the business cycle the economy is currently in.

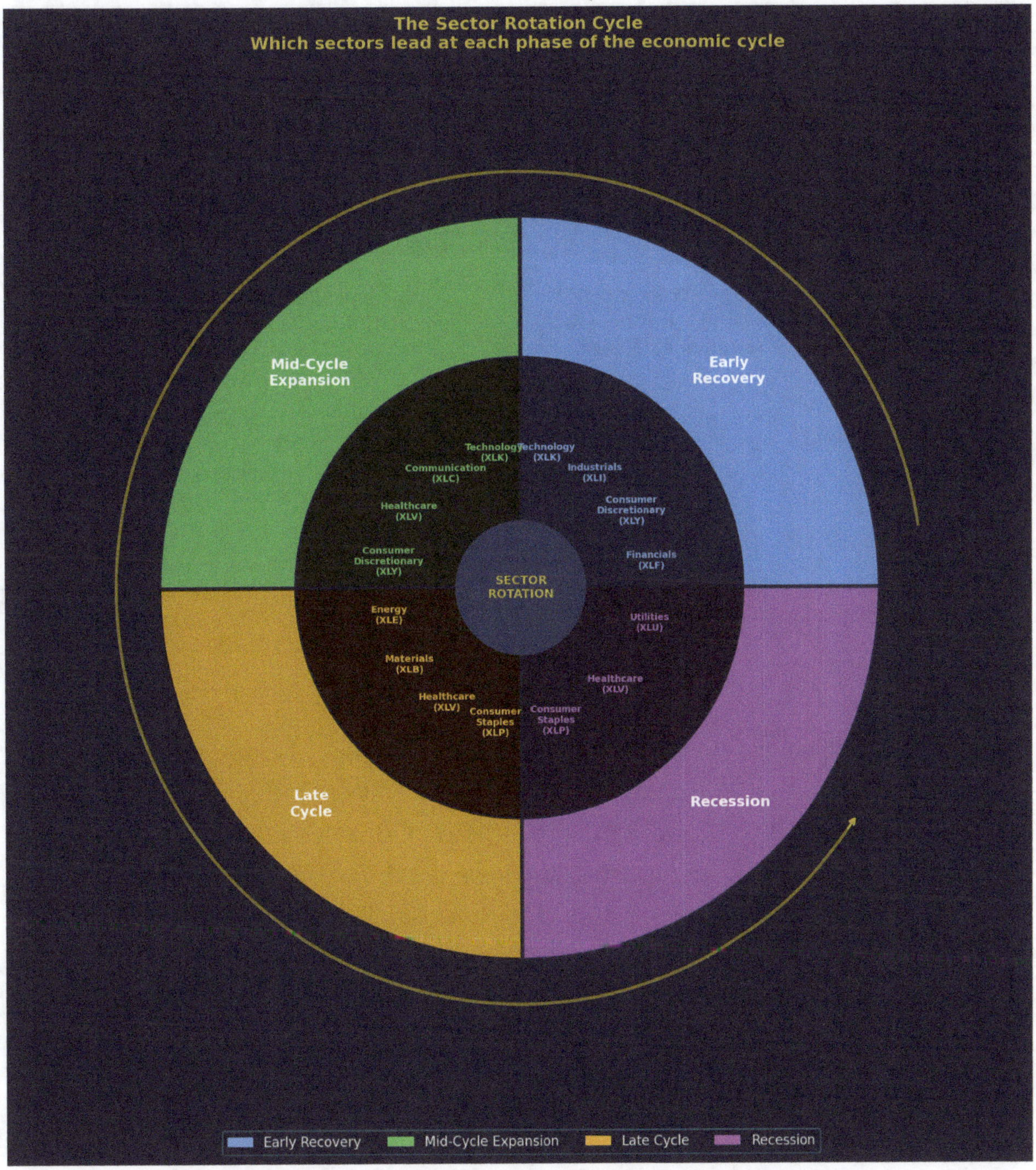

Figure 12.5 — The Sector Rotation Cycle: Different sectors lead at each phase of the economic cycle.

Economic Phase	Typical Sector Leaders	Rationale
Early Recovery (rates falling,	Financials (XLF), Consumer Discretionary (XLY),	Lower interest rates reduce borrowing costs for businesses and consumers. Cyclical

Economic Phase	Typical Sector Leaders	Rationale
growth accelerating)	Industrials (XLI), Technology (XLK)	sectors with high economic sensitivity tend to lead as growth accelerates from a trough.
Mid-Cycle Expansion (sustained growth, moderate inflation)	Technology (XLK), Communication Services (XLC), Healthcare (XLV), Consumer Discretionary (XLY)	The longest and most productive phase for equities. Growth stocks outperform as earnings expand broadly. Technology in particular tends to compound well during sustained expansions.
Late Cycle (growth slowing, inflation rising)	Energy (XLE), Materials (XLB), Healthcare (XLV), Consumer Staples (XLP)	As growth peaks, commodity-related sectors benefit from rising input prices. Defensive sectors attract capital as investors rotate away from cyclicals into more stable cash flows.
Recession (contraction, falling interest rates)	Consumer Staples (XLP), Healthcare (XLV), Utilities (XLU)	Demand for food, medicine, and essential utilities is relatively inelastic. These sectors generate stable earnings regardless of economic conditions and often pay reliable dividends.
Early Recovery begins again	Financials (XLF), Industrials (XLI) lead the next cycle	The cycle repeats. Understanding where the economy is in the cycle does not require perfect prediction. Even rough positioning in the right sectors adds meaningful return over time.

The practical implementation of sector rotation in your portfolio: use the Compare tool in StockTradesApp.com to overlay the major sector ETFs (XLK, XLV, XLF, XLE, XLY, XLP, XLI, XLU, XLB, XLC, XLRE) with a 3MO and 6MO time frame. The sectors showing the strongest relative performance over both periods are currently in favor. Direct a higher proportion of your individual stock satellite toward names within those leading sectors. Underweight or avoid stocks in the sectors showing the weakest relative performance.

This top-down approach does not guarantee outperformance, but it does ensure that you are trading in the direction of institutional money flows rather than against them. A stock with an excellent individual setup in a sector that is currently out of favor faces a significant headwind that a stock with an equally good setup in a leading sector does not.

12.6 Introduction to Options: What Every Stock Trader Should Understand

Options are financial contracts that give the buyer the right, but not the obligation, to buy or sell an underlying security at a predetermined price before a specified expiration date. They are among the most powerful and most frequently misused instruments in the retail investing universe.

The purpose of this section is not to make you an options trader. Options trading, particularly complex multi-leg strategies, requires significant additional study beyond this book. The purpose is to give you sufficient understanding of two options strategies that are directly relevant to stock traders: the covered call (for generating income from existing stock positions) and the protective put (for insuring existing stock positions against large losses). Both are covered in the table below alongside the foundational vocabulary you need to understand how options work.

A CRITICAL WARNING BEFORE READING FURTHER

Options involve significant risk and are not appropriate for all investors. Unlike stocks, options can expire worthless, resulting in the total loss of the premium paid. Certain options strategies involve unlimited or very large potential losses.

Before trading options in a live account, you must apply for and receive options trading approval from your broker. Brokers require you to demonstrate knowledge and financial suitability before granting options access. Most brokers offer options approval levels from Level 1 (covered calls and cash-secured puts only) to Level 4 (naked options, which carry unlimited risk).

This chapter covers options at the introductory level. Before implementing any options strategy with real capital, study the OCC's (Options Clearing Corporation) publication "Characteristics and Risks of Standardized Options" (available free at theocc.com), and consider completing a structured options education course from your broker or from the CBOE Institute (cboe.com). This book is not a substitute for that specialized education.

With that important context established, the following table covers the nine most essential options concepts for stock traders, each explained in plain English with a concrete Apple (AAPL) example.

Options Concept	Plain-English Definition	Example
Call Option	The right (not obligation) to BUY 100 shares of a stock at a specific price (the strike price) by a specific date (the expiration date). Buyers of calls	You buy a call option on AAPL with a \$200 strike price expiring in 30 days, paying a \$3.00 premium per share (\$300 total for 100 shares). If AAPL rises to

Options Concept	Plain-English Definition	Example
	profit when the stock rises above the strike price. Sellers of calls collect premium income in exchange for the obligation to sell shares if exercised.	$210 before expiration, your call is worth at least $10 per share ($1,000 total), a gain of $700. If AAPL stays below $200, the option expires worthless and you lose the $300 premium.
Put Option	The right (not obligation) to SELL 100 shares of a stock at the strike price by the expiration date. Buyers of puts profit when the stock falls below the strike price. Puts are often used as portfolio insurance.	You buy a put option on AAPL with a $190 strike price expiring in 30 days, paying a $2.50 premium ($250 total). If AAPL falls to $175, your put is worth at least $15 per share ($1,500 total), a gain of $1,250. If AAPL stays above $190, the put expires worthless and you lose the $250 premium.
Strike Price	The pre-agreed price at which the option gives the buyer the right to buy (call) or sell (put) the underlying stock.	An AAPL $200 call has a strike price of $200. If you exercise this call, you buy AAPL at $200 per share regardless of the current market price.
Expiration Date	The date on which the option contract expires. After this date, the option is worthless if not exercised or sold. Options exist in weekly, monthly, and LEAPS (up to 2-year) maturities.	A "30-day option" typically refers to a contract expiring at market close on the third Friday of the current or next month. As expiration approaches, time value erodes (theta decay).
Premium	The price the buyer pays to the seller for the option contract. The premium is determined by intrinsic value (how far the option is in-the-money) plus time value (how much time remains) plus implied volatility.	An AAPL $200 call expiring in 30 days might trade at a premium of $3.00 per share, or $300 for one contract covering 100 shares. This $300 is the maximum loss for the buyer and the immediate income for the seller.
Covered Call	Selling a call option on shares you already own. Generates premium income in exchange for capping your upside above the strike price. The strategy works best in flat or slowly rising markets.	You own 100 shares of AAPL at $190. You sell one $200 call expiring in 30 days and collect $300 in premium. If AAPL stays below $200, you keep the $300 and your shares. If AAPL rises above $200, your shares are called away at $200, but you still keep the $300 premium plus the gain from $190 to $200.
Protective Put	Buying a put option on shares you already own, functioning as portfolio insurance. Limits your downside below the strike price in exchange for the premium cost.	You own 100 shares of AAPL at $190. You buy one $180 put expiring in 60 days, paying $250 in premium. If AAPL falls to $150, your put limits your loss to $10 per share (from $190 to $180) plus the $250 premium, rather than the full $40 decline you would experience without the put.
In-the-Money (ITM)	A call is in-the-money when the stock price is ABOVE the strike price. A put is in-the-money when the stock price is BELOW the strike price. ITM options have intrinsic value.	An AAPL $180 call when AAPL trades at $195 is $15 in-the-money. The intrinsic value is $15 per share.

Options Concept	Plain-English Definition	Example
Out-of-the-Money (OTM)	A call is out-of-the-money when the stock price is BELOW the strike price. A put is out-of-the-money when the stock price is ABOVE the strike price. OTM options have zero intrinsic value, only time value.	An AAPL $220 call when AAPL trades at $195 is $25 out-of-the-money. The entire premium is time value and implied volatility premium.

The Covered Call: The Most Conservative Options Strategy for Stock Owners

Of all the options strategies available, the covered call is the one most directly relevant to the stock trader who has followed the process in this book. It is the only options strategy that is purely income-generating rather than speculative, and it is the only strategy that requires only existing stock holdings, not additional capital.

The mechanics: you own 100 shares of a stock. You sell one call option contract at a strike price above the current stock price, collecting the premium. If the stock stays below the strike price through expiration, the option expires worthless and you keep both your shares and the premium, which represents additional income on top of any dividends the stock pays. If the stock rises above the strike price, your shares may be called away (purchased by the option buyer at the strike price), but you still keep the premium plus the gain from your purchase price to the strike price.

The covered call is appropriate in one specific market environment: when you own a stock you are happy to hold for the medium term, when you do not expect a dramatic near-term price move, and when you would be satisfied selling the stock at the strike price if the option is exercised. It is not appropriate for stocks you believe are about to make a significant move upward, because the covered call caps your upside at the strike price and eliminates your participation in gains above it.

The Protective Put: Portfolio Insurance for Stock Owners

The protective put is the purchase of a put option on shares you already own, functioning as insurance against a significant price decline. Like any insurance, it costs a premium, and like any insurance, it only pays off in a scenario you hope does not occur.

The appropriate use of a protective put: you hold a significant stock position heading into a high-risk event (an earnings report, a regulatory decision, a macro catalyst) where the potential downside is large but you do not want to sell the position because you believe in the long-term thesis. A put at a strike price 5 to 10% below the current price gives you a defined floor below which your loss cannot exceed, regardless of how far the stock falls.

The cost of this insurance (the put premium) is the trade-off. If the stock does not fall, the put expires worthless and the premium represents a cost. If the stock falls significantly, the put provides meaningful protection. Whether this cost is justified depends on the specific risk event, the cost of the put relative to the position size, and your overall risk tolerance.

OPTIONS AND STOCKTRADESAPP.COM

The StockTradesApp.com Terminal currently supports analysis of the underlying stocks and ETFs on which options are traded. The platform's Blended Signal, RSI, MACD, and trend analysis can inform your assessment of the underlying stock's direction, which is the most important input to any options decision.

For dedicated options analysis (pricing, Greeks, options chains), you will need the options tools available within your live brokerage account. Fidelity, Schwab, and E*TRADE all provide comprehensive options chain data and options analysis tools within their platforms. Interactive Brokers and thinkorswim (Schwab) are particularly well-regarded for advanced options analysis.

As your skills develop and your account grows, the StockTradesApp.com analysis provides the stock-level conviction layer, while your brokerage's options tools provide the options-specific execution layer. This two-platform workflow mirrors how most professional individual traders operate.

12.7 Building Toward a Complete Portfolio Strategy

Chapter 12 has introduced three significant expansions to your trading and investing framework: the role of ETFs and index funds, the introduction of covered calls and protective puts, and the sector rotation discipline that bridges individual stock selection and portfolio-level management. The question now is how these pieces fit together with everything you have learned across the previous eleven chapters.

The answer is a tiered, integrated portfolio strategy that allocates capital based on evidence of edge, manages risk at the portfolio level rather than only at the position level, and evolves systematically as your skills and account size develop.

Tier 1: The Foundation (Core ETF Portfolio)

The core ETF portfolio forms the foundation. It holds 60 to 80% of your total investable capital in two or three broad index ETFs (VTI or VOO for U.S. equity market exposure, and optionally an international fund such as VXUS for global diversification). It is managed passively: no active trading, only periodic rebalancing (once or twice per year) to maintain target allocations. It competes with your active satellite for capital, so any expansion of the satellite reduces the core and vice versa.

Tier 2: The Active Satellite (Individual Stocks)

The active satellite holds 20 to 40% of total capital in individual stock positions selected through the systematic process of this book. It is managed actively using all the tools from Chapters 5 through 9: fundamental research, technical analysis, systematic watchlist management, risk management rules, and weekly performance review. Every position in the satellite represents a deliberate bet that your analytical edge has identified a stock that will outperform the broad market over the holding period.

Tier 3: Options Overlay (Income and Protection)

As your stock positions in Tier 2 mature and your understanding of options deepens (through the additional study recommended in Section 12.6), a selective options overlay can be added. Covered calls on larger positions in flat market environments generate premium income. Protective puts on significant positions heading into high-risk events limit catastrophic loss. This tier is optional and should be implemented only after completing dedicated options education.

Chapter 12 Exercise: Building Your Integrated Portfolio Framework

Step 1: CORE ETF ALLOCATION: Determine what percentage of your total investable capital you will allocate to the core ETF portfolio. Write this down as a specific target. For most beginning traders with under two years of live trading experience, this should be at least 70%. Identify which one or two ETFs will serve as your core: VTI for total U.S. market exposure, VOO for S&P 500 exposure, or a combination.

Step 2: SATELLITE SIZING: Determine what percentage of total capital will form your active satellite. This should not exceed 30% for beginning live traders. Confirm this allocation is consistent with your risk tolerance and with the maximum drawdown your portfolio can absorb if the satellite experiences a 20% drawdown.

Step 3: SECTOR ROTATION ASSESSMENT: Open the Compare tool in StockTradesApp.com and add the major sector ETFs: XLK, XLV, XLF, XLE, XLY, XLP, XLI. Set the time frame to 6MO. Identify the top two and bottom two sectors by relative performance. Record your sector rotation view: which sectors are you overweighting in your individual stock satellite and which are you underweighting?

Step 4: ETF ANALYSIS PRACTICE: Search for SPY, VOO, and QQQ in the StockTradesApp.com Terminal. For each, review the Blended Signal, the chart with SMA overlays, and the AI Signal banner. Compare their current technical postures. Are all three aligned in the same direction? Record your observations as context for the broader market environment.

Step 5: OPTIONS AWARENESS: Review the options vocabulary table in Section 12.6. Identify whether you currently own any stock positions in your paper trading or live portfolio that would make a covered call logically sensible (stock you hold, flat or slightly rising market, happy to sell at a slightly higher price). Calculate what premium income a hypothetical covered call 5-10% above the current price would generate. Note this as a future tool to explore when you have completed dedicated options education.

Step 6: PORTFOLIO DOCUMENTATION: Write a one-page Portfolio Strategy Statement that captures your current core-satellite allocation, your sector rotation view, your active satellite watchlist tier structure from Chapter 7, and your risk management parameters from Chapter 8. This document is your evolving investment policy statement, the written framework that governs how you allocate and manage capital across all three portfolio tiers.

Chapter 12 Summary

Chapter 12 has expanded your toolkit beyond individual stocks into the broader landscape of exchange-traded funds, sector rotation, and options. Here is what you now carry forward:

- **The Case for ETFs is Empirically Strong:** 92% of actively managed large-cap funds underperformed the S&P 500 over 15 years after fees (SPIVA 2023). Low-cost index ETFs represent the most reliable way to capture market returns for capital not being managed with a genuine, documented active edge.
- **ETFs vs. Mutual Funds:** ETFs offer intraday tradability, lower minimums, generally superior tax efficiency, and full daily transparency. Mutual funds offer simplicity in dollar-cost averaging and are well-suited for tax-advantaged retirement accounts. For active traders with taxable brokerage accounts, ETFs are generally the better choice for any pooled investment.
- **Ten Core ETFs to Know:** SPY (S&P 500, maximum liquidity), VOO (S&P 500, lowest cost for long-term investors), QQQ (NASDAQ-100, technology focus), VTI (total U.S. market), IWM (small caps), GLD (gold), TLT (long-duration bonds), XLK (technology sector), XLV (healthcare sector), and DIA (Dow Jones). These ten cover

the instruments you will encounter most frequently in analysis and portfolio construction.

- **Expense Ratios Compound Over Time:** The difference between 0.03% and 1.0% annual expense ratio on $100,000 over 30 years exceeds $220,000 in terminal value. Always minimize expense ratios in passive portfolio components.
- **The Core-Satellite Framework:** 60-80% in passive index ETFs (the core), 20-40% in actively selected individual stocks (the satellite). The core provides stable market returns and a psychological anchor during active trading drawdowns. The satellite is where your analytical edge generates potential alpha.
- **Sector Rotation Integrates Macro and Stock Selection:** Four economic cycle phases (Early Recovery, Mid-Cycle Expansion, Late Cycle, Recession) correspond to different sector leadership patterns. Aligning your individual stock satellite with currently leading sectors reduces headwinds and increases the probability that institutional money flows support your positions.
- **Options: Two Strategies for Stock Traders:** The covered call generates premium income on existing stock positions in flat or slowly rising markets, at the cost of capping upside above the strike price. The protective put insures existing positions against large declines before high-risk events, at the cost of the put premium. Neither should be implemented without dedicated options education beyond this chapter.

CHAPTER 13

The Lifelong Trader: Building a Sustainable Daily Practice

"The secret of getting ahead is getting started. The secret of getting started is breaking your complex, overwhelming tasks into small manageable tasks, and then starting on the first one."

— Attributed to Mark Twain

There is a version of trading education that ends with a set of analytical tools and risk management rules and leaves the reader to figure out the rest. This book takes a different approach. Chapter 13 is devoted to the practice layer that makes all the technical knowledge in previous chapters actually work over time: the daily routine, the journaling discipline, the continuous education habits, the community and mentorship structures, and the long-term mindset that separates traders who steadily improve over years from those who plateau after their initial learning phase.

Mastery in trading is not a state you reach. It is a direction you travel. The tools, the rules, the frameworks, and the psychological infrastructure you have built across twelve chapters are not a destination. They are the foundation of a practice. How consistently and deliberately you maintain that practice determines where your trading journey takes you over the next decade.

This chapter gives you the structure to maintain that practice. It is the chapter about the work after the reading is done.

> *"In my experience, the single most important factor separating the traders who made it from those who did not was not intelligence, capital, or access to information. It was consistency. The ones who showed up with the same discipline every single day, in good markets and bad, in winning months and losing months."*
>
> — **Jack D. Schwager**, *Market Wizards series (1989-2012): based on interviews with over 50 of the world's most successful traders*

13.1 Why Routine Is the Foundation of Consistent Performance

Every professional in a complex, performance-driven domain, from elite athletes to surgeons to concert musicians, maintains a structured daily routine. Not because the routine itself produces excellence, but because the routine creates the consistent conditions under which excellence can be practiced and developed. Trading is no different.

Without a structured daily routine, trading becomes reactive: you check prices when something feels interesting, you research stocks when you happen to have time, you review performance when the results are good enough to look at, and you journal occasionally when a trade feels worth documenting. This reactive approach produces an inconsistent skill development trajectory. The knowledge compounds slowly because the practice is fragmented.

A structured trading routine does four things: it ensures that preparation always precedes action, it creates regular feedback loops through systematic review, it builds the habitual processes that eventually operate automatically rather than requiring conscious effort, and it protects against the psychological degradation that occurs when traders engage with markets impulsively rather than intentionally.

Session Block	Time Allocation	Activities
Pre-Market Preparation	15-20 minutes before 9:30 AM ET	Review Dashboard equity and open positions. Check Watchlist Live Signals for overnight changes. Read macro news headlines (Fed, economic data, earnings). Check Alerts for any triggered overnight levels. Write the session intention: what are you watching for today and under what conditions will you act?
Active Session Monitoring	As needed during 9:30 AM to 4:00 PM ET	Honor stop alerts within five minutes. Check Tier 1 watchlist stocks at logical intervals (not every price tick). Avoid new entries in the first and last 30 minutes of the session unless a pre-planned setup triggers. Execute exactly one discretionary research task during the session.
Post-Market Review	15-30 minutes after 4:00 PM close	Journal any trades placed or closed today. Run one AI Screener prompt to refresh the Tier 2/3 watchlist pipeline. Complete one Terminal deep-dive on a candidate. Update stop alerts for any positions that moved significantly intraday.

Session Block	Time Allocation	Activities
Weekly Deep Research	45-60 minutes, one session per week	Full sector rotation review via Compare tool. Performance metrics review on Dashboard. Pre-trade documentation for any Tier 1 setups planning for the coming week. Read one financial chapter or research paper. Update Portfolio Strategy Statement if any allocation changes are warranted.
Monthly Performance Audit	90-120 minutes, once per month	Formal performance review using the Chapter 9 framework. Behavioral pattern diagnosis. Strategy refinement assessment. Compare live trading metrics to paper trading baseline. Update Investor Identity Statement. Set the single most important process improvement goal for the coming month.

The total active time commitment in this routine is approximately 30 to 45 minutes on standard trading days, 45 to 60 minutes on days with significant positions or market events, and one 45 to 60 minute weekly session. This is not a part-time job. It is a disciplined practice that fits alongside any full-time career.

THE MINIMUM VIABLE ROUTINE FOR BUSY PROFESSIONALS

Not every trader has 45 minutes available before the market opens. For professionals with highly constrained schedules, the minimum viable routine is: five minutes on the Dashboard each morning to check alerts and equity, one limit order set the previous evening for any planned entry, and one 20-minute weekly review session on Saturday or Sunday.

This stripped-down routine sacrifices some analytical depth in exchange for sustainability. A routine you maintain every week for two years produces more skill development than an ambitious routine you maintain for three weeks and then abandon.

The goal is to find the minimum routine you can realistically sustain seven days a week, not the maximum routine you can sustain for one exceptional week.

13.2 The Trading Journal: Your Most Valuable Long-Term Asset

If you ask experienced traders to identify the single practice that contributed most to their long-term development, the trading journal is cited more frequently than any other. More than reading books. More than watching markets. More than conversations with other traders. The journal is the practice that closes the learning loop between action and improvement.

The reason the journal is so powerful is that it externalizes and makes permanent the internal reasoning process behind each trade. Without a journal, the reasoning behind every trade, the thesis, the entry logic, the exit plan, evaporates within hours or days of the trade closing. The journal preserves that reasoning as a data point that can be compared against outcomes, analyzed for patterns, and applied to future decisions.

Research on reflective learning, particularly work by Harvard Business School professor Giada Di Stefano and colleagues published in Psychological Science (2016), found that individuals who spent time reflecting on what they had learned after a task performed 23 percent better on subsequent identical tasks than those who simply practiced the task repeatedly without structured reflection. The trading journal is the structural implementation of this finding.

Journal Entry Type	What to Record and Why
Pre-Trade Documentation	Ticker, date, entry price, stop price, target price, risk per trade ($), R:R ratio, share count, total position value, Blended Signal at entry, the fundamental thesis in 2-3 sentences, the technical setup description (stage, trend, support level, indicator readings), and the one condition that would invalidate the thesis.
Post-Trade Review (Win)	Actual exit price, actual profit in dollars and percentage, number of R-multiples captured, how the actual outcome compared to the pre-trade plan. Did you exit at the target, or early? If early: what emotional state prompted the early exit? What would the outcome have been had you held to the target?
Post-Trade Review (Loss)	Actual exit price, actual loss in dollars and percentage. Was the stop honored immediately? Was the loss within the 1% rule? Was the stop at the original structural level or was it moved? One sentence on what the chart was telling you that you may have missed in the pre-trade analysis.
Market Observation Entry	A daily note (3-5 sentences) on current market conditions: the S&P 500 trend, sector rotation observations from the Compare tool, any significant macro news, and the overall trading environment. This creates a longitudinal record of market conditions that gives context to future trade reviews.
Pattern Recognition Note	When you notice a setup, indicator reading, or market behavior pattern that you want to remember and study further. These notes become your personal pattern library, an evolving record of what you are learning to see in markets.
Monthly Strategy Reflection	A longer entry (one to two pages) reviewing the month: what worked, what did not, what behavioral patterns emerged, what you learned, and what the single most important development priority is for the coming month. This is your most valuable journal entry type because it forces synthesis rather than mere record-keeping.

PLATFORM FEATURE: Using Your Research Notes Alongside StockTradesApp.com

StockTradesApp.com's Dashboard and Terminal provide real-time data, but your personal research notes (maintained separately in a notebook, digital document, or dedicated journaling app) provide the narrative context that performance data alone cannot capture.

Many experienced traders use a split-screen approach during their review sessions: the Dashboard open on one side of the screen showing performance metrics and equity curve, and their personal research notes open on the other side. This pairing of quantitative data with qualitative narrative produces the richest possible post-trade analysis.

For the monthly strategy reflection, export or screenshot your Dashboard PERFORMANCE metrics as a baseline record for that month. Attach or reference this screenshot in your monthly journal entry so that future readings have the exact performance data from that period alongside the narrative context you wrote at the time.

13.3 Continuous Education: The Compounding Knowledge Base

The analytical landscape of financial markets is not static. Monetary policy regimes shift. New industries emerge and old ones decline. Regulatory frameworks change. The statistical patterns in price data evolve as more market participants adopt the same analytical frameworks. The trader who stops learning when they finish this book will find their edge eroding within two to three years, not because their skills declined, but because the market environment around those skills changed.

Continuous education is not the same as continuous information consumption. Reading every financial article, watching every market commentary video, and following every market commentator on social media is information consumption, not education. True education is deliberate, focused, and designed to expand specific aspects of your analytical or psychological capabilities.

> *"I am not a genius. I am just passionately curious."*
>
> — **Albert Einstein**, *widely attributed, reflecting the disposition that characterizes the world's most effective continuous learners*

The Three Levels of Continuous Education

- **Level 1: Foundational Depth.** Rereading and deepening your understanding of the core texts that underpin your strategy. Returning to The Intelligent Investor after twelve months of live trading experience will reveal insights you could not access as a beginner. Rereading this book after your first year of live trading will produce a completely different reading experience. Foundational texts yield new understanding at every stage of development.
- **Level 2: Domain Expansion.** Adding new analytical tools and instruments to your repertoire in a deliberate, sequential manner. Options study after mastering individual stocks. Sector analysis in greater depth. Macroeconomic frameworks for understanding interest rate cycles. Each addition should be motivated by a specific gap in your current framework, not by general curiosity or novelty.
- **Level 3: Market History.** Studying historical market cycles, crashes, bubbles, recoveries, and the conditions that produced them. The trader who has studied the 1929 crash, the dot-com bubble, the 2008 financial crisis, and the 2020 pandemic selloff and recovery has a pattern library of extreme market behavior that no amount of recent price chart study can provide. Market history is the compressed experience of a century of collective human behavior in financial markets.

The recommended reading list below covers the ten books most directly relevant to the framework you have built in this book. These are not supplementary reading. They are the next layer of a compounding knowledge base that will deepen and refine your understanding over the coming years.

Book	Author / Year	Why It Belongs in Every Trader's Library
The Intelligent Investor	Benjamin Graham (1949)	The foundational text of value investing and margin of safety. Warren Buffett has called it "by far the best book on investing ever written." Chapter 8 (The Investor and Market Fluctuations) alone is worth the entire book.
How to Make Money in Stocks	William J. O'Neil (1988)	The definitive guide to the CAN SLIM growth stock methodology. Practical, data-driven, and directly applicable to the technical and fundamental framework you have built in this book.
Market Wizards	Jack D. Schwager (1989)	Interviews with the greatest traders of the 20th century: Paul Tudor Jones, Ed Seykota, Richard Dennis, Marty Schwartz, and others. Invaluable

Book	Author / Year	Why It Belongs in Every Trader's Library
		for understanding the diversity of successful approaches and the psychological threads common to all of them.
Trading in the Zone	Mark Douglas (2000)	The most widely recommended book on trading psychology. Addresses the gap between knowing a strategy and executing it consistently under real-money conditions.
Trade Your Way to Financial Freedom	Dr. Van K. Tharp (1998)	The definitive text on position sizing, expectancy, and system development. The source of the 1% rule, portfolio heat concepts, and expectancy framework used throughout this book.
One Up on Wall Street	Peter Lynch (1989)	Lynch's investment philosophy grounded in everyday consumer observation and fundamental analysis. Accessible, practical, and a masterclass in finding great businesses before Wall Street does.
The Little Book of Common Sense Investing	John C. Bogle (2007)	Bogle's definitive case for index funds. Essential counterbalance to active trading enthusiasm. Every active trader should understand the argument they are competing against.
Technical Analysis of the Financial Markets	John J. Murphy (1999)	The standard reference text of technical analysis. Comprehensive, rigorous, and the intellectual foundation of Chapters 6 and beyond in this book.
Reminiscences of a Stock Operator	Edwin Lefevre (1923)	The fictionalized memoir of Jesse Livermore. Over a century old and still the most instructive narrative account of trading psychology ever written.
Common Stocks and Uncommon Profits	Philip Fisher (1958)	The qualitative counterpart to Graham's quantitative approach. Fisher's fifteen questions for evaluating a business remain the gold standard for qualitative fundamental analysis.

StockTradesApp.com's Learn Hub as a Continuous Reference

The Learn Hub (navigation menu: Learn) serves as your in-platform continuous education resource. Its seven categories (Market Basics, Stocks, ETFs and Funds, Options, Retirement, Personal Finance, and Glossary) are refreshed by AI as market knowledge evolves, providing current, jargon-free explanations of concepts at every level of sophistication.

A practical continuous education habit: each week, identify one concept from your trading activity (a technical indicator reading you are less certain about, a fundamental metric you want to understand more deeply, a market event you want to contextualize) and search for it in the Learn Hub. Read the relevant lesson, then verify and expand your understanding against one of the foundational texts in the reading list above. This two-layer approach, platform lesson plus authoritative text, produces faster and more durable learning than either source alone.

13.4 Community, Mentorship, and Peer Learning

Trading is largely a solitary activity, and the isolation that comes with independent decision-making under uncertainty is one of the underappreciated psychological challenges of the profession. The trader who learns and practices entirely in isolation misses one of the most powerful accelerants of skill development: exposure to the analytical frameworks, decision-making patterns, and hard-won experience of other serious practitioners.

Finding the Right Community

The retail trading community spans an enormous quality range, from highly disciplined, evidence-based practitioners who will sharpen your analytical thinking to momentum-chasing social media communities that will actively damage your development by promoting impulsive, high-risk behaviors. Choosing the right community is as important as choosing the right books.

The characteristics of a high-quality trading community are consistent. Members discuss process rather than outcomes: they talk about what they looked for before entering a trade, not just whether it worked. They acknowledge losses openly and analyze their causes. They cite evidence for their views rather than asserting confident predictions. They demonstrate awareness of their own biases and limitations. They engage with opposing views thoughtfully rather than dismissing them.

Communities built around trading education platforms, investing books, and structured skill development (rather than around hot stocks, recent performance, or social media influencer figures) tend to produce these characteristics. The American Association of Individual Investors (AAII), the CFA Institute community for those pursuing formal credentials, and book-focused communities such as the Bogleheads forum represent examples of the quality range to aim for.

The Value of a Mentor

A mentor with genuine, long-term trading experience represents the single highest-leverage investment a developing trader can make in their education. A skilled mentor can identify patterns in your decision-making that your own journaling and performance review cannot surface, because they have an external perspective on your process that you inherently cannot have yourself.

Finding a genuine trading mentor requires the same research discipline as finding any other high-quality resource. Look for someone with a documented, multi-year track record rather than a recent winning period. Look for humility about their limitations alongside confidence in their approach. Look for someone who emphasizes process and risk management as much as returns. Be skeptical of anyone who charges high fees for "trading signals" or who emphasizes winning percentages without discussing losing trade management.

GIVING BACK: TEACHING ACCELERATES LEARNING

One of the most consistently documented accelerators of learning in complex domains is teaching what you know to others. Richard Feynman, the Nobel Prize-winning physicist, developed what became known as the Feynman Technique: to truly understand something, try to explain it in simple terms as if teaching a child. The gaps in your explanation reveal the gaps in your understanding.

For developing traders, teaching manifests as explaining a trade setup to a peer before entering it, writing up analysis for a trading study group, or mentoring someone who is earlier in their development journey than you are. Each of these activities forces a level of clarity and precision in your thinking that solitary study does not.

StockTradesApp.com's WALKTHROUGH tab in the Terminal is, in a sense, a built-in teaching tool: it explains the logic behind the current signal step by step. Reading it and then trying to explain that logic in your own words to another person, or in your trading journal, is one of the most effective ways to deepen your analytical vocabulary.

13.5 Adapting to Market Cycles: The Long-Term Perspective

Every trading strategy that works does so within a specific market regime: a set of conditions (trend direction, volatility level, interest rate environment, liquidity conditions) that favor the approach. No strategy works equally well in all market environments. Understanding this is not a limitation to be frustrated by. It is a reality to be managed through adaptability.

The most durable trading practitioners are not those who found a perfect strategy and executed it unchanged for decades. They are those who developed a deep enough understanding of market structure and their own psychological patterns that they could adapt their approach as conditions evolved, without abandoning their core principles of risk management, systematic process, and continuous improvement.

> *"The markets are always changing, and the successful trader needs to adapt to these changes. The key is to remain humble, remain curious, and remain disciplined. The moment you think you have figured it all out is the most dangerous moment of your career."*
>
> — **Ray Dalio, founder of Bridgewater Associates**, *widely paraphrased from Principles (2017) and various interviews*

Four Market Regimes and Their Implications

- **Trending Bull Market (sustained upward price movement with low volatility):** The most favorable environment for momentum-based growth stock strategies. CAN SLIM setups and breakout entries work well. The challenge is not finding opportunities but not overextending during the inevitable corrections within the broader uptrend.
- **Choppy or Sideways Market (no clear trend, high false breakout frequency):** The most challenging environment for trend-following strategies. Breakouts fail frequently. Range-bound conditions favor mean-reversion approaches and more conservative position sizing. Recognize this regime quickly and reduce trading activity rather than forcing setups that do not meet your criteria.
- **Trending Bear Market (sustained downward price movement):** Individual stock strategies become extremely difficult. Capital preservation takes priority. The core ETF portfolio provides a natural hedge (by going to cash within the core allocation during severe declines) and patience becomes the primary skill. Some traders switch to cash-rich defensive positions or reduce the satellite to near zero during confirmed bear markets.
- **High-Volatility Event-Driven Market (sharp moves triggered by macro events):** Requires reduced position sizes (smaller than your normal 1% risk per trade) to account for wider-than-normal stop distances. Pre-planned entries become essential because emotional decision-making during high-volatility events is particularly costly. The post-loss cooldown protocol from Chapter 10 is most important in this regime.

The regime awareness practice: during your weekly review session, classify the current market environment into one of these four categories based on the S&P 500 chart and the Blended Signal of ^GSPC in the StockTradesApp.com Terminal. Note the classification in your weekly journal entry. Over time, you will build a longitudinal record of regime changes and your strategy's performance across each, which becomes the most powerful data for your long-term strategy evolution.

13.6 The Five-Year Development Arc

To close Chapter 13, it is worth painting the trajectory that consistent application of this book's framework typically produces over a five-year period. This is not a guarantee or a prediction. It is a calibrated expectation based on the documented development patterns of traders who combine systematic education, deliberate practice, disciplined risk management, and rigorous performance review.

- **Year 1: Foundation and Discipline.** The paper trading phase generates your initial edge assessment. Live trading begins at minimum position sizes. The primary development goal is consistent rule compliance: every pre-trade checklist completed, every stop honored, every position correctly sized. Returns may be modest or even slightly negative. The goal is building the process infrastructure, not generating returns.
- **Year 2: Edge Clarification and Scaling.** The first meaningful sample of live trading data clarifies which specific setups and market conditions your strategy handles best. Position sizes begin to scale toward the 1% rule consistently. Win rate and profit factor stabilize. The satellite allocation grows modestly as documented performance supports it.
- **Year 3: Strategy Refinement and Consistency.** The strategy is refined based on two years of live data. Secondary skills (options basics, sector rotation) are incorporated deliberately. The daily routine becomes habitual rather than effortful. Monthly performance reviews are faster and more diagnostic. The gap between intended behavior and actual behavior narrows significantly.
- **Year 4: Performance Maturation.** Above-market returns become measurably consistent over rolling 12-month periods. The satellite allocation has grown in proportion to documented performance. Mentorship becomes bidirectional: you begin contributing to others' development. The psychological challenges of live trading are familiar rather than surprising.

- **Year 5 and Beyond: Compounding Mastery.** The combination of compounding capital, compounding skills, and compounding pattern recognition produces a self-reinforcing upward spiral. The portfolio architecture evolves to match your specific strengths. The daily practice is sustainable enough to be maintained indefinitely, not as a burden but as a genuinely engaging professional discipline.

THE HONEST CAVEAT: NOT EVERYONE FOLLOWS THIS ARC

This five-year arc describes the trajectory available to traders who maintain consistent process discipline, conduct genuine performance reviews, adapt their strategy based on evidence, and manage their psychology with the tools from Chapter 10. It does not describe the trajectory of all traders.

Research consistently shows that the majority of retail traders do not maintain this level of consistency. They abandon strategies during losing streaks, increase position sizes during winning streaks, skip the performance review process, and allow emotional reactions to override their rules. These are the traders who plateau.

The single most reliable predictor of which trajectory a developing trader follows is not intelligence, market access, or starting capital. It is the consistency of the practice habits described in this chapter. The daily routine. The journal. The weekly review. The continuous education. These habits are the mechanism through which knowledge converts into skill.

13.7 Chapter 13 Exercise: Building Your Personal Practice System

The following exercise builds the structural components of your long-term trading practice. Each step produces a tangible document or system that you will use from this point forward in your trading career.

Personal Practice System Exercise

Step 1: DESIGN YOUR DAILY ROUTINE. Based on your actual schedule, write a realistic daily trading routine using the five session blocks from Section 13.1 as a template. Be honest about your time constraints. Define the minimum viable version of each block that you can realistically sustain every single day. Write this routine as a concrete schedule and post it somewhere visible near your trading workspace.

Step 2: SET UP YOUR JOURNAL SYSTEM. Choose your journal format: a physical notebook, a digital document (Notion, Word, Google Docs), or a dedicated journaling application. Create the six entry types from Section 13.2 as templates: pre-trade documentation, post-trade review (win), post-trade review (loss), market observation, pattern recognition, and monthly strategy reflection. Complete one entry of each type today, using a recent paper or live trade and your current market observations.

Step 3: BUILD YOUR READING QUEUE. From the ten-book reading list in Section 13.3, select the two books you will read first. Order them or locate them at your local library. Set a reading goal of at least 20 pages per week. Write the book titles and your start date commitment in your journal.

Step 4: IDENTIFY YOUR COMMUNITY. Research two or three communities of serious investors that meet the quality criteria in Section 13.4. Consider the AAII (aaii.com) for structured investment education, the Bogleheads forum for index investing community, and any structured trading education community you have access to. Commit to active participation (asking questions, sharing analysis, engaging with others' ideas) in at least one community consistently.

Step 5: ASSESS YOUR CURRENT MARKET REGIME. Open the StockTradesApp.com Terminal and search for ^GSPC (S&P 500). Review the 6-month chart. Based on the price structure, moving average position, and Blended Signal, classify the current market regime using the four categories from Section 13.5. Write a two-paragraph regime assessment in your journal, noting which aspects of your strategy are most and least well-suited to the current environment.

Step 6: WRITE YOUR FIVE-YEAR INTENTION STATEMENT. Write one page describing where you intend to be in your trading and investing practice in five years. Be specific about your target portfolio size, your target active satellite allocation, the specific skills you intend to develop, and the role trading will play in your broader financial life. Keep this document alongside your Investor Identity Statement from Chapter 2. Return to both documents annually to assess progress and revise intentions.

Chapter 13 Summary

Chapter 13 has given you the practice infrastructure that converts analytical knowledge into compounding skill over a career. Here is what you now carry forward:

- **Routine Is the Foundation:** A structured daily routine of five session blocks (pre-market, active session, post-market, weekly deep research, monthly audit) creates the consistent conditions for deliberate practice. The minimum viable routine (five minutes daily, one 20-minute weekly session) is more valuable than an ambitious routine that gets abandoned.
- **The Journal Is Your Most Valuable Asset:** Six entry types (pre-trade documentation, win review, loss review, market observation, pattern recognition, and monthly reflection) create a longitudinal record of your reasoning and its

outcomes. Research by Di Stefano et al. (Psychological Science, 2016) confirms that structured reflection after practice produces 23% better performance on subsequent identical tasks.

- **Continuous Education Has Three Levels:** Foundational depth (rereading core texts at each new experience level), domain expansion (deliberate addition of new analytical tools), and market history (studying historical cycles and extreme market events). The ten-book reading list provides a structured starting point for this lifelong curriculum.
- **Community and Mentorship Accelerate Development:** High-quality communities discuss process rather than outcomes, acknowledge losses openly, and cite evidence for their views. A genuine mentor with a documented multi-year track record provides an external perspective on your process that solitary journaling cannot. Teaching others accelerates your own learning through the Feynman Technique.
- **Four Market Regimes Require Different Approaches:** Trending bull (momentum-friendly), choppy sideways (reduce activity), trending bear (capital preservation), and high-volatility event-driven (reduce position sizes). Classifying the current regime in your weekly journal creates a longitudinal record of performance across different market environments.
- **The Five-Year Development Arc:** Year 1 (foundation and discipline), Year 2 (edge clarification and scaling), Year 3 (strategy refinement), Year 4 (performance maturation), Year 5 and beyond (compounding mastery). The trajectory is available to traders who maintain the practice habits in this chapter. The single most reliable predictor of trajectory is not intelligence or capital but consistency of practice.

CHAPTER 14

Advanced Strategies: Options, ETF Trading, and Expanding the Toolkit

"Options are not inherently risky. What is risky is not understanding what you own."

— Lawrence McMillan, Options as a Strategic Investment (1993): the standard reference text of options trading

Chapter 12 introduced options and ETFs at the conceptual level, giving you enough vocabulary and framework to make informed decisions about whether these instruments belong in your evolving strategy. Chapter 14 goes significantly deeper. It is designed for traders who have completed their first year of documented live trading, who have met the three readiness thresholds from Chapter 9, and who are ready to expand their analytical toolkit beyond individual stocks.

This chapter covers seven options strategies in a structured framework, the five options Greeks that every serious options trader must understand, five specific ways to trade ETFs as active instruments rather than passive holdings, and a structured approach to deciding when and how to incorporate each of these advanced tools into your existing strategy. The goal is depth over breadth: enough understanding to trade each strategy safely, not a superficial survey that leaves you unable to apply what you have read.

One important reaffirmation: the risk warning from Chapter 12 remains fully in force. Options involve significant risk and require broker approval. Before trading any options strategy beyond a covered call or protective put in a live account, complete the OCC's Characteristics and Risks of Standardized Options (theocc.com) and your broker's options education curriculum. This chapter is educational preparation, not a substitute for that structured pre-approval education.

14.1 The Options Prerequisite: What You Must Know Before Trading

Before studying options strategies and Greeks, it is worth being explicit about the knowledge and experience prerequisites that make options trading safe and productive rather than dangerous and expensive.

- **Individual Stock Proficiency:** You should have a documented track record of at least 50 live stock trades with positive expectancy over a meaningful period. Options involve an additional layer of complexity (expiration, Greeks, implied volatility) that compound any weaknesses in your underlying stock analysis. An unreliable stock selection process becomes even more unreliable as an options strategy.
- **Position Sizing Mastery:** Your 1% rule application should be automatic, not effortful. Options risk is expressed differently from stock risk (maximum loss is the premium for buyers, potentially much larger for sellers), which requires confident fluency with position sizing concepts before adding options-specific sizing complexity.
- **Broker Approval:** Most brokers tier their options approvals. Level 1 (covered calls, cash-secured puts) requires the least experience. Level 2 (long calls and puts) requires more. Level 3 and 4 (spreads, naked options) require the most. Apply for the approval level appropriate to the strategies in this chapter and complete your broker's required education before executing any live options trade.
- **Dedicated Options Education:** Beyond this chapter, complete at minimum the CBOE Institute's free options education curriculum at cboe.com and read the OCC's Characteristics and Risks of Standardized Options. Consider Lawrence McMillan's Options as a Strategic Investment for comprehensive depth.

THE OPTIONS APPROVAL PROCESS: WHAT TO EXPECT

When you apply for options trading approval at your broker, you will be asked to provide information about your investment experience (years of investing, types of investments held), your financial situation (income, net worth, liquid net worth), and your investment objectives (income, growth, speculation).

Based on your responses, the broker assigns you a tier level (typically Level 1 through 4, though nomenclature varies by broker). Level 1 typically allows covered calls and cash-secured puts. Level 2 adds long calls and puts. Level 3 adds spreads. Level 4 adds naked short options, which carry unlimited theoretical risk and are not appropriate for retail traders at any experience level.

The strategies in this chapter are appropriate for Level 1 and Level 2 approval. The spreads (bull call spread, bear put spread) in the strategies table require Level 3 at most brokers. Apply for the level that matches your documented experience and financial profile honestly.

14.2 Seven Options Strategies: A Structured Framework

Chapter 12 introduced the covered call and protective put as the two options strategies most immediately relevant to stock traders. This section expands that foundation to seven strategies, organized from the most conservative and income-focused to the more directional and leverage-oriented. Each strategy has a specific market outlook it is designed to express and a defined risk profile that makes it appropriate or inappropriate for a given situation.

Strategy	Position Type	Market Outlook	Risk Profile
Long Call	Buy a call option	Bullish: expect stock to rise significantly above strike price before expiration	Limited loss (premium paid). Unlimited profit potential above the strike. High probability of total loss if stock does not move sufficiently.
Long Put	Buy a put option	Bearish: expect stock to fall significantly below strike price before expiration	Limited loss (premium paid). Large profit potential if stock falls sharply. Often used as portfolio insurance on existing holdings.
Covered Call	Own 100 shares + sell 1 call	Neutral to mildly bullish: stock expected to be flat or rise slowly	Income generation (premium collected). Upside capped at strike price. Downside is owning the stock (same as without the option, minus the premium cushion).
Cash-Secured Put	Sell 1 put, hold cash to cover assignment	Neutral to mildly bullish: willing to buy the stock at the strike price	Income generation (premium collected). If stock falls below strike, you are obligated to buy 100 shares at strike price. Best used on stocks you genuinely want to own at the strike price.
Protective Put	Own 100 shares + buy 1 put	Uncertain or bearish in short term, bullish long term	Insurance: limits downside below the strike price. Cost is the premium, which reduces net return from the stock

Strategy	Position Type	Market Outlook	Risk Profile
			position. Acts as a floor on potential losses.
Bull Call Spread	Buy 1 lower strike call + sell 1 higher strike call	Moderately bullish: expect stock to rise to but not far above the higher strike	Lower cost than a long call (premium received from the sold call offsets cost of the bought call). Maximum profit capped at the spread between strikes. Maximum loss is the net premium paid.
Bear Put Spread	Buy 1 higher strike put + sell 1 lower strike put	Moderately bearish: expect stock to fall to but not far below the lower strike	Lower cost than a long put. Maximum profit capped. Maximum loss is the net premium paid. Useful when you expect a moderate decline rather than a collapse.

Strategy Selection: Matching the Tool to the Market View

The most common error beginning options traders make is selecting a strategy based on its complexity or its potential profit rather than its alignment with their specific market view. The correct approach is the reverse: start with a clear view on the stock's direction and magnitude of expected move, then identify which strategy expresses that view most efficiently given the current implied volatility environment.

- **Strongly bullish with a defined time horizon:** Long call option or bull call spread (if you want to reduce cost).
- **Strongly bearish with a defined time horizon:** Long put option or bear put spread (if you want to reduce cost).
- **Neutral to mildly bullish, income-focused, stock already owned:** Covered call.
- **Neutral to mildly bullish, income-focused, would happily buy stock at lower price:** Cash-secured put.
- **Existing position needs insurance before a specific risk event:** Protective put.

The bull call spread and bear put spread in the table represent a meaningful step up in complexity from the single-leg strategies. They involve two option legs (buying one option and selling another simultaneously) and require Level 3 approval at most brokers. Their primary advantage is reduced cost compared to a single long call or put.

Their primary limitation is that profit is capped at the spread between the two strike prices. They are appropriate when you have a moderate directional view and want to reduce the premium cost of expressing it.

14.3 The Options Greeks: Understanding What Drives Option Prices

One of the most common mistakes beginning options traders make is buying an option on a stock that subsequently moves in the right direction, only to find that the option barely increased in value or actually decreased. This confusion disappears once you understand the Greeks: the five mathematical sensitivities that determine how an option's price responds to changes in the underlying stock, time, and volatility.

The Greeks are not abstract academic concepts. They are the practical inputs that determine whether an options trade is structured efficiently for its intended purpose. A trader who does not understand Theta will repeatedly overpay for options that decay rapidly. A trader who does not understand Vega will be repeatedly caught by volatility collapses after earnings announcements.

Greek	Symbol	What It Measures and Why It Matters
Delta	Δ (Delta)	The rate of change in option price per $1 move in the underlying stock. A delta of 0.50 means the option moves approximately $0.50 for every $1 the stock moves. Call deltas range from 0 to 1.0; put deltas range from -1.0 to 0. At-the-money options have deltas near 0.50. Deep in-the-money options approach 1.0. Delta is also roughly the probability that an option expires in-the-money.
Theta	Θ (Theta)	Time decay. The rate at which an option loses value each day purely due to the passage of time, holding all else constant. Theta is negative for option buyers (time works against you) and positive for option sellers (time works in your favor). An option with a theta of -0.05 loses approximately $0.05 per day from time decay alone. Theta accelerates dramatically in the final 30 days before expiration.
Gamma	Γ (Gamma)	The rate of change in Delta per $1 move in the underlying stock. High gamma means your position's delta changes rapidly as the stock moves, making the position more sensitive to large moves. At-the-money options near expiration have the highest gamma. Gamma risk is the primary reason why very short-dated options (weekly options) carry dramatically more risk than longer-dated ones for the same premium.

Greek	Symbol	What It Measures and Why It Matters
Vega	ν (Vega)	Sensitivity to implied volatility. For every 1% increase in implied volatility, Vega shows how much the option price changes. Long option positions benefit from rising implied volatility (your option becomes more valuable). Short option positions are hurt by rising implied volatility. Understanding Vega is essential for avoiding the trap of buying options just before a volatility collapse (such as immediately after an earnings release).
Rho	ρ (Rho)	Sensitivity to interest rate changes. For most short-dated retail options strategies, Rho is the least important Greek and can generally be ignored in early-stage options learning. It becomes relevant for longer-dated options (LEAPS) and in high-interest-rate environments.

The Three Most Important Greeks for Beginning Options Traders

While all five Greeks matter, three deserve particular focus for traders in their first year of options use.

Delta is your first priority because it tells you how much your option moves per dollar move in the stock. It is the most direct connection between your stock analysis (which is strong) and your options position (which is new). When you buy a call with a delta of 0.40, you need the stock to move more than the premium cost divided by 0.40 to profit at expiration.

Theta is your second priority because it represents the constant, daily erosion of your purchased option's value. Every day that passes without the expected move occurring costs you money. Beginning options buyers systematically underestimate theta's impact, particularly when buying options with less than 30 days to expiration. As a general guideline for option buyers: prefer options with at least 45 to 60 days to expiration to give your thesis adequate time to develop without losing excessive value to time decay.

Vega is your third priority because it explains the "volatility crush" phenomenon that regularly destroys option buyers who purchase options before earnings announcements without understanding implied volatility dynamics. Before a known catalyst (earnings, FDA decision, product launch), implied volatility rises, inflating option premiums above their fair value. Immediately after the catalyst, implied volatility collapses regardless of the stock's direction, causing option prices to fall sharply even if the stock moved in the direction you expected. This "buy the rumor, sell the news" effect in options pricing is one of the most expensive education taxes beginners pay.

THE IMPLIED VOLATILITY RULE FOR EARNINGS TRADES

The most reliable rule for beginning options traders around earnings announcements: do not buy options in the final week before earnings. The implied volatility premium embedded in the option price is almost always too high relative to the actual move that occurs, resulting in a loss even when your directional prediction is correct.

If you want to trade a stock around earnings, consider a defined-risk spread (buying one strike, selling another) rather than a single long option, as the spread structure partially hedges the volatility crush. Better still, wait until after the earnings announcement for the implied volatility to normalize, and then use standard technical analysis to find your entry in the stock itself rather than through options.

Your StockTradesApp.com Terminal's AI Earnings Briefing button (available on the Terminal page for any stock) provides a plain-English summary of the most recent earnings report, which is valuable input for assessing whether a post-earnings options entry makes sense based on the quality and surprise factor of the results.

14.4 Advanced ETF Trading: Five Active Strategies

Chapter 12 introduced ETFs primarily as passive portfolio components: buy-and-hold instruments for the core portfolio allocation. This section introduces five ways to trade ETFs actively, applying the same technical analysis framework from Chapter 6 and the same risk management rules from Chapter 8 to ETF price action rather than individual stock price action.

Active ETF trading offers several advantages over individual stock trading that make it particularly valuable for certain situations: elimination of single company fundamental risk (earnings surprises, management failures, product failures), higher liquidity and tighter spreads than most individual stocks, and the ability to express macro or sector views without the research burden of individual stock selection.

ETF Trading Strategy	Description and Application
Index ETF Trend Following	Using SPY or QQQ as a direct trading vehicle rather than purely as a benchmark or portfolio holding. When the S&P 500 is in a confirmed Stage 2 uptrend (above its 50-day and 200-day SMA, Blended Signal positive), a long position in SPY captures broad market gains with a single, highly liquid instrument. Risk management rules (1% position sizing, structural stop below the 50-day SMA) apply identically to ETF trades as to individual stocks.

ETF Trading Strategy	Description and Application
Sector ETF Rotation Trading	Rather than selecting individual stocks within a leading sector, buying the sector ETF directly. If Technology (XLK) is showing the strongest relative performance on the Compare tool and the sector is in a Stage 2 uptrend, buying XLK provides diversified exposure to the entire sector without single-stock risk. The entry, stop, and target logic from Chapters 6 and 8 applies directly.
Volatility-Adjusted Sizing for ETFs	Because broad ETFs like SPY have lower volatility than individual stocks, the same percentage stop distance covers less absolute dollar risk, allowing for larger share counts within the 1% rule. An 8% stop on an individual stock represents normal position risk. An 8% stop on SPY would be unusually wide given the index's historical volatility. Adjust stop distances to reflect the ETF's actual typical range.
ETF Pair Trading (Compare Tool Application)	Using the Compare tool to identify a leading sector ETF and a lagging one, then going long the leader and reducing exposure to the lagger. This relative-strength approach captures the rotation between sectors without requiring prediction of absolute market direction. StockTradesApp.com's Compare tool makes this analysis straightforward with its normalized percentage return view.
Bond/Equity Rotation	Monitoring TLT (long-term Treasury bonds) alongside SPY on the Compare tool. When the economy is decelerating and the Fed is cutting rates, TLT tends to rise as SPY falls. Rotating a portion of the core portfolio from equity ETFs to TLT during confirmed risk-off periods is a macro-driven defense strategy used by institutional investors and accessible to retail traders through the same simple ETF mechanics.

🖥️ PLATFORM FEATURE: ETF Analysis on stocktradesapp.com

The StockTradesApp.com Terminal supports full technical analysis of all major ETFs. Type any ETF ticker in the search bar and the Terminal loads the price chart with SMA20 and SMA50 overlays, RSI (14), MACD (12,26,9), AI Signal banner, Blended Signal score, and News panel.

For sector rotation analysis, open the Compare tool (navigation menu: Compare) and add XLK, XLV, XLF, XLE, XLY, XLP, XLI, and XLU. Set the time frame to 3MO and 6MO. The normalized return chart immediately shows which sectors are leading and lagging.

Add SPY, QQQ, and any actively traded ETFs to your Watchlist alongside your individual stock positions. The Watchlist Live Signals panel on the Dashboard shows all of them together with their current Blended Signals, giving you a holistic view of your monitored universe across both individual stocks and ETFs.

14.5 Retirement Accounts: Roth IRA, Traditional IRA, and 401(k) Strategy

Chapter 11 introduced the major account types and recommended a taxable brokerage account as the primary vehicle for your active trading. This section revisits retirement accounts with greater depth, because a complete advanced investment strategy integrates active trading in a taxable account with disciplined, long-term wealth building in tax-advantaged retirement accounts.

The two most powerful retirement account vehicles for most U.S. investors in their working years are the Roth IRA and the 401(k) with employer match. They serve complementary purposes and together form the foundation of a complete wealth-building strategy that exists alongside, not instead of, active trading.

The Roth IRA: Tax-Free Growth

Contributions to a Roth IRA are made with after-tax dollars, meaning you receive no tax deduction in the year of contribution. The power of the Roth is what happens afterward: all growth and qualified withdrawals are completely tax-free. A $7,000 contribution to a Roth IRA at age 25 that grows to $75,000 by age 65 (at 6% annual return) produces $68,000 in completely tax-free growth. There is no required minimum distribution, which makes the Roth an exceptional vehicle for long-term wealth compounding.

The strategic use of the Roth IRA for active traders: some traders use their Roth IRA for longer-term, fundamentally strong stock positions (one to three year holds) where the tax-free growth compounds most powerfully. This does not mean day trading inside a Roth, which generates frequent short-term gains that forfeit the long-term compounding advantage. It means holding genuinely high-conviction positions for longer than you might in a taxable account, because there is no capital gains tax on the eventual sale.

Income limits apply to direct Roth IRA contributions. As of 2025, the ability to contribute directly begins phasing out at $150,000 in modified adjusted gross income for single filers ($236,000 for married filing jointly). Above these thresholds, the Backdoor Roth IRA conversion strategy is available but requires consultation with a CPA due to the pro-rata rule. Verify current limits with your financial advisor.

The 401(k) with Employer Match: The Immediate Return

The 401(k) employer match is the highest guaranteed return available to any investor. If your employer matches 50% of your contributions up to 6% of your salary, every dollar you contribute receives an immediate 50% return before it is invested. No investment strategy produces this kind of guaranteed, immediate gain on capital.

The fundamental rule: always contribute enough to your 401(k) to capture the full employer match before allocating any additional capital to active trading. This is not a philosophical preference. It is a mathematical certainty. No active trading result has ever consistently matched the risk-adjusted return of a 50% or 100% employer match on the first dollars contributed.

Beyond the match, 401(k) investment options are typically limited to a fund menu selected by the employer. For most investors, the optimal strategy within the 401(k) is three-fund simplicity: a total U.S. stock market index fund, an international stock index fund, and a bond index fund in proportions appropriate to your time horizon and risk tolerance. Keep the 401(k) passive and let your active satellite in the taxable brokerage account do the active work.

14.6 Chapter 14 Exercise: Integrating the Advanced Toolkit

The following exercise integrates the concepts from this chapter into your existing strategy framework. Complete each step only if you meet the prerequisites from Section 14.1. If you have not yet met those prerequisites, bookmark this exercise and return to it after completing your first year of live trading.

Advanced Toolkit Integration Exercise

Step 1: OPTIONS APPROVAL ASSESSMENT: Log in to your live brokerage account and check your current options approval level. If you do not yet have options approval, review the broker's application requirements and determine whether your documented experience and financial profile qualify you for Level 1 or Level 2 approval. Complete any required broker education modules before applying.

Step 2: PAPER TRADE A COVERED CALL: In StockTradesApp.com's Paper section, identify a stock in your paper portfolio where you hold 100 or more virtual shares. Research the options chain for that stock in your brokerage account (or a financial data source). Identify a call option 5-10% above the current price expiring in approximately 30 days. Calculate the premium income that selling this call would generate. Record the delta, theta, and premium in your journal as a paper trade observation (you cannot place the option in StockTradesApp.com paper trading, but you can document and track it manually).

Step 3: ETF TREND ANALYSIS: Open the Terminal and search for SPY. Apply the Chapter 6 pre-trade checklist to SPY as if it were an individual stock. What stage is SPY in? Where is it relative to its 50-day and 200-day SMA? What are the RSI and MACD reading? What would a 1% risk trade in SPY look like (entry, stop at the 50-day SMA or below recent support, position size calculation)?

Step 4: SECTOR ROTATION DEEP DIVE: Open the Compare tool and add all 11 sector ETFs (XLK, XLV, XLF, XLE, XLY, XLP, XLI, XLU, XLB, XLC, XLRE). Set the time frame to 6MO. Rank the sectors from strongest to weakest relative performance. Write a two-paragraph sector rotation assessment: which two sectors are you overweighting in your individual stock satellite based on this analysis, and which two are you underweighting?

Step 5: RETIREMENT ACCOUNT AUDIT: Review your current retirement account status. Are you contributing to a 401(k)? Are you capturing the full employer match? Do you have a Roth IRA open and funded? Calculate how much additional annual contribution you could make to tax-advantaged accounts within IRS limits. Write a one-paragraph retirement account action plan identifying any gaps between your current contributions and the optimum described in Section 14.5.

Step 6: ADVANCED STRATEGY SELECTION: For each of the five ETF active trading strategies in Section 14.4, write one sentence explaining whether and why each strategy fits your current skill level, risk tolerance, and market view. For each that you identify as appropriate for your next six months, write a specific plan: which ETF, what trigger condition, what position size, what stop level.

Chapter 14 Summary

Chapter 14 has expanded your toolkit into the advanced instruments that characterize a mature, diversified investment and trading strategy. Here is what you now carry forward:

- **Options Prerequisites First:** Individual stock proficiency with a documented track record, position sizing mastery, broker approval at the appropriate level, and completion of the OCC and CBOE Institute education curricula. Options compound the consequences of any weaknesses in your underlying stock process.
- **Seven Options Strategies:** Long Call, Long Put, Covered Call, Cash-Secured Put, Protective Put, Bull Call Spread, and Bear Put Spread. Each is matched to a specific market outlook and risk profile. The selection principle: start with your market view

and find the strategy that expresses it most efficiently, not the strategy that seems most sophisticated.

- **Five Options Greeks:** Delta (price sensitivity), Theta (time decay), Gamma (rate of delta change), Vega (implied volatility sensitivity), and Rho (interest rate sensitivity). Delta, Theta, and Vega are the three most important for beginning options traders. The Vega warning: buying options before earnings announcements without understanding implied volatility crush is one of the most common and expensive beginner errors.
- **Five Active ETF Strategies:** Index ETF trend following, sector ETF rotation trading, volatility-adjusted sizing, ETF pair trading via the Compare tool, and bond/equity rotation. All apply the same technical analysis and risk management framework from earlier chapters. ETF trading eliminates single-company risk while retaining directional and sector exposure.
- **Retirement Accounts as a Parallel Strategy:** The 401(k) employer match is the highest guaranteed return available: always maximize it before allocating to active trading. The Roth IRA provides tax-free growth for long-term positions. Keep retirement accounts passively managed with index funds; let the active satellite in your taxable brokerage account do the active work.

CHAPTER 15

The Mastery Mindset: Trading as a Lifelong Discipline

"The more I learn, the more I realize how much I don't know."
— **Albert Einstein, widely attributed**

You have reached the final chapter of Stock Trades: From Beginner to Mastery. Over the preceding fourteen chapters, you built the complete architecture of a disciplined, systematic trading and investing practice: the foundational knowledge of how markets work, the analytical tools of fundamental and technical analysis, the systematic research process of a professional watchlist, the risk management framework that protects capital through inevitable adversity, the performance review discipline that converts experience into improvement, the psychological infrastructure of live trading, the practical mechanics of brokerage accounts and tax awareness, and the advanced instruments of ETFs, options, and sector rotation.

Chapter 15 does not introduce new tools. It introduces the frame within which all those tools operate for a lifetime: the mindset of mastery. Mastery in trading is not a credential you earn or a level you reach. It is a posture you adopt toward the practice itself: one of permanent curiosity, honest self-assessment, disciplined process adherence, and genuine respect for the difficulty and depth of what you are doing.

This chapter is the most personal in the book. It is about why you are doing this, what kind of trader and investor you are becoming, and how to sustain the practice long enough for compounding to work its transformative effects on both your capital and your capability.

> *"There are no secrets to success. It is the result of preparation, hard work, and learning from failure."*
> — **Colin Powell**, *My American Journey (1995)*

15.1 What Mastery Actually Means in Trading

The word mastery carries cultural associations that can mislead: the master as someone who has completed their learning, who performs without error, who no longer faces significant challenges. None of these associations apply to trading mastery.

In trading, mastery is not the absence of losses. Every master trader loses on a substantial percentage of their trades. It is not the absence of uncertainty. Markets are irreducibly uncertain, and the best traders acknowledge rather than deny this. It is not the achievement of a specific return target. Exceptional returns are achieved in some years and not in others by even the greatest practitioners.

Trading mastery is something more practical and more durable: the consistent application of a sound, evidence-based process across all market conditions, combined with the psychological stability to maintain that process under the emotional pressures of real money, genuine uncertainty, and the inevitable adversity of losing streaks. It is competence plus character. It is knowing what to do and being reliably able to do it when the conditions make it hardest.

> *"I have learned through bitter experience the one cardinal rule of saving face: to wit, if you must be wrong, be wrong as quickly as possible."*
> — **Paul Tudor Jones**, *Market Wizards by Jack D. Schwager (1989)*

This definition of mastery has a specific practical implication: it is achievable. Not because trading is easy, but because the process of building it is clear, the evidence base for what works is substantial, and the primary obstacles are behavioral rather than intellectual. The ideas in this book are not secrets known only to professionals. They are well-documented, widely available principles that most retail traders do not apply consistently. The gap between knowing these principles and applying them consistently is where mastery is built.

15.2 The Seven Principles of the Mastery Mindset

The following seven principles are not additions to the technical framework you have built. They are the philosophical foundation that makes the technical framework sustainable over a lifetime of practice. Each represents a deeper understanding of a concept that appeared in earlier chapters, elevated from a rule to follow to a belief to embody.

Mastery Principle	The Deeper Understanding
Process Precedes Outcome	Every profitable trade that resulted from a flawed process is a debt to be repaid. Every losing trade that resulted from a sound process is tuition paid on the path to mastery. Evaluating your trades by outcome alone is the most reliable way to remain a beginner. Evaluating them by process fidelity is what produces compounding improvement.
Humility Is Operational	The market is always right. Your thesis is always provisional. The moment you become certain about what a stock will do, you have stopped being an analyst and started being an advocate. The most dangerous words in trading are "I know this is going to work." The most protective words are "based on current evidence, this is the most probable outcome, and if I am wrong, here is where I will exit."
Losses Are Information	A stop-loss that fires is not a failure. It is the risk management framework working exactly as designed. Every stop-loss honestly honored removes a would-be catastrophic loss from your future. The traders who avoid all losses are the traders who let losses grow unchecked. The traders who honor every stop convert inevitable losses into the manageable, defined expenses of running a trading business.
Patience Is a Strategy	Most of the alpha in active trading comes from a small number of high-conviction setups. Waiting for those setups without forcing trades in between is not passivity. It is the most active form of discipline available. Jesse Livermore, one of the greatest traders in history, wrote that "it was never my thinking that made the big money for me. It was always my sitting."
Volatility Is Not Risk	True risk is permanent loss of capital: holding a deteriorating position past your stop because you cannot accept the loss. The short-term price volatility of a well-managed position with a defined stop is not risk. It is the normal noise of markets doing what markets do. Confusing volatility with risk leads to premature exits from well-structured positions and to the disposition effect that plagues most retail traders.
The Market Will Always Be There	One of the most productive beliefs a trader can internalize is that there will always be another setup. Missing a trade, whether because you were too cautious or because you did not act fast enough, is not a loss. It is an opportunity deferred. The traders who chase missed setups, who increase position sizes to compensate for missed gains, or who take substandard entries because they fear missing more opportunities, consistently underperform those who accept with equanimity that not every opportunity will be captured.
Continuous Improvement Compounds	A 1% improvement in win rate, maintained consistently, compounds over hundreds of trades into a dramatically different performance trajectory. A 1% reduction in average loss size, maintained consistently, compounds into a dramatically lower maximum drawdown. The goal is not perfection in any single period. The goal is measurable improvement from each period to the

Mastery Principle	The Deeper Understanding
	next, repeated until the aggregate improvements produce the results you intend.

These seven principles share a common thread: they all involve a shift from outcome-focused thinking to process-focused thinking. This shift is the defining psychological achievement of trading mastery. It is what allows a trader to honor a stop-loss without despair, to miss a winning trade without regret, to experience a losing streak without strategy abandonment, and to sustain a disciplined practice through market conditions that would break a trader whose identity was tied to short-term results.

15.3 Financial Independence: The Longer Vision

Throughout this book, the primary focus has been on developing trading skill. But trading skill exists within a larger financial life, and the most important measure of success is not how well you trade in any given year. It is whether the compounding effects of your skill, your capital, and your time move you steadily toward financial independence.

Financial independence, defined for our purposes as the state in which your passive and active investment income is sufficient to cover your living expenses without requiring active employment, is the natural long-term aspiration of a serious investor and trader. It is not achieved through a single dramatic trade or a single exceptional year. It is achieved through the same compounding mechanism that John Bogle spent his career documenting: consistent contribution, disciplined risk management, and the patience to let time do its work.

> *"Financial freedom is freedom from fear."*
> — **Robert Kiyosaki**, *Rich Dad Poor Dad (1997): the book that introduced financial education to millions of readers who had never thought systematically about money*

The Three Compounding Engines

The complete financial strategy implied by this book operates through three simultaneously compounding engines, each reinforcing the others.

- **Engine 1: Capital Compounding.** The mathematical compounding of returns over time. At 8% annual returns, $100,000 becomes $466,000 in 20 years and $1,000,000 in 30 years without any additional contributions. Add consistent monthly contributions and the numbers become dramatically larger. This is the engine that makes starting early irreplaceable.
- **Engine 2: Skill Compounding.** The analytical skills, pattern recognition, and psychological discipline you build through practice compound in value over time. The trader in year five sees setups the trader in year one cannot see. The discipline maintained through a difficult year two makes year three significantly more profitable. Skills compound through deliberate practice in ways that cannot be accelerated beyond the rate at which experience is genuinely absorbed and reflected upon.
- **Engine 3: Knowledge Compounding.** Every book read, every trade reviewed, every market cycle studied adds to a growing base of market understanding that makes each subsequent analysis richer and more reliable. The trader who has read The Intelligent Investor, Market Wizards, and Trade Your Way to Financial Freedom approaches a chart with a different depth of context than one who has read only stock tips on social media. Knowledge compounds: each new understanding builds on and enriches the prior base.

The integration of these three engines is the vision that makes the daily discipline of trading practice worth sustaining. The hours spent on your pre-market routine, your weekly performance review, and your continuous education are not costs. They are investments in all three engines simultaneously.

15.4 The Trader You Are Becoming

At the beginning of Chapter 1, you were invited to understand what a stock is. By the end of Chapter 15, you understand the complete ecosystem within which stocks exist: the markets, the participants, the analytical tools, the risk frameworks, the psychological dynamics, the tax structures, the instruments, and the philosophical foundations of a practice that can generate real wealth over a serious lifetime of engagement.

More important than what you know is what you now know how to do. You know how to research a stock using fundamental analysis. You know how to read a chart using technical analysis. You know how to build a systematic watchlist. You know how to size a position correctly. You know how to set a stop-loss at a structural level. You know how to review your performance honestly. You know how to manage the emotional pressures of live trading. You know how to select a broker, fund an account, and execute your first real trades. You know how to build a portfolio that combines active trading with passive index investing. You know how to use ETFs and options as additional instruments in a mature strategy.

These are not abstract understandings. They are practical competencies built on the most widely tested, most authoritative research and practitioner wisdom available. They were built by Benjamin Graham and Warren Buffett, by William O'Neil and Peter Lynch, by Jack Bogle and Philip Fisher, by Jesse Livermore and Paul Tudor Jones, by Daniel Kahneman and Van Tharp. You stand on a century of accumulated knowledge about how markets work and how human beings interact with them.

Now comes the part that no book can do for you: the application. The daily practice. The honest performance review. The patient discipline through adversity. The continuous learning. The willingness to be wrong quickly, to learn from losses, and to improve measurably from one period to the next.

> *"An investment in knowledge pays the best interest."*
> — **Benjamin Franklin**, *widely attributed across Franklin's writings on self-improvement and education*

15.5 Your Complete Framework: A Final Integration

Before closing, it is worth reviewing the complete integrated framework you have built across fifteen chapters in a single, consolidated view. This is not a summary of chapter content. It is a map of how every element connects to every other element in the practice of a disciplined, systematic trader and investor.

The Research Layer: Chapters 1-6

Your analytical foundation. Understanding what stocks are and how markets work (Chapter 1). The psychological and goal-setting framework (Chapter 2). The platform you use for all analysis (Chapter 3). The language of price that every chart speaks (Chapter 4). The fundamental analysis of companies through financial statements and key ratios (Chapter 5). The technical analysis of price and volume through charts, patterns, and indicators (Chapter 6). These six chapters form the analytical vocabulary that every subsequent action in your trading practice draws upon.

The Strategy Layer: Chapters 7-9

Your systematic execution framework. Building and maintaining a tiered watchlist through systematic sourcing, the AI Screener, and the Compare tool (Chapter 7). Managing risk through the 1% rule, position sizing, structural stops, and minimum R:R requirements (Chapter 8). Analyzing performance through the Dashboard metrics, equity curve, behavioral pattern diagnosis, and the weekly review process (Chapter 9). These three chapters convert analytical knowledge into actionable, repeatable trading decisions.

The Transition Layer: Chapters 10-11

The bridge from paper to live trading. The psychological infrastructure of emotional management, cognitive bias defense, and pre-live preparation (Chapter 10). The practical mechanics of broker selection, account funding, order types, tax awareness, and the structured first 30 days of live trading (Chapter 11). These two chapters address the specific challenges of the transition that paper trading alone cannot fully prepare you for.

The Expansion Layer: Chapters 12-14

The advanced toolkit. The core-satellite portfolio architecture integrating passive ETFs and active stocks (Chapter 12). The daily practice structure, journaling discipline, continuous education system, and five-year development arc (Chapter 13). The advanced strategies of options beyond covered calls and puts, active ETF trading, and retirement account optimization (Chapter 14). These three chapters expand the framework developed in the first eleven chapters into a complete, mature investment practice.

The Mastery Layer: Chapter 15

The philosophical foundation that makes everything else sustainable: the seven mastery principles, the three compounding engines, the long-term vision of financial independence, and the daily practice of becoming the trader you intend to become.

THE SINGLE MOST IMPORTANT SENTENCE IN THIS BOOK

Every concept, every tool, every rule, every framework in this book is in service of a single goal: to help you make more informed, more disciplined, more consistently profitable decisions in financial markets over a long and productive investing lifetime.

That goal is not achieved on the day you finish reading. It is achieved, gradually and measurably, through the daily practice of applying what you have read. Through the pre-market routine you maintain even when you do not feel like it. Through the performance review you complete honestly even when the results are difficult to face. Through the stop-loss you honor immediately even when every emotional instinct tells you to hold. Through the patience you exercise in waiting for the right setup rather than forcing a trade that does not qualify.

The reading ends here. The practice begins now.

15.6 Your Final Chapter Exercise: The Letter to Your Future Self

There is a tradition in personal development literature of writing a letter to your future self: a document that captures your current understanding, your current commitments, your current intentions, and your honest assessment of where you are in your development. It serves as a time capsule of your thinking at this moment, and a contract with the person you are becoming.

This final exercise asks you to write that letter. It is not graded, not shared with anyone, and not evaluated by any external standard. It is a private conversation between the trader you are today and the trader you intend to become. Write it with the same honesty and precision you have been building through your performance reviews and your trading journal.

The Letter to Your Future Self: Writing Prompts

Step 1: WHERE YOU ARE TODAY: Describe your current trading and investing knowledge and skill level honestly. What analytical tools do you feel genuinely competent with? Where do you still feel uncertain or underdeveloped? What is your current paper trading performance showing you about your edge?

Step 2: WHAT YOU HAVE LEARNED THAT SURPRISED YOU MOST: Reflecting on the fifteen chapters of this book, identify the single concept or insight that most changed how you think about trading and investing. Why was it surprising? How has it already changed your behavior?

Step 3: YOUR SPECIFIC COMMITMENTS: Write three to five specific, measurable commitments you are making to your future self about how you will practice trading. Not general aspirations ("I will trade better") but specific behavioral commitments ("I will complete the full pre-trade checklist before every trade for the next 90 days without exception").

Step 4: YOUR BIGGEST PSYCHOLOGICAL CHALLENGE: Based on your honest self-assessment from Chapter 10 and your paper trading behavioral pattern analysis from Chapter 9, identify the single psychological challenge that poses the greatest risk to your live trading consistency. What is your specific structural defense against it?

Step 5: YOUR FIVE-YEAR VISION: Describe specifically where you intend to be in your trading and investing practice in five years. Be specific about portfolio size targets, skill development goals, income contributions from trading, and the role this practice plays in your broader financial and personal life.

Step 6: WHAT YOU WILL DO DIFFERENTLY: What is the single most important thing you will do differently starting tomorrow, based on everything you have learned in this book? What has been the most significant gap between how you have approached markets in the past and how you will approach them from this point forward?

Step 7: A NOTE OF ENCOURAGEMENT TO YOURSELF: Write three to five sentences of genuine encouragement to your future self for the inevitable difficult period that lies ahead, whether it is a losing streak, a challenging market environment, or a moment when the practice feels thankless. What would you want to hear in that moment to help you maintain your discipline and your perspective?

Seal this letter (either physically or in a locked digital document) and set a reminder to open and read it in exactly one year. Compare where you are then to where you said you would be now. Revise your commitments, update your vision, and write a new letter for the next year. Repeated annually, this practice becomes one of the most powerful tools for maintaining long-term perspective and intentional development in the history of your trading career.

Chapter 15 Summary and Closing Thoughts

Chapter 15 has given you the philosophical framework that makes everything else in this book sustainable. Here is what you now carry forward from this final chapter, and from the entire journey of Stock Trades: From Beginner to Mastery:

- **Mastery Is a Posture, Not a Destination:** The consistent application of a sound process across all market conditions. Not the absence of losses. Not certainty. Not a specific performance threshold. Mastery is competence plus character, maintained day after day, especially in the days when it is hardest.

- **Seven Mastery Principles:** Process precedes outcome. Humility is operational. Losses are information. Patience is a strategy. Volatility is not risk. The market will always be there. Continuous improvement compounds. These principles are the philosophical foundation that sustains disciplined practice through adversity.
- **Three Compounding Engines:** Capital compounding (returns on returns over time), skill compounding (analytical capability growing through deliberate practice), and knowledge compounding (each new understanding enriching all prior knowledge). All three operate simultaneously and reinforce each other.
- **The Complete Integrated Framework:** Research layer (Chapters 1-6), Strategy layer (Chapters 7-9), Transition layer (Chapters 10-11), Expansion layer (Chapters 12-14), and Mastery layer (Chapter 15). Every element connects to every other. The framework is a unified system, not a collection of independent techniques.

A FINAL WORD

The market has been the greatest school of character, patience, discipline, and self-knowledge available to any human being willing to engage with it seriously. It rewards preparation and punishes assumption. It demands humility and destroys arrogance. It teaches patience to those who stay long enough to learn it.

You now have the framework. You have the tools. You have the knowledge of those who came before and did this well.

What happens next depends entirely on what you do with them.

Go trade well. Review honestly. Improve continuously. Protect your capital.

stocktradesapp.com

STOCK TRADES: FROM BEGINNER TO MASTERY

REFERENCES AND BIBLIOGRAPHY

The following bibliography lists all sources cited, referenced, or directly drawn upon in Stock Trades: From Beginner to Mastery. Sources are organized by category and presented in a modified Chicago/APA hybrid format appropriate for practitioner texts. Where a source is a landmark work widely available in multiple editions, the original publication year is noted alongside the edition most commonly in print. All website sources reflect content accessible as of 2025-2026.

Part I: Foundational Investment and Trading Books

Value Investing and Fundamental Analysis

Graham, Benjamin. The Intelligent Investor: The Definitive Book on Value Investing. Originally published 1949. Revised edition with commentary by Jason Zweig. HarperCollins, 2006. Cited in Chapters 2, 5, 15. Source of margin of safety concept, Mr. Market parable, and defensive vs. enterprising investor framework.

Graham, Benjamin, and David L. Dodd. Security Analysis. Originally published 1934. Sixth edition. McGraw-Hill, 2008. Foundational text of quantitative fundamental analysis. Framework underlying Chapter 5.

Fisher, Philip A. Common Stocks and Uncommon Profits and Other Writings. Originally published 1958. John Wiley and Sons, 1996. Source of qualitative analysis framework and fifteen questions methodology. Cited in Chapter 7 (opening quote). Referenced in Chapter 15 reading list.

Lynch, Peter, with John Rothchild. One Up on Wall Street: How to Use What You Already Know to Make Money in the Market. Simon and Schuster, 1989. Source of "turn over rocks" approach to stock sourcing. Lynch quoted in Chapter 7. Referenced in Chapter 15 reading list. Lynch managed Fidelity Magellan Fund to 29.2% average annual returns 1977-1990.

Lynch, Peter, with John Rothchild. Beating the Street. Simon and Schuster, 1993. Source of the "13 minutes" quote on economic analysis cited in Chapter 7.

Buffett, Warren E. Berkshire Hathaway Annual Shareholder Letters, 1977-2024. Berkshire Hathaway Inc. Available at berkshirehathaway.com. Foundational source of business quality analysis framework referenced throughout Part I.

Greenblatt, Joel. The Little Book That Beats the Market. John Wiley and Sons, 2005. Framework for return on capital and earnings yield as valuation tools.

Technical Analysis

Murphy, John J. Technical Analysis of the Financial Markets: A Comprehensive Guide to Trading Methods and Applications. New York Institute of Finance, 1999. The standard reference text of technical analysis. Framework underlying Chapter 6. Cited for volume analysis (1.5x ADV threshold). Referenced in Chapter 15 reading list.

Edwards, Robert D., and John Magee. Technical Analysis of Stock Trends. Originally published 1948. Eleventh edition, with W.H.C. Bassetti. CRC Press, 2018. Classic foundational text on chart pattern analysis.

Nison, Steve. Japanese Candlestick Charting Techniques. New York Institute of Finance, 1991. Cited in Chapter 6 for candlestick history and introduction of Japanese candlestick methods to Western markets.

Wilder, J. Welles, Jr. New Concepts in Technical Trading Systems. Trend Research, 1978. Original publication introducing the Relative Strength Index (RSI). Cited in Chapter 6.

Appel, Gerald. Technical Analysis: Power Tools for Active Investors. FT Press, 2005. Original developer of the MACD indicator. Cited in Chapter 6.

Weinstein, Stan. Secrets for Profiting in Bull and Bear Markets. McGraw-Hill, 1988. Source of the four-stage market cycle framework (Stage 1 Accumulation through Stage 4 Decline) cited in Chapters 6 and 7.

George, Thomas J., and Chuan-Yang Hwang. "The 52-Week High and Momentum Investing." Journal of Finance 59, no. 5 (2004): 2145-2176. Academic source cited in Chapter 4 for the psychological significance of the 52-week high and low as reference points.

Growth Stock Investing

O'Neil, William J. How to Make Money in Stocks: A Winning System in Good Times and Bad. Originally published 1988. Fourth edition. McGraw-Hill, 2009. Source of the CAN SLIM methodology cited and applied in Chapters 7 and 15. Named by the American Association of Individual Investors as the top-performing investment strategy from 1998 to 2009. Referenced in Chapter 15 reading list.

Part II: Trading Psychology and Skill Development

Trading Psychology

Douglas, Mark. Trading in the Zone: Master the Market with Confidence, Discipline, and a Winning Attitude. Prentice Hall Press, 2000. Cited in Chapter 10 (losing streak management quote). Widely considered the definitive text on trading psychology. Referenced in Chapter 15 reading list.

Elder, Alexander. Trading for a Living: Psychology, Trading Tactics, Money Management. John Wiley and Sons, 1993. Chapter 10 opening quote source: "The goal of a successful trader is to make the best trades. Money is secondary." Referenced throughout trading psychology sections.

Schwager, Jack D. Market Wizards: Interviews with Top Traders. HarperBusiness, 1989. Source of Ed Seykota quote (Chapter 8 opener), Paul Tudor Jones quotes (Chapters 8, 10, 15), and Schwager's observation on consistency (Chapter 13 opener). Referenced in Chapter 15 reading list.

Schwager, Jack D. The New Market Wizards: Conversations with America's Top Traders. HarperBusiness, 1992. Additional interviews with exceptional traders providing context for Chapters 10 and 13.

Schwager, Jack D. Market Wizards series (1989-2012). All volumes cited collectively in Chapter 13 for the observation that consistency is the defining differentiator between successful and unsuccessful traders.

Kahneman, Daniel, and Amos Tversky. "Prospect Theory: An Analysis of Decision under Risk." Econometrica 47, no. 2 (1979): 263-291. Foundational academic paper establishing loss aversion as a robust feature of human decision-making. Cited in Chapters 2 and 10.

Kahneman, Daniel. Thinking, Fast and Slow. Farrar, Straus and Giroux, 2011. Comprehensive treatment of the dual-process theory of cognition underlying the cognitive biases discussed in Chapter 10.

Tetlock, Philip E. Expert Political Judgment: How Good Is It? How Can We Know? Princeton University Press, 2005. Cited in Chapter 7 for evidence that financial expert forecasters perform only marginally better than chance.

Tetlock, Philip E., and Dan Gardner. Superforecasting: The Art and Science of Prediction. Crown Publishers, 2015. Extended treatment of forecasting accuracy cited in Chapter 7.

Trading-Setup.com Research Team. "Mastering Trading Psychology: The Ultimate Guide." Trading-Setup.com, 2026. Source of the resilience and structural distance quote cited in Chapter 10.

BIS Behavioural Finance Review, cited by EBC Financial Group. "Retail Trading Psychology Research." EBC Financial Group research compilation, 2025. Source of the 70-80% retail trading loss rate statistic and 30% higher survivability with psychological training, cited in Chapter 10 stat box.

NBER Working Paper on paper vs. live trading behavior. Referenced in Chapter 10 for the finding that paper trading and live trading behavior show scant correlation across multiple psychological dimensions, particularly in risk-taking and emotional decision-making. Specific paper referenced: experimental research on day trader training programs.

Position Sizing and System Development

Tharp, Van K. Trade Your Way to Financial Freedom. McGraw-Hill, 1998. Most cited work in this book's risk management chapters. Source of the 1% rule framework, position sizing formula, portfolio heat concept, expectancy calculation, minimum 30-trade sample size requirement, and "position sizing is THE number one skill" quote. Cited in Chapters 8, 9, 13.

Tharp, Van K. Peak Performance Trading research. Widely paraphrased across trading education sources. Source of "emotional discipline" quote cited in Chapter 10.

Part III: Behavioral Finance and Academic Research

Academic Research on Active vs. Passive Management

S&P Dow Jones Indices. SPIVA U.S. Scorecard, Year-End 2023. S&P Global, 2024. Source of the 92% statistic: the percentage of actively managed large-cap U.S. funds that underperformed the S&P 500 over a 15-year period after fees. Cited in Chapter 12. Available at spglobal.com/spdji.

S&P Dow Jones Indices. SPIVA series (1998-2024). Ongoing research program comparing active fund performance to benchmark indices across global markets and asset classes.

Barber, Brad M., and Terrance Odean. "Trading Is Hazardous to Your Wealth: The Common Stock Investment Performance of Individual Investors." Journal of Finance 55, no. 2 (2000): 773-806. Foundational academic paper demonstrating that frequent trading reduces retail investor returns.

Odean, Terrance. "Are Investors Reluctant to Realize Their Losses?" Journal of Finance 53, no. 5 (1998): 1775-1798. Academic source for the disposition effect: the tendency to sell winners too early and hold losers too long, referenced in Chapter 9.

Di Stefano, Giada, Francesca Gino, Gary P. Pisano, and Bradley R. Staats. "Making Experience Count: The Role of Reflection in Individual Learning." Harvard Business School Working Paper 14-093. Published in Psychological Science, 2016. Source of the 23% improvement statistic from structured reflection cited in Chapter 13.

Applied Finance Research

Applied Finance Letters. "CAN SLIM Screening Methodology Performance Analysis." Applied Finance Letters, 2023. Academic validation of simplified CAN SLIM screens producing consistent index outperformance over multi-year test periods. Cited in Chapter 7.

American Association of Individual Investors (AAII). CAN SLIM screen research and strategy performance tracking, 1998-2009. Source of AAII naming CAN SLIM the top-performing investment strategy from 1998 to 2009. Cited in Chapter 7.

QuantVPS.com. Quantitative trading survival research: position sizing and account longevity. QuantVPS.com research compilation, 2025. Source of the 85%/88% survival rate statistics at 1-2% vs. 10% risk per trade. Cited in Chapter 8 stat box.

NerdWallet, Bankrate, The Motley Fool. Broker review and comparison research, June 2026. Collective source for the broker comparison table in Chapter 11. Individual broker specifications verified against broker websites. Not a financial endorsement of any broker.

Part IV: Index Fund, ETF, and Portfolio Construction Literature

---

Bogle, John C. Common Sense on Mutual Funds: New Imperatives for the Intelligent Investor. Originally published 1999. Updated edition. John Wiley and Sons, 2009. Source of multiple Bogle quotes throughout Chapters 2, 9, and 12. Framework for cost-minimization and passive investing philosophy.

Bogle, John C. The Little Book of Common Sense Investing: The Only Way to Guarantee Your Fair Share of Stock Market Returns. John Wiley and Sons, 2007. "Don't look for the needle" quote source. Cited in Chapters 12 and 15 reading list.

Index Fund Advisors (IFA). "Quotes by John Bogle." IFA.com. Comprehensive collection of Bogle quotations. Available at ifa.com/quotes/john_bogle. Referenced for Bogle quote sourcing.

The Motley Fool. "Who Is John 'Jack' Bogle?" The Motley Fool website, updated 2025. Source for Bogle biography and investing philosophy summary cited in Chapter 12.

CFA Institute Research Foundation. "A Comprehensive Guide to ETFs, 2nd Edition." CFA Institute, 2025. Source for ETF structure, creation/redemption mechanism, and expense ratio data. Available at rpc.cfainstitute.org.

Morningstar. "SPY vs. VOO: Which S&P 500 ETF Should You Own?" Morningstar.com, July 2025. Source for expense ratio comparison and investor guidance. Cited in Chapter 12 ETF reference table.

Yahoo Finance. "SPY, VOO, or QQQ: Discover Which ETF Reigns Supreme for U.S. Investors." Yahoo Finance, March 2025. Source for QQQ AUM data ($312 billion) and annualized return comparisons cited in Chapter 12.

ETF.com. ETF data, flows, and expense ratios. etf.com. Ongoing reference for ETF market data cited in Chapter 12.

Vanguard. "Vanguard S&P 500 ETF (VOO)." Vanguard.com. Fund profile and expense ratio data. Available at investor.vanguard.com.

SPDR. "SPDR S&P 500 ETF Trust (SPY)." State Street Global Advisors. Fund profile and liquidity data. Available at ssga.com.

Part V: Options Education Literature

McMillan, Lawrence G. Options as a Strategic Investment. Originally published 1993. Fifth edition. Prentice Hall Press, 2012. Chapter 14 opening quote source. Standard reference text of options trading. Cited for comprehensiveness and depth on options strategy.

Options Clearing Corporation (OCC). "Characteristics and Risks of Standardized Options." OCC, current edition. Required reading before trading options. Available free at theocc.com. Cited in Chapters 12 and 14 as prerequisite reading.

CBOE Institute. Options education curriculum. Chicago Board Options Exchange, ongoing. Cited in Chapters 12 and 14 as recommended options education resource. Available at cboe.com.

Barchart.com. "QQQ Put/Call Ratio for Invesco QQQ Trust." Barchart.com, June 2026. Reference for options flow data and implied volatility concepts. Available at barchart.com.

Part VI: Regulatory and Platform References

FINRA (Financial Industry Regulatory Authority). BrokerCheck database. Available at brokercheck.finra.org. Cited in Chapter 11 as the required verification tool for broker registration and disciplinary history.

SIPC (Securities Investor Protection Corporation). "What SIPC Covers and Does Not Cover." sipc.org. Official SIPC protection guidance. $500,000 coverage limit and $250,000 cash sublimit cited in Chapter 11.

U.S. Securities and Exchange Commission. SEC.gov. Reference for securities regulations, Pattern Day Trader rule, and investor protection framework cited in Chapter 11.

Internal Revenue Service (IRS). "Topic No. 409 Capital Gains and Losses." IRS.gov. Source for short-term and long-term capital gains tax treatment discussed in Chapter 11.

IRS. "Publication 550: Investment Income and Expenses." IRS.gov, current year. Source for wash sale rule explanation in Chapter 11.

StockTradesApp.com. Platform documentation and in-product copy, 2026. Primary source for all platform feature descriptions, navigation items, button names, signal explanations, and Learn Hub content throughout this book. Screenshots analyzed and described in Chapter 3 and all subsequent platform callouts were captured from the live platform in June 2026.

StockTradesApp.com. "QT Stock Trades Learn Hub." stocktradesapp.com/learn. Source for Learn Hub category structure (7 categories, 43 lessons, Glossary) and lesson titles cited in Chapters 3 and 13.

Part VII: Practitioner Quotes and Attributed Sources

The following quotes are cited directly in the text. Where a quote is widely attributed but not confirmed to a specific original publication, the most commonly cited attribution is used and noted accordingly.

Dalio, Ray. Principles: Life and Work. Simon and Schuster, 2017. "The markets are always changing" paraphrase cited in Chapter 13. Dalio is founder of Bridgewater Associates, the world's largest hedge fund by assets under management.

Drucker, Peter F. The Practice of Management. Harper and Row, 1954. "What gets measured gets managed" quote cited in Chapter 9. Foundational management text.

Einstein, Albert. "The more I learn, the more I realize how much I don't know." Widely attributed to Einstein across multiple sources. Cited in Chapter 15. No single confirmed original publication.

Franklin, Benjamin. "An investment in knowledge pays the best interest." Widely attributed across Franklin's writings on self-improvement and education. Cited in Chapter 15. Specific source: The Way to Wealth (1758) and Poor Richard's Almanack, various editions.

Jones, Paul Tudor. Quotes cited in Market Wizards by Jack D. Schwager (1989). "The most important thing in making money is not letting your losses get out of hand" cited in Chapter 8. "Do not focus on making money; focus on protecting what you have" paraphrase cited in Chapter 11.

Kiyosaki, Robert T., with Sharon Lechter. Rich Dad Poor Dad: What the Rich Teach Their Kids About Money That the Poor and Middle Class Do Not! TechPress, 1997. "Financial freedom is freedom from fear" cited in Chapter 15.

Powell, Colin L. My American Journey. Random House, 1995. "There are no secrets to success" cited in Chapter 15.

Seykota, Ed. Quote in Market Wizards by Jack D. Schwager (1989). "There are old traders and there are bold traders, but there are very few old, bold traders" cited as Chapter 8 opener.

Twain, Mark. "The secret of getting ahead is getting started." Widely attributed to Mark Twain. Specific source unconfirmed; cited in Chapter 13 opener with attribution notation.

Traditional coaching maxim. "An amateur practices until he gets it right. A professional practices until he cannot get it wrong." Widely cited in coaching, surgery, athletics, and performance literature. No single confirmed originator. Cited in Chapter 9.

Part VIII: General Financial Education References

Arnott, Robert. "In investing, what is comfortable is rarely profitable." Widely quoted from Research Affiliates research. Robert Arnott is founder and chairman of Research Affiliates. Cited in Preface.

Elder, Alexander. Trading for a Living. 1993. Cited throughout Chapters 10 and 13 for trading psychology framework.

Lefevre, Edwin. Reminiscences of a Stock Operator. George H. Doran Company, 1923. Fictionalized memoir of Jesse Livermore. "It was never my thinking that made the big money for me. It was always my sitting" cited in Chapter 15 Mastery Principles table. Referenced in Chapter 15 reading list.

Livermore, Jesse L. How to Trade in Stocks. Duell, Sloan, and Pearce, 1940. Livermore's own account of his trading methodology and principles.

Zweig, Jason. Your Money and Your Brain: How the New Science of Neuroeconomics Can Help Make You Rich. Simon and Schuster, 2007. Cited for behavioral finance insights. Zweig is personal finance columnist at the Wall Street Journal.

DALBAR, Inc. Quantitative Analysis of Investor Behavior (QAIB). Annual study showing the average investor underperforms the market due to timing decisions. The 6.8% average investor return statistic versus index returns cited in Chapter 2. DALBAR research has tracked investor behavior since 1994.

End of References

stocktradesapp.com

STOCK TRADES: FROM BEGINNER TO MASTERY

Glossary of Key Terms

This glossary defines every Key Term introduced in the body of this book. Entries are listed alphabetically. Each definition corresponds to the Key Term box in the chapter where the term was first introduced.

1% Rule. A position sizing principle that limits the maximum risk on any single trade to 1 percent of the total trading account balance. Applied to the dollar difference between entry price and stop-loss price, not to total position value. A 0.5% rule is appropriate for beginning traders; 2% is acceptable for experienced traders with a proven edge.

52-Week Range. The highest and lowest prices at which a stock has traded during the preceding 52-week period. Displayed in the Terminal quote grid as two values in red (low) and green (high) with a position indicator showing where the current price falls within the range.

ATR (Average True Range). A technical indicator measuring the average daily price movement of a security, accounting for gaps. Used as the basis for volatility-based stop-loss placement and for comparing the typical price noise of different stocks.

Blended Signal. The primary rating on StockTradesApp.com's Terminal. Combines a Technical score (RSI, MACD, momentum, trend), a Fundamentals delta (adjustment from balance sheet and earnings data), and a News delta (sentiment from headline analysis) into a composite BUY, HOLD, or SELL rating with a numeric score. The component breakdown is always shown.

Bull Call Spread. An options strategy involving buying one call at a lower strike and selling another at a higher strike simultaneously. Reduces cost vs. a single long call; caps maximum profit at the spread width.

CAN SLIM. A seven-criteria growth stock screening methodology developed by William J. O'Neil (1988). Acronym for: Current quarterly earnings, Annual earnings growth, New product/service/management, Supply and demand, Leader vs. laggard, Institutional sponsorship, Market direction. Named the top-performing investment strategy 1998-2009 by the American Association of Individual Investors.

Capital Gain. The profit realized when a security is sold for more than its purchase price. Short-term capital gains (held under one year) are taxed at ordinary income rates. Long-term capital gains (held over one year) are taxed at preferential rates of 0%, 15%, or 20% depending on income.

Composite Signal. A circular gauge on the StockTradesApp.com Terminal showing the overall conviction level of the Blended Signal, displayed as BUY (green), HOLD (amber), or SELL (red) with a CONFIDENCE percentage.

CAN SLIM. A seven-criteria growth stock screening methodology developed by William J. O'Neil (1988). Named the top-performing investment strategy from 1998 to 2009 by the American Association of Individual Investors.

Covered Call. An options strategy where the owner of 100 shares sells one call option at a strike price above the current stock price. Generates premium income in exchange for capping upside above the strike. Appropriate in flat or slowly rising market environments.

Death Cross. A technical signal produced when the 50-day Simple Moving Average crosses below the 200-day Simple Moving Average. Associated with bearish longer-term momentum. The opposite of a Golden Cross.

Disposition Effect. The documented behavioral tendency of investors to sell winning positions too early (to lock in gains) and hold losing positions too long (to avoid realizing losses). Identified by Odean (1998). Produces a high win rate combined with poor risk-reward ratios.

Drawdown. The peak-to-trough decline in account equity from any given high point. Measured in both dollars and percentage. The Max Drawdown metric on the Dashboard shows the largest drawdown experienced since the start of the paper trading account.

Equity Curve. A chart showing the cumulative change in a trading account's value over time, with each completed trade updating the curve. Shown on the Dashboard with the strategy line (green) plotted against the SPY benchmark (gray).

ETF (Exchange-Traded Fund). A type of investment fund holding a collection of securities that trades on a stock exchange like an individual share. Combines the diversification of mutual funds with the intraday tradability of stocks. The first ETF, SPY, was launched by State Street Global Advisors in January 1993.

Expectancy. The average amount a trading system earns or loses per dollar risked per trade, measured across a meaningful sample. Calculated as: (Win Rate x Average Win) minus (Loss Rate x Average Loss). Positive expectancy indicates a sustainable edge.

Expense Ratio. The annual fee charged by an ETF or mutual fund to cover management costs, expressed as a percentage of assets and deducted daily from the fund's value. Ranges from 0.03% for broad index ETFs to 1.5%+ for actively managed funds.

FINRA (Financial Industry Regulatory Authority). A self-regulatory organization authorized by Congress to oversee U.S. broker-dealers. Operates BrokerCheck at brokercheck.finra.org where investors can verify any broker's licensing status and disciplinary history.

Free Cash Flow (FCF). Operating cash flow minus capital expenditures. Represents the cash a business generates after maintaining and expanding its asset base. Often considered the most reliable fundamental metric for assessing a company's financial strength and ability to fund growth.

Golden Cross. A technical signal produced when the 50-day Simple Moving Average crosses above the 200-day Simple Moving Average. Associated with bullish longer-term momentum. The opposite of a Death Cross.

In-the-Money (ITM). An options term. A call option is in-the-money when the stock price is above the strike price. A put option is in-the-money when the stock price is below the strike price. In-the-money options have intrinsic value.

Live Trading Readiness. The state of documented, evidence-based preparation to transition from paper trading to real-money trading. Three minimum thresholds: 50 completed paper trades with documentation, Profit Factor of 1.3 or above for 4 consecutive weeks, and zero stop-loss violations in the most recent 20 trades.

MACD (Moving Average Convergence Divergence). A momentum indicator developed by Gerald Appel. Calculated as the difference between a 12-period EMA and a 26-period EMA, with a 9-period EMA signal line. Displayed in the Terminal as MACD (12,26,9). Used to identify momentum changes and potential crossover signals.

Margin of Safety. A fundamental analysis concept introduced by Benjamin Graham. The difference between a security's calculated intrinsic value and its current market price. A larger margin of safety provides greater protection against errors in valuation assumptions.

Market Capitalization. The total market value of a company's outstanding shares, calculated as share price multiplied by total shares outstanding. Categories: mega-cap (over $200 billion), large-cap ($10-200 billion), mid-cap ($2-10 billion), small-cap ($300 million to $2 billion), micro-cap (under $300 million).

Out-of-the-Money (OTM). An options term. A call option is out-of-the-money when the stock price is below the strike price. A put option is out-of-the-money when the stock price is above the strike price. OTM options have zero intrinsic value and consist entirely of time value.

Pattern Day Trader (PDT) Rule. A FINRA regulation requiring that any trader who executes four or more day trades within a five-business-day rolling period in a margin account maintain at least $25,000 in account equity. Does not apply to cash accounts.

Portfolio Heat. The total dollar risk across all open positions simultaneously, expressed as a percentage of the account. Calculated by summing the maximum loss (entry minus stop, times share count) across all open trades. Professional standard cap: 6% of account equity.

Profit Factor. Total gross profit divided by total gross loss across all closed trades. A Profit Factor above 1.0 indicates net profitability. A Profit Factor above 1.5 is considered viable; above 2.0 is strong. Displayed in the Dashboard PERFORMANCE section.

Protective Put. An options strategy where the owner of shares purchases a put option on those shares, functioning as downside insurance. Limits loss below the strike price in exchange for the put premium cost.

RSI (Relative Strength Index). A momentum oscillator developed by J. Welles Wilder (1978). Measures the speed and change of price movements on a scale of 0 to 100. Readings above 70 are considered overbought; below 30 are oversold. Displayed in the Terminal as RSI (14), using a 14-period calculation window.

Risk-Reward Ratio (R:R). The ratio of potential profit to maximum risk on a trade. Calculated as (Price Target minus Entry) divided by (Entry minus Stop Price). Minimum professional standard: 2:1. A 2:1 R:R means the potential gain is twice the potential loss.

Sector Rotation. The systematic practice of overweighting sectors expected to outperform in the current economic environment and underweighting those expected to underperform. Based on the observation that different sectors of the economy lead at different phases of the business cycle.

SIPC (Securities Investor Protection Corporation). A nonprofit organization created by Congress in 1970 that protects customers of SIPC-member brokerage firms if the firm fails. Protects up to $500,000 per customer ($250,000 in cash). Covers custody of assets, not investment performance or market losses.

Sharpe-Like Score. A risk-adjusted return metric displayed on the StockTradesApp.com Dashboard. Modeled after the professional Sharpe Ratio; measures return relative to the volatility of results. A score above 1.0 indicates adequate risk-adjusted performance; above 2.0 is strong.

SMA (Simple Moving Average). The arithmetic mean of a security's closing prices over a specified number of periods. The Terminal displays SMA20 (20-day) and SMA50 (50-day) on every chart. The SMA200 is the standard long-term trend indicator and the basis for Golden/Death Cross analysis.

Stage Analysis. Stan Weinstein's four-stage framework for identifying where a stock is in its price cycle: Stage 1 (Accumulation/base-building), Stage 2 (Advancing/uptrend), Stage 3 (Distribution/topping), Stage 4 (Declining/downtrend). Optimal entries are at Stage 1-to-2 transitions.

Stop-Loss Order. An order to automatically sell (for long positions) a security when its price reaches a specified level. Converts a potentially open-ended loss into a defined, pre-calculated maximum loss. On StockTradesApp.com, managed manually via the Alerts section's Crosses Below feature.

Support and Resistance. Price levels on a chart where buying pressure (support) or selling pressure (resistance) has historically been sufficient to halt or reverse price movement. Role reversal principle: former support often becomes new resistance when broken, and vice versa.

Trailing Stop. A stop-loss that automatically adjusts upward (for long positions) as the stock price rises, maintaining a fixed percentage or dollar distance from the current high. Locks in progressively more profit while allowing positions to run during strong trends.

Wash Sale Rule. An IRS regulation that disallows a capital loss deduction when the investor sells a security at a loss and purchases the same or substantially identical security within 30 days before or after the sale. The disallowed loss is added to the cost basis of the repurchased shares.

STOCK TRADES: FROM BEGINNER TO MASTERY

INDEX

This index covers the primary analytical concepts, strategies, platforms features, regulatory terms, and named individuals referenced throughout the book. Chapter numbers are indicated for each entry. Italic chapter numbers indicate that the subject appears in a table or visual element rather than body text.

A

B

C

S

T

www.ingramcontent.com/pod-product-compliance
Lightning Source LLC
LaVergne TN
LVHW080031210926
848481LV00011B/3154
* 9 7 9 8 9 9 9 4 1 0 3 6 8 *